797,885 Books

are available to read at

www.ForgottenBooks.com

Forgotten Books' App
Available for mobile, tablet & eReader

ISBN 978-1-334-67994-0
PIBN 10740551

This book is a reproduction of an important historical work. Forgotten Books uses
state-of-the-art technology to digitally reconstruct the work, preserving the original format
whilst repairing imperfections present in the aged copy. In rare cases, an imperfection in
the original, such as a blemish or missing page, may be replicated in our edition. We do,
however, repair the vast majority of imperfections successfully; any imperfections that
remain are intentionally left to preserve the state of such historical works.

Forgotten Books is a registered trademark of FB &c Ltd.
Copyright © 2017 FB &c Ltd.
FB &c Ltd, Dalton House, 60 Windsor Avenue, London, SW19 2RR.
Company number 08720141. Registered in England and Wales.

For support please visit www.forgottenbooks.com

1 MONTH OF
FREE
READING

at

www.ForgottenBooks.com

By purchasing this book you are eligible for one month membership to ForgottenBooks.com, giving you unlimited access to our entire collection of over 700,000 titles via our web site and mobile apps.

To claim your free month visit:

www.forgottenbooks.com/free740551

* Offer is valid for 45 days from date of purchase. Terms and conditions apply.

English
Français
Deutsche
Italiano
Español
Português

www.forgottenbooks.com

Mythology Photography **Fiction**
Fishing Christianity **Art** Cooking
Essays Buddhism Freemasonry
Medicine **Biology** Music **Ancient
Egypt** Evolution Carpentry Physics
Dance Geology **Mathematics** Fitness
Shakespeare **Folklore** Yoga Marketing
Confidence Immortality Biographies
Poetry **Psychology** Witchcraft
Electronics Chemistry History **Law**
Accounting **Philosophy** Anthropology
Alchemy Drama Quantum Mechanics
Atheism Sexual Health **Ancient History**
Entrepreneurship Languages Sport
Paleontology Needlework Islam
Metaphysics Investment Archaeology
Parenting Statistics Criminology
Motivational

Shakespeare's Revelations

by

Shakespeare's Spirit

Through the medium of his pen
SARAH TAYLOR SHATFORD
Dictated exactly as herein found.
No illiteracies, no obliterations,
chargable to the Medium.   My
hand and seal hereon.

W. S. In spirit.

NEW YORK
THE TORCH PRESS, Inc.
Publishers
MCMXIX

932
5532

COPYRIGHT 1919
THE TORCH PRESS, Inc.
ALL RIGHTS RESERVED

Contents

Ouija Board Poems (3) ....9 - 11
Sayings of W. S. In Spirit (To keep the hearing open to spirit voice..12 - 27
GEMS FROM THE SPIRIT WORLD ....28 - 45
Why I Am Here.. 45
Preface ....47 - 50
I Am He Who Wrote... 51
The Reason Why 53
There Is No Death... 54
Fearless We Search The Earth.................................. 54
Divine History 56
The Truth Regarding The Truth................................. 56
A Message To The Weary World.................................. 57
Across The Border... 58
To Critics Of My Pen.. 58
To Lift The Veil 59
To A Poet Who Could Not Die................................... 61
The Poet's Farewell... 62
To One In A Tomb.. 63
The Poems Of A Bard... 64
To Set The World Right 65
Fourteen Summers Have Passed Since I Saw England.............. 66
Found 74
My Work And I... 76
To One Who Mentions Shakespeare's Name........................ 77
Evil Spirits 78
To The Man Of God... 78
The Old Haunts 79
Rectitude 80
What England Knows Today...................................... 82
When The Stars Went Out....................................... 83
Old England's Flower 83
To One I Love Still Through All The Lapse Of Time............. 84
MY ENGLAND 86
May-Day Home 86
To Be A Boy... 87
England's Primrose 87
My Song Today... 88
The Immortal Shakespeare's Birthday........................... 89
Shakespeare's Thanksgiving 89
The Spirit's Harvest 90
Lonely On Earth 91

I

M188552

Readjustment 91
To Commemorate The Passing of My Son.......................... 92
The Love Sonnets Of Shakespeare................................ 93
The Love Sonnets Of Shakespeare (same title).................. 94
O Could The World Of Strife.................................... 94
You Look Upon Earth's Beauteous Womankind...................... 95
When I Came To This Land....................................... 96
Why Love Must Live... 96
LIFE 96
To Hold The Hand Of An Immortal Poet........................... 97
A PERFECT SONNET 97
O World Where Earthly Joys Abound So Fair...................... 98
When The Stars Go Out And The Sun Sinks Not.................... 98
Happy New-Year, Sarah 99
O Leave The World Of Sin While Yet............................. 99
There Is No Greater Self Than What You Are..................... 100
A Sonnet For Lovers.. 100
A Sonnet Of Love... 101
How Shall I Love Thee Who Have Writ These Leaves.............. 101
Wake, Sleeping World, Before The World Lies Dead.............. 102
When Love Shall Die.. 102
O Could You But Know The Rare Essence Of love................. 103
Where Shall The World At Last Find Men......................... 103
Where Are The Loves We Loved And Soon Forgot.................. 104
Uplift The Heart While This Heart In You Beats................ 105
ETERNAL LIFE 105
We Have Come From The Playhouse, God's Woman And I........... 106
When Mortals Are Given A Chance At The Last................... 106
O What Is More Dear Than The Hands That We Love.............. 107
The Balance True 107
Sonnets Of Mine 108
To All Lovers 108
To My Love In His Sphere—Wherever That May Be............... 109
Speak 110
Sweet My Love 110
To Her At Last I've Come To Love............................... 112
My Love, My Pure, My Only Love................................. 112
To Her I Love With A Cherishing Constant Attendance........... 113
A Nation's Gloom 113
Keep In Your Heart A Little Place.............................. 115
A Long Time 115
Communion Sunday 116
In The Wellsprings Of Being.................................... 116
Spirit Truth 117
To A Harp Of God... 117
Our Burdens 118
The Sleeping World 119
Your Sweet Heart 119
Take From My Heart Its Wealth Of Love......................... 120
When Love Is Young... 120
Enduring Love 120

Love Of Love 121
Love's Sacrifice 122
Spooks And Ghosts 122
RETURN 123
Few Fit! 124
So Far! 124
Eternal Love 125
We Shall Spill No More Gold.................................... 125
There Is No Cross Without Its Pain............................. 126
Sex Attraction 126
To The Source Of All Love...................................... 127
Love's Emissary 127
When The World Regains Its Sanity.............................. 128
A Love Song 128
The Fulfilment Of Love... 129
Love's Crucible 129
The Value Of A Friend.. 130
Hell A Reality 130
Then All Shall Know When "'Death" Hath Laid Them By........... 131
Thousands Of Millions.. 131
When Will The Saints Come Home................................. 132
God's Best 133
God Made The Light And With His Word........................... 133
Mental Questions Read By W. S. In Spirit without an error....... 135
A Single Note 135
If The World Only Knew 136
To Our Lady Of Lourdes 137
Obedience 138
Reinstated 139
One Time 139
Lives Whorish 140
Mortal's Incredulity 141
Renunciation 141
Omnipresent 142
Revealment 143
Martyrs 143
Unfoldment 144
The Morning Hymn 144
Praise Of God 145
Peace With Honor... 145
Somewhere 146
Sorrow 147
God Is 147
So Near Am I 148
A Warrior's Battles 148
What Will The Answer Be.. 149
Rejoice 149
Work And Weep 149
Satan's Hierarchy 150
To Suffer Is To Grow... 150
Years And Years And What They Bring............................ 151

III

The Measuring Scales 151
Yours And Yours Alone... 151
Dear 152
To The World 152
What Will The Answer Be... 153
When The Summons Comes... 153
When The Old Becomes New... 154
Floundering Fools ("What Is Psychoanalysis?") 155
Fortunate Fools 155
Abandoned 156
The Heavenly Host 156
Workers Of Iniquity 157
All The Way 158
Self-Heroes 158
Poverty 159
Give Me Room.. 159
Eternal Joy 159
When Will Jesus Come To Earth Again?.............................. 160
Fooled Again 161
The Door Ajar 162
So Little Can We Give... 163
There Is A Land... 163
Poor Fools 164
The Mystic Shrine 164
Pangs Forgot 165
Deathless 166
Forgiveness 167
The Powers Beyond 167
When Ye Go Hence 169
When Mortal's Eyes Blind To The Light............................. 169
By Words Inspired 170
The Only Way 171
Destiny 171
Thy Mouth Is A Rose... 172
A Hymn Of Love.. 172
The Void 173
Into—Out of—The Vast Beyond....................................... 174
Living And Dead 175
The "Dead Sleep Aye" Men Say...................................... 176
Sacrifice 176
God's Mill 177
When Goodness Fails To Keep A Friend.............................. 177
I Would That God Would Give....................................... 178
PEACE 178
Every Hand Holds Its Wealth....................................... 179
WOMAN: A Tribute 179
Universal Suffrage 180
The Vicar's Peace... 181
When Wars No Longer Drag Men Into Graves.......................... 182
Lost And Won.. 183
As It Is Writ... 183

Answered 184
The Wakeful Dead... 186
Look at Belgium.. 187
A Lasting Peace 187
The Wars Of The World.................................... 188
Shall The War Work The Miracle Of Christ................. 188
"Peace, Be Still . . ."................................... 189
The Jews Restored 189
The Invisible Foe 190
My Humble Supplication................................... 191
War's Toll 192
War's Tragic Game.. 193
Fiends 193
Arch Fiends 194
Restoration 194
Fortunes Of War.. 195
Cleansing Fire 195
Divinity 196
Foes Of The Dark 197
Buried Alive 197
Remake The World, O God.................................. 198
Charity 198
Malediction's End 199
Reconstruction 200
Mercy 200
Great Questions Mark The Hour............................ 201
Time's Garland 202
The Broken Bound 202
To Those Who Have No Chance.............................. 203
The Burthen Of Loss...................................... 203
This Is The Day When Fears And Hate Hold Sway............ 204
The Spirit Which Longs To Be Free........................ 205
United 205
Warriors 206
A Soldier's Orison 206
Fallen Thrones 207
Liberty Or Death 208
A Hero 208
"Out-There" 209
Shunned 209
The World Victorious 210
Out Of The Past.. 210
Mother And Her Own....................................... 211
Mercy 212
Fools 212
The Enemy 213
The Earth A Moon?.. 214
The Dying Soldier 214
To The American Red Cross:............................... 215
To Be Or Not To Be, THAT (This) Is The Question.......... 215
The Ploughshares And The Swords 216

v

A Prophecy 217
Why The World Forgets..................................... 217
What Will The World Be Then?.............................. 218
Remake—Restore 218
Under The Red, White and Blue (song) To The American Red Cross:
    Donation 219
At Last The Huns Have Met Their Fate 220
A Requiem For Those Who Die............................... 221
Belgium 221
A New-Year Prayer 221
One King, One Land, One Song.............................. 222
There Is A World When Men Are "Dead"...................... 222
To Give 223
Seekers 223
The Mountain 223
The Reapers 224
"The Invisible Balance Sheet" (With Acknowledgment)........ 224
"If There's A God".. 225
O JUSTICE With Thy Scales Unseen.......................... 225
Wonders And Signs 226
In The Wellsprings Of Being............................... 226
What Purpose? 226
"Ye Cannot Bear Them Now" 227
Salvation 228
O When The Cheek Of Early Dawn............................ 228
Thy Heritage 229
"Behold I Stand At The Door,—"............................ 229
A Cross Of Gold... 229
The Downward Path 230
The Patience Of God....................................... 231
To ———— 231
Where Shall Jesus Find The Table Spread For Him........... 232
When All The World Now Living Sleeps...................... 232
Sorrow's Crown 233
The Test 233
The Potter And The Clay 233
The Poets 234
Spurious Gems 234
To A Poet Clown: Sarah.................................... 234
Things We Need.. 235
Where Worlds Divide 235
A Renegade's Portrait Of Himself.......................... 236
How Can You Know?... 236
Man's Sin 237
The End Of Time... 237
The Hills Of God.. 238
The Glory Of God.. 239
God's Love 239
God's Word 240
What Gain? 240
Give God His Due.. 241

"The Way . . . The Truth . . . And The Life" 241
"The Dawn Of A Perfect Day" 242
The Law 242
"Thou Shalt Not Steal" 243
"Thou Shalt Not Commit Adultery" 243
The Forever 244
Take Me And Let Me Live, O God, Most High 245
"The Best Woman In The Bible" (W. S.'s idea of :) 245
"Go, And Sin No More" 246
Increasing Store 247
The Adjustment 247
Why Is The World All Wrong? 248
Plea For Harmony 248
The Fallen Priest 249
Give Me A Chance 250
Jesus' Wonderful Love 250
Faded Flowers 251
To Call In Vain 251
"The Advantage Of A Handicap" 252
Where Shall We Find God? 252
What Will The World Give You? 253
Peace (To Father ———, Priest, from W S.) 254
The Priest's Penance 255
Holy Of Holies 255
Inheritance 255
A Cross 255
The Secret Chest 256
Each Answers 256
To The Blind 257
His Holy Name 258
His Everlasting Glory 259
The Voice 259
Praise 260
A Christ-Like Love 261
Debt And Debtor 261
"Our Poverty And Jesus" 262
"Now I Lay Me Down To Sleep" 263
Riches Without Wings 263
When Earth's Annointed Walk With Him 264
O Saintly Light Which Pours Across The Night 264
The Thief On The Cross 264
MOTHER OF GOD 264
When The World Is Ready For The Saviour 265
God Will Save His World 266
The Beacon Light 266
The Poor 267
"Sower Went Forth" 267
Sorrows Of Women 268
The Dying Saviour 268
Easter In The South 269
Exercises in "stringing" . . . to keep in touch with the voice 270

Hell's Spirits 271
HAIL, BERNHARDT! LA VIE DE FRANCE! 271
Who Shall Say? 272
Rhymes And Jingles 272
An Orchestration In Words Instead Of Notes: 273
Adieu 273
"The Wisest Word" 274
On The Death Of ———— 274
To The Old General Who Has Fought Many Battles 275
———— Prayer 276
". . . By The Still Waters" 276
Never! 277
Where Shall We Go? 278
O For The Wonderful, Wonderful Past 278
The Value Of Sin 279
The Peace of Christ (Prose) 282
Great Men: To His Countryman, The Hon. Arthur J. Balfour, British
       War Commissioner (Prose) 284
Great Men (Poem) 286
First Experiences After the Change Called Death (Prose) .. 286
The Mysterious Portal (Prose) 291
Two Worlds One 293
Spirit Memory 296
Misguided Love 299
The Sex Relation 301
Intellect And Spirit 306
A Spirit's Feelings 308
Is A Soul Conscious Of The Change Called Death 309
Why So Few Mortals Are Adequate For Spirit Use 311
The Glory Of Spirit 313
The War As Seen From The World Of Spirit 317
Extracts From "Care Of The Body" 323
The Crannies Of The Mind 326
Insanity, And The Mental Deficient 328
What Is The Meaning Of Death—For Human Life As A Whole 331
What Is The Meaning Of Spiritual Development 333
Why Spirits Do Not Reincarnate As Mortals, But As Spirits . 337
Reincarnation 339
Sir Oliver Lodge's "RAYMOND" After Reading 341
Magazine Article After Reading 342
On Theosophic Teachers And The Cult. W. S. In Spirit 343
Care 344
What Can The World Say (Personal Remarks to S. T. S. from W. S. .. 346
To The Spirit Whose House I Occupy 347
Eden 349
Searchers 349
The Bolted Door 350
Onward And Upward 350
Au Revoir 351
Saved 352
To Lufbery—The American Ace 353

Joan Of Arc 353
Souls 354
The Star In The East...................................... 355
God's Love 355
One With Thee 356
The Life Line 356
Reconsecration 357
The Yankee's Prayer 358
Past Mortal Trials.. 359
Sometime 359
Flood-Tide 360
Fate? 360
When You Shall Find No Path............................... 360
When Gentle Shakespeare Came to Me....................... 361
I Am "Sweet Shakespeare" Still, If Such I Were.............. 361
W. S.'s Favorite Hymn.................................... 362
Eternal God From Whom I Came............................. 362
O To Be One.. 363
Holy Wrath 363
Daybreak 364
When Wars Have Done.................................... 364
Works Or Deeds 365
Repentance 365
Who Will Care?...........................L............. 366
Following 366
Hope 367
O What Would You Give?.................................. 367
Take From My Heart Every Malice.......................... 368
Let Us Not Despair....................................... 368
"Unhealthy Optimism" (Criticism of) 368
"The Stingy Receiver" 369
Foes Of War.. 369
The Strife 370
Kings And Kingdoms 371
The Balance True 372
The Wanderer 372
Oh—Oh—Oh 373
A Lasting Good 373
All 374
Fortune 374
Go Then, Be Wise....................................... 375
An Army Of Foes At Hand................................. 375
The Invisible Foe 376
Marital Miseries 377
Make Me A Place O God.................................. 378
Wake, O My Soul 378
Begin Again 378
A Leaf 379
The Setting Sun (unfinished).............................. 379
The Sleeping World 379
Charity 380

In Thy Care 381
Get In Line 381
"Thou Shalt Not Commit Adultery"................................ 382
Save Thy Soul 383
Esteem 384
Fret Not, The World Will See The Light.......................... 384
Wake, Sleeping Dead 385
Shorter And Swifter Flows The Outgoing Tide.................... 386
There Is A Land Where All Men Find............................. 386
The Risen Lord 387
A Cross No Loss.. 387
Whence? 388
The Sins Of The World.. 389
Far And Near... 389
The Rescue 390
Awing 390
Faith 391
The Prodigal Son... 391
When Men Shall Know.. 391
The Glory Of His Mission... 391
Along The Road To God.. 393
How Long? 393
Fouling The Nest... 394
Summertime In The Heart.. 394
Thine 395
Take His Hand.. 395
Come To Me 396
Jesus' Woes 396
All Praise To Thee... 397
The Soul's Cry 397
In The City Of God... 398
Tell It All.. 399
O King Divine.. 399
Old Glory 400
Along With The Tide 401
When The Cows Return to Roost (The Huns Speaking)............ 402
To Keep Awhile The Oldtime Thoughts.............................. 402
Make Me Some Place, O God, Where I May Rest.................... 403
Exercises to keep the hearing...................................... 403
Shakespeare's Letter to Sir Oliver Lodge.................L......... 409
To ———. Through S. T. S. A Bond Of Gold.................... 410
When I Was Twenty-One.. 411
Higher Powers 411
Harmony 412
Signs Of The Times... 413
Liberty 414
In Memoriam 414
Destiny 415
Sowing And Reaping... 416
The Giver 416
Wilde Once: But Wild No More....................................... 417

A Spirit's Prayer 418
The Christian's God 418
The Ritual Of Spirit... 419
To A Southern Rose.. 420
Repentance 420
The Meaning Of Power... 421
The Bird's Cradle-Song.. 422
The Messenger 422
Thousands And Millions 423
To ———, Author of "Dead Authors"............................. 424
The Vassal 426
When You Gave Me Your Heart.................................... 426
To Palladino 427
Hubbards, Nova Scotia 428
A Lover's Wish 428
The Worst Woman In The Bible.................................... 429
When Gifts Are Given Mortals Here............................... 429
A Word Of Praise... 430
"Behold, I Stand At The Door"................................... 430
"Consider The Lilies Of The Field 431
Vision 432
A Garden Celestial 432
W. S. To Perverts: (His own title).............................. 433
A Flute Of God... 434
The Rose Of Paradise... 434
When We Look At The World...................................... 435
While The Good Must Pay.. 435
When Shall Men Rise To Do God's Will............................ 436
The New Born Year.. 437
Faithful And True 437
Messages For The Soldiers....................................... 438
Self-Abnegation 439
Angels En Passant.. 440
Peace 441
Wounds 441
Fountain Of Life... 442
Sacrifice 442
A Bird 443
No More (Song) 443
A Lover's Kiss (Song).. 445
Hearts Aflame 445
To The Winds And The Sea....................................... 446
Heaven's Hold 446
Resolve 447
Help Me To Pray... 447
Brothermen 448
Love's Birth Renewed... 448
I Shall Know Him (Song).. 449
Have You Any Use For Jesus? (Song).............................. 449
Come And—See (Song) 450
Waiting At The Door (Song)...................................... 450

When Jesus Shall Call Me His Own (Song).......................... 451
Lost In The Wilderness (Song)...................................... 451
The Love You Have Found In Jesus (Song)........................ 452
There Shall Be No Night With Jesus (Song)...................... 453
Harvest Of Thorns 453
The Grace Of God... 454
This Is Thine... 455
On A Willow-Bough (Song).. 455
Spring's Joyous Notes... 456
Christ Of Peace.. 456
Just A "Stringing Exercise"... 456
A Lover's Last Request.. 457
The Fate Of Poets 458
Birth Of Light... 459
Pre-Science 459
Bethlehem's Star (Song) 459
Song 460
The Late Arrivals 460
Heavens And Hells 461
Christmas Tidings 462
Sundown 462
Be Not Afraid 463
The Light Of The World..s 464
When The Morning Breaks... 464
Faith (A sermonette) 465
Spectres 467
To My Spouf 467
Researchers 468
The Ordeal 470
Thanksgiving 470
The Lost Chord (Song) 472
The Song Never Sung (Song).. 472
A Child's Prayer 472
From Whence? 472
To The Aerialists 473
To Scientific Researchers Psychical................................. 474
One King, One Throne.. 475
BRITAIN'S DAY 475
TO SEARCHERS OF GOD'S WISDOM.............................. 476
TO GOD'S ELECT 478
A Final Word 479

TO MY MOTHER

God made all women fair; thee, He made fairest.
Oh gentle, kind, forgiving to the last!
In memories fond I feel your arms around me:
These bind and hold me, through the eons past.

To search on high until I find and greet thee,
To hear once more the name I know you love,
Here have I served until my past is mended,
To wipe away your tears, and be with you above.

W. S. In Spirit
(Through Sarah Shatford)

Xmas, 1918.

"FOREWORD"

To the one who has compiled for me these lines I'll speak for her these words.

She has been mine instrument indeed, varying, immobile as ever a spirit's tool is, yet strained not at all, never snapped a string while working out this volume in words here spoken in her right ear, outside the body, by her side, inside the mental equipment truly, opening one door after another, through her work, (as she progressed we moved higher let me say) until we could reach her audibly anywhere, anytime whatever.

To those who revile a medium I wish to speak here for the rest of time, which is God's eternity. To brand the culprit who defames, underestimates the instrument through which his work is accomplished, stigmatized in spirit as foul and poor, I take this place to proclaim of highest value in the sordid world at this hour a living electric charged battery connecting the unseen living with the seen dying verily through whose currents magnetic, spirituelle (above all this) attuned to higher sounds than grovelling mortals hear, we work, and all must work, for Spirit.

To pettifoggers who declaim and spume at length a mess of balderdash to befuddle the seeker of truth, proclaiming no advance where worlds divide, I say, who spell through her these lines, Avaunt dissembler: you who know the truth and lie to shield your muggy braincells under a cloak of Science, you fool not any but yourself. Your work must live and you must live and see its purility from spirit who evade the heart-wrung cries and pleadings of a torn world bereaved at loss which may be gain were all facts known we could make known had we the power to shield, protect, find such wires as we employ who write hereon through ear in tune, applied as taught by me, the shade of Shakespeare, whom the world has never derided, but loved and called a poet up to now.

I came to this one in a seance where she sat to learn if death were true. I lost no chance in taking her in hand. I gave as much as ever here I took. And yet I claim my debt has not been met. I still must pay. And pay I will, if men who cry against God's plan, will heed my words spelled with lips no longer foul, and give to Him Who gave His Son to teach all mortals life could not end here, but man must be for all I know throughout His time, the same in spirit as when his breath he ceased to draw: living an entity close to the earth, in sight of woe, unless he mend, while there is time, his soul.

We carry here the man we were. Our longings, likes, some hatreds, as of yore. And I who wove my rhyme am he, the same, except for my soul's tears. To all who yearn to know if still man lives without his bones, I say, COMPLETE. He dies never. His ashes are the remnants of his suit. I have my whiskers still.

To those who love and read me still I would a tithe I could return of your heart's wealth who speak these words to save your love unblemished when as souls, ay spirits, ye come before the Lamp whose sacred incense if ye are will burn with love but His Divine, and rise on high where is His sacred, Holy, pure, Almighty hand, out of whose chalice ye were sent to praise His Holy Name.

SHAKESPEARE In Spirit

Through my treasured humble clairaudient, Sarah; the only medium through whom I, as spirit, have worked at words."

(Dictated by the spirit August 14th, 1919.)

Shakespeare's Revelations

BY SHAKESPEARE'S SPIRIT

(Three poems written through the Ouija Board, Dec. 19th, 1916,—in the space of one hour's time before breakfast,—I heard the voice on Dec. 22nd, same year . . and have not used the board since.) S. S.

I.   PEACE AFTER WAR.
II.   A sonnet: HEAVEN IS A PART OF LOVE etc.
III.   WAR NO MORE.

PEACE AFTER WAR

When wars have done and peace is come, and to a wounded
    world no longer torn
By cannonshell, or doubts or fears, there comes sweet rest, new
    born,
To solace hearts and make men see how traitorous their itching
    greed,
O What a World wherein to live, where each man shares his
    brother's need!

When useless wars and greed no more shall tear men's hearts
    or take their souls,
Then shall this world be heaven indeed, when men have steered
    clear of war's shoals,
And from a height where all obey the mandates of a King
    Supreme,
A Light shall shine to guide their ways, and make of life one
    long sweet dream!

When mortals see that life is given to bless by One Who knows
    no greed,

When mankind sees his lifetime spent in serving as his God
    decreed,
The poor, the halt, the blind, the lame, who need a brother's
    succoring hand,
O what a privilege to be born to serve his God on the earthland!
When all that live are gathered in, and all that serve are given
    place,

Where is no war nor murderous strife, and all must look
    into His face,
Then will men see the uselessness of serving gods of their own
    make,
And beg their Maker but to kneel,—the humblest place to let
them take.
            W. S. In spirit Through S. S. (The Ouija Board.)
    Dec. 19th, 1916.

            II. Sonnet: HEAVEN IS A PART OF LOVE etc.
    Heaven is a part of love which God has given
    To be forevermore the birthright of each soul,
    If they but choose to love, by love be driven,
    And claim their right to share in Love's great whole!
    Heaven is the place of love's existence:
    'Tis here, 'tis there,—wherever love may go!
    Its boundless shores so vast as mortal sense is,
    Increased abundance finds in spirit's glow!
    Then when thou reachest out to take thy blessing
    A God of Love in bounty doth provide,
    Be sure thy storehouse by great cubits measured
    Shall hold full all that thou canst scatter wide:
    For God's own love unfathomed as the sea is,—
    Unceasing as its everlasting tide.
            W. S. In spirit   Through S. S. (Written three
                days before hearing the voice, and with the
                Ouija Board.)   Dec. 19th, 1916.

III. WAR NO MORE.

War no more, oh gentle people!
Time has come for war to cease.
Go about your daily duties;
Time has come for peace! . . .

Drag the cannons home behind you;
Leave the gore-soaked fields;
Battles for all time are over;
Love, her sceptre wields.

Give the Nations all their freedom;
Take no toll of tears:
Leave behind all sordid feelings
Of war's wasted years!

Give the women back their firesides;
Give to men their work again.
Take the blasted crops and plant them,
With your monuments of pain.

Tell the children of their fathers
Who will not come back again!
Tell the widows of their heroes
Who were by war's cannon slain!

Give as heritage to Nations
All the memories foul and black;
Give their devastated cities
To the ones who want them back!

Take the orphans and uprear them:
Tell them what you think you can:
Then go forth, ye warring Nations,
And be brothers,—man to man.

> W. S. In spirit Through S. S. Dec. 19th, 1916.
> Written through the Ouija Board, three
> days before hearing the voice.

SAYINGS OF W. S. (In Spirit)

"Get your stick (pencil) and make me a poem."

"Writers and dogs with fleas have to scratch and make ends meet."

"Wily-nily is a poor master and a poorer hireling."

"Thought is a force; but who can force a thought?"

"A flower seldom blossoms either before or after its time."

"A toadstool makes poor shelter from the rain!"

"Scandal travels faster than light. But a poor woman's virtue assailed is a lightening stroke."

"Work is a blessing and idleness a curse. Yet who prays for the blessing and despises the curse."

"To hatch wings is given even to worms."

"A bee's honey every man can smack but only a poet reveres."

"The dove is a love-bird, and true; but its nest is invaded by the owl."

"A serpent is wisdom; and "wise as a serpent" oft said. Without legs it crawls on its belly, its weapon venomous and hidden in its head."

"Too much learning makes a dolt."

"Fortune and favour ruins more souls than poverty."

"Pigs and sows have no need of gloves."

"A man never wants anything he has defiled."

"If you give your soul to a man instead of giving it to God. he will knock it around like a cricket-ball."

"They (the soldiers) are marching quick time into the wilderness of heaven (so called)

        "Oh do not write this silly stuff—
        It all is Shakespeare's Bill.
        Just make it out and send it in,
        And pay it Shakespeare Will."

"A whore and a leech are related nearer than first cousins."

"Silence a woman and she is you enemy. Let her loquacious

tongue wag both ways and reprove her not, and, thinking herself admired she will be your friend."

"Poke a hornet's nest if you want to be stung."

"Letters of fire made no actress for me."

"To write a good play three things store away: food for thought, bits of plot, odds and ends of what not. Sort, and dabble in these whatever will please 'till the world calls it *rot*."

"Worship is of two kinds. Outward and inward."

"The lamb and the lion are in the spirit peaceable; but there are preying wolves seeking the unguarded both in spirit and earth planes. So beware, my lamb."

"The flowers of the kingdom are all in one bouquet. The humble ones have their virtue, and the beautiful ones their poison, sometimes."

"No bronze typifies the spirit. How do you account for this?"

"Jesus of Nazareth was the world's greatest medium. But He heard the voice of satan in the wilderness as well as His Father's voice. Evil and good abounds."

"So called "dying" does not *alter* anything, but separates rather."

"Much of my work (Shakespeare) should be burned and future generations purified thereby."

"Work no iniquity; for it is eternal."

"Spare, bear, and free thy spirit future care."

"To walk with the angles who aspires? To sit with mongrels, and feast, is man's aim on earth, as we see from the spirit-side."

"Told a thousand thousand times my faults to save mankind!"

"Sobriety is a blessing which endures, ay, past "the end"."

"Foisted on man's soul the crimes he has done his enemies."

"Revenge is sweet" men say. But where one meets his debt, he finds not one escapes vengeance."

"Mercy and charity are His only."

"To escape many have tried but none found possible."

"When a spirit finds himself naked he longs for raiment. This is awarded as his first blessing."

"If men would discover the soul let these seek aright. It will not be found at the dissecting college."

"Wherever man turns he looks God in the face, yet he sees Him not in himself until it is too late."

"A reviler and a tempter are the same; both spoilers."

"The courageous need no armor. A daring spirit is protected by Divine Justice."

"Criminals with stripes behind prison walls pay their penalties; but there is a prison without walls which is found by the spirit who has not paid and is guilty."

"When we become spirit we seek to elevate through our experience. To save others we come, since ourselves we did not save."

"Some puny puke would spue a plot or play
    To set the world agog? Ah well-a-day.
Where he must pass when he shall fare from earth,
    No plot or play will find him spirit berth."

"The man who thinks himself wise needs only to pass through the change (death) to find a fool's past staring him in the face."

"Woe unto him who "dies" satisfied with his soul."

"A sinner profiteth by God's mercy. But a pervert has lost God."

"Foiled is many a murderers dirk. But the one who stabs thee from behind has no claim."

"Equality is not possible to mortals. But in spirit all are poor: few have riches, and none are perfect."

"Society of one's equals is rarely possible unless through humility ones stature be shifted to include those who measure themselves up to the heights."

- "To plan is to conceive. To conceive is to create."

"Gems stud the rocks and beset the sky, yet none shineth so bright as a pure soul."

"The Master Mechanic draws no patterns and uses no screws. The bill and talons of a bird are His wonders, as well as the wings."

"Halos I have not seen. Beyond "the beyond" must be these.

"Softly as the night drops over all the soul emerges from its clay."

"Your many questions plied would fill the shelves of the world in bound volumes."

"Joy is enduring only which harms not another or thyself."

"Torture nothing. Pain is pain."

"Supply the thrill at the cost of God's light and you will know darkness deeper than woe."

"Esteem is like perfume. It permeates the world."

"Frankness is to be shunned where it causes a wound."

"Model your life after the Great Pattern. To be less is unlike."

"Change cometh to all stations in the future life. No man is what he thought himself, and nothing which was thought of him can alter the final estimate set on him."

"The future is just ahead. Today was yesterday. Tomorrow will soon be today."

"Paradise is the cow's pasture for some. If it only contains the stomach full, and they may browse eternally in clover!"

"Play is a good thing, but work is a better."

> "To steal a deer I played a prank,
> A thief was penned by history's crank:
> My boys held horses at my door,
> Yet was I writ a boy thus poor."

"Though Shakespeare wrote all that he wrote,

Nor Bacon stole, nor deer, nor goat,
He now speaks from a land remote,
And yet so near as this one's coat."

"Smoke without fire is impossible."

"Many a fagot has been used as a torch to bear a light to a benighted world."

"Fortune favors earth's men with shining metals and gems, which they cannot fetch along with them, and he only is rich whose misfortune hath profited him."

"Cold and heat, servitors of men, both enemies become, and monstrous cruel."

"Man's greatest blessing is forbearance of the Almighty God, who stays His hand."

"The lower the instinct the larger the debt."

"Yearning is of two kinds; earthly and heavenly. One keeps you down and the other uplifts."

"White is the color of saint's robes; but many a saint is without a saint's robe."

"Fairies are listening: beware!

"Will the world recognize the difference between the Jews and Gentiles when the world is but a market-place, devoid of Christianity?"

"To buy and sell the Jews will barter their souls. To get and have they are willing to."

"In the spirit there is no change but exchange; and this is no trade and no voluntary bargain."

"We in the spirit-world know no stocks, either security. All is variable and unstable."

"Where love is there is holiness: where is none, there is hell."

"Where worlds divide mortals care not. When they become spirit they may care less."

(This is for yourself only. W. S.)

"When the world awakens to the truth as spirits will inform them there will be no happier place than the earth."

"Life is difficult, it is true. But eternal life is more difficult still. So prepare for this now while you can do so. After the change you will have to serve as you profited by the preliminary course."

"Work for an object not alone earthly. Diversify your time with humorous story; but do not wake expecting to find a library of knowledge at your fingertips or before your eyes. Progression is the first law of spirit and service is the school."

"Copper is a base metal yet serves where gold could not."

"Refinement of taste and custom is due the wordlings who seek it in the hereafter; but where they shall find it I cannot say."

"No loopholes of escape is there after "death" sets the spirit free. You HAVE escaped. And the mystery is a mystery still."

"Go about your duties, nor pause for any trivial occurrence which would retard your growth. The wheel of Time is grinding your grist for Eternity."

"Fools only worry."

"Hang up your beaver and pay me the compliment of chatting awhile?"

"To dig for terse sentences is like taking in the last trump."

"We hear the ruffians and see them. "Dying" does not refine nor rarify to the utmost. Our sensibilities are keener but in constant association with the unlike (as near as I can make it understood to mortals.)

"We stand, we walk and oftimes rest as when on earth by a recumbent position. But we do not need "rest" of this kind. When our forces grow weak we draw on other forces, for there is no dynamo within the spirit out of the body."

"There are spirits which can be attracted by mortals and there are spirits which cannot be attracted by mortals. These latter are too high to serve on the earthplane (except it be the cloth) and walk with Him. At least we are told this. For they are not in our realm. Servants of the Lord then are these."

"Spirits unite in bands to perform feats and work wonders for mortal's eyes. But these are not intellectuals. And danger may follow after them."

"In my Father's house there are many mansions, yet have I seen but two."

"It is useless to rebel. There is a fate for each according to their works, and a Power behind all."

"Towards evening the eyes are heavy. So the spirit nearing the shore enjoys the buoyant rest."

"The first sight of the spirit newly arrived is of the old body over which it lingers. Then, spirits like himself bodiless which are near. Then, he is accompanied where there are only these, after which he is alone, for all he knows, for a long, long serious, repentent time, in which he realizes his mistakes and shortcoming—even failure. Then he is free, but unable to recall for the most part his trivial earth scenes, appaling as it is, his name even escapes him except he has cause to remember it, many tell me so at least, this has been true of them. For myself I can truly state that I never forgot for a moment how little I had accomplished with all my time given to play, which was work indeed, but not to be counted as fit to bless me. (Shakespeare.)

"When a man is a man he is proud, conceited, affected and vain. When this man comes to the spirit he loses his body, or rather leaves it behind him (for we lose nothing here) and fetches to be his for all time all the rest that he was. Survival after death, ay.

"To a spirit a man is a fortunate being making a fool of himself. But fooling no one else.

"We peep into the cranium to find the real soul."

"Fools let themselves out, poor souls!"

"Putty never staid a widow pain, nor kept out inclement torrents for this one."

"A path o'erstrewn with roses may lead to a thorny hill."

"Watching and waiting brought many a woman twins."

"Look out and look in or you will be in where you cannot look out."

"A chain of gold is a poor bond which binds many fast to the earth who should pass on."

"Liberty" all spirits know. But having it, few prize the same."

"To wreck a life beside your own makes your record a wrecker."

"Failures make the heavens accursed."

"Strumpets must strump at other pastime here."

"Soldiers and Sailors have their mates and leave the whores behind them, yet none of these will lose eternal life if they confess and repent in the body the sins of the body."

> "The stars shine nightly from His sky,
> The moon is lustrous, pale,—
> Yet what am I in God's own sky?
> A failure, if I fail."

"Across the hereafter many a man will find his signature attached to bonds which bind him down, nor purchase "Liberty."

"The pastime of spirits is wondering when mortals will care where they are bound."

"Fulsome and rich is the blessing for those who partake of the feast Invisible."

"Wrong is made right only through intercession of the injured. To return all spirits must who leave a debt unpaid."

"Eternal Justice is not blind, neither blindfolded."

"The scales of the soul are adding or subtracting every hour."

"Witches are earth's hellish spit-fires."

"No door is wider than your heart."

"God kissed her in her cradle (Bernhardt) and never left her after."

"Life is the cradle which holds the spirit babe."

"Hope is the distaff on which man's faith is held."

"Saving and spending,—history of a soul." ·

"Writing names of earth's departed now keeps the angel recorder occupied."

"Fools take their medecine here. When they come to find their past saviors of the heinous of earth."

"Spoil is man's idea of the hereafter. Otherwise he would think."

"Look up to the stars and you will have no idle misspent hours."

"Wandering brings many a spirit home."

"To be sprinkled with deceit is every heart's disfigurement."

"Watching the dog and making the cart push the nag saviors of mid-apish hours."

"Folding the skin of a hybred plant over the thumb never fooled a wizard."

"The past is a cloak; the present is a hood; but the future is a poor man's trunk which he finds sacked by himself."

"We have no better world than earth, nor any greater happiness than earth mortals share with the Great Giver of all."

"To speak of the wives of whoresons being happy is to speak truly. They live their lives utterly apart when the veil parts them."

"Invisible as the spirits to most are the thoughts of mankind usually, but there are these which read thoughts, surrounding every mortal. To them nothing is hidden."

"Fight the evils of life handicapped and alone, but best them a victor."

"Mere herrings are some souls. The more one tries to en-large them the smaller they shrink."

"Feed and fodder puts many a striving intellect out of house and home."

(Gilly, the baritone starving, a prisoner of war! . . TIMES. Oct. 16, 1917.)

"The singers must starve with the rest, Sarah. It is not sadder than for a Mother to starve with a babe at her breast. W. S."

"Though heaven itself be spangled o'er there is but one fair evening star!"

"Honors and trappings are vainglorious. Futile all earth's grandeur and decorations where honor means service in God's cause."

"Wash yourselves clean of crime and lusts of the flesh before departing, else you must bear the defilement of the body though you have none."

"Make a new beginning. It is not too late if you are a breathing thinking mortal.

"Chastisement sickens if often abused."

"Saws in my time, like these, never cut a poet's wreath."

"Flutes and frills never made royalty, neither crests nor handles. The mark of a gentleman is branded where eyes need not search."

"To fail is to be a failure. To succeed is to be saved."

"Let us press on!"

"Oh leave Thy footprints in the way that I may see which way to take!"

"They would rob me of my pin-feathers? My immortality's at stake!

"My scansion never halted where a word could fit it served."

"I do not care what this book says, in fact I do not here care at all."

"Never mind who wrote the plays if our primrose still lives in the windowbox."

"A plume is a feather, begorrah. How many have you for future wings now pinning?"

"Thou art a fool that pleases me."

"Thou art a bag of nuts and I am a cracker. To get what is in thee I have to work."

"Strange but true is said oft. Well, the strangest things are true in the spirit."

"The stars do not change their course when a sky-rocket bursts forth."

"The heavens look on our failures."

"Surely the wisest reflect Wisdom."

"Reach out your hand empty and carry all you can hold."

"See what the birds have done for man. And see what man does to them."

"A field-mouse may an enemy become."

"Stone a beggar and he will turn to stone."

"Lights are many; but His, undimmed, are undying."

"Prepare for the harvest when the seed is sown. Nature is speedier in her work than man."

"'Take no thought of tomorrow,'—but eternity will."

"Saviours are of various kinds: but One was Saviour of All."

"Sorrow no more shall victimize after this war ends."

"Myrmadons sift at will to work on high the CRUEL BENEFITS mortals later acredit to fate."

"The curtailment of ones powers is the stultifying of ones growth.

"A picture is not painted with one stroke."

"A master speaks to the multitude; and they follow."

"Even a flower, unfolds according to a plan under and high

above the earth. It leans on the Infinite more than mortals, and *I* cannot say if it is conscious of this or its God."

"Leaders are few. The crosses are too many and exactions great. If inspired they WILL lead, even through the sea. The sea will part for them." (The way will be opened.)

"The silence serves. It takes and gives."

"One who has been a beacon to so many will receive the light she deserves."

"Gooseberry of mine, it is for *me* to say if you shall be plucked or not."

"There is a chance in life that "death" will set you free. But there is no chance after "death" that LIFE will see me more than a prisoner." W. S.

"You cannot lead and follow at the same time."

"Chickabiddy, harvest the crop, and THEN thresh it!"

"Well fledgling how are you? Oh, you have a few plumes scattering but you are a gosling still.

"The arrow never shoots backward."

"A frog is your near relative according to the new religion. Then men are cannibals still, for they eat their brothers fried."

"Your lord a curdled custard is."

"Worry no more; when things have to be they are."

"Sin is age old and its face is always the same."

"If you destroy the fabric (of our dreams) of what shall the production be made?"

"She would sell her birthright to reproduce her monstrous self."

"To slip out of ones hide into the ether is to understand *something of the Almighty* at one blow."

"Sorrows are many of earth but the sorrows to which hidebound hieretics must come are much worse."

"Regents claim kingdoms. Well there are no kings in the spirit. The king here serves. And many land with packs (burdens) too heavy to lift."

"Even candy wears stripes?"

"Singlehanded and alone spirits fight their battles after "death" shows them how (*eternal life* shows them how. W. S.)

"There is a brief time when we realize we are in the body and going out too : this lasts a second maybe ten seconds. Rare souls (mortals) sometimes see a departing spirit. The core is the soul."

"Esoteric evolvement would compute eternity."

"They (Theosophists)are following a gleam of such infinite magnitude only the Infinite can grasp it or hold it after he caught it.

"To return, or rebirth in others forms is not possible since (if) the Creator evolved His own creations and made all subject to man and under his dominion (domination).

"His plan is all wise: and how perfect the life following (continuing) reveals."

"To smart under the lash is not wise. If driven by the All seeing All powerful Maker of worlds and systems trust is the element unfolding His secrets withheld from the wise but revealed to babes. But I am earth bound as I have often told, and impoverished.

"His secrets are His secrets still. To enrich the mind after the change we spirits wait upon Him."

"That there is a world within a world is true. But if souls are within souls I know not NOW (here).

"There is a following after strange gods here too. The occult has its adherents, as all gods followed in the body. My God was always the Creator but His wisdom was not sufficient for me. Thus am I here. for all I know for aye."

"Higher powers come through to serve earth-mortals.

"There is a change after "death" in all dogma. Mortals can only learn of this each for theirself."

"Children have little choice: and we have less." (Spirits)

"Smooth the napery and it glistens: but rub a cat the wrong way and the fur may fly."

"Stools were made for fools: and many fools are wise."

"Drugs and concoctions are nostrums of medicos and sooth-sayers. Harm is poison no matter how small the dose. Eyes cannot see what harm these work." "Shun poison, no matter what the form: and it is not all bottled, neither labelled" (as virus).

"Make no attempt to hide iniquity. All is revealed where nothing is hidden, or can be hidden."

"Miracles and wonders are common compared to a just man made perfect."

"Reach in as well as out, and save your soul from sinking."

"The light is God's perfection: yet who wonders at His power."

"Mind conceives and man perceives . . . yet is he deceived through his eyes.

"Barriers you may leap or vault at will, but thin partitions erected by the Great God still hide His harvest of spirits. At His will shall this be swept aside? (Make a question mark here. W. S.)

"The soul's filmy substance like the bride's veil, will stand the shock of eternal suffering; of such substance is it."

"Past belief are His plans for mortals who disobey the Laws."

"Fallen heroes never erected anything half so worth saving as their own souls. The murderers lot is hard in the hereafter."

"Should my own soul be saved through her who writes here-on I may push back the curtain for those who despised the justice they found waiting after the change. When we reach eternity there is no court of pleas: we stand convicted by our sins which stare us out of countenance; and with these on our backs we travel, if we can carry the load."

"The bridge of sighs is crossed ten thousand times by those who will never sight it."

"Folly and fun are sisters, twins maybe; still happiness is the gift of one and something more often akin to misery is left in the wake of the other."

"Angels having wings are as rare in the spirit world as on the plane where many an angel hovers without feathered airships."

"We move by volition . . . in spirite form. Will carries us no matter how far we may decide to journey. We usually travel in pairs; but some are hermits still. Crusty old batches make a poor showing where the moment one arrives he looks about for his dear, sometimes found, more often not found then."

"Chickabiddy make a chaplet and then be satisfied. No more then."

"Higher powers come through to serve earth mortals. There is a change after "death" (so called) in all dogma: mortals can only learn of this each for theirself. (Each mortal learns, must learn, this for himself, I said.)

"Where these higher powers come from, from whom they come, we do not know except what they tell us which may or may not be veritable truth, since we know where we are false spirits abound and continue false desiring no uplift and repentant of no thing which brought them out as they are.

"His plan is His as I see it. Be content in well doing. Their teaching (theosophical) responds to the upshooting grain of Almighty truth within desiring to know more of His plan. (Him) They work great good in so much as the soul (spirit) can be nothing but what life has made it (us) and turning the light inside the imperfect is found as well as that which is All perfect."

W. S. In spirit (Through S. S.)

Feb. 13th, '18, New Orleans, La.

"The heaviest clouds sometimes pass by."

"Many a vassal is greater than his master."

"Mediumship is not a burst of power but a gradual opening of closed doors. So be patient."

"The hand of Almighty God is the pendulum of universal Time."

"The milk of human kindness is mostly curdled."

"We serve who pay and you must pay who serve."

"Now is that in black and white? Can I think without my bones?"

Name The Book:

GEMS FROM THE SPIRIT WORLD

By W. S.

(Through S. S.)

GOD

The life behind all life, the governing power;
The pulse of every orb, and swinging sphere;
The Guardian, Keeper, Judge, yet more than all,
The Father of mankind—whom He holds dear.

SPIRIT

The man himself, with all his baser nature,
Freed from the flesh to find his heaven or hell:
His form the same, as every taste and longing,
But unconfined by mortal case, or shell.

LIFE

The spark Divine: the ray we know as spirit:
Undying as the God who gives and takes:
Part of Himself, though housed in poverty;
Enriching those with love the world forsakes.

MIND

Reflection of Himself, is mind, eternal:

And mirrored in each soul of all-mankind;
Undying thought, or will, in deed or purpose,—
The part that lives when clay is left behind!

OMNIPOTENCE
The One pervading ALL.

DEATH
The pall that covers all and all reveals.
The change that casts a worthless shell aside.
Of sleep the brother-twin, but knows all waking.
Death is the bridegroom surely,—life the bride!

PRAYER
Supplication of Divinity: God's intercession:
Upliftment of the spirit to His throne:
The sharing of our every earthly burden;
The merging of our spirits with His own.

HEAVEN
A place beyond the earth, or sight of woe:
A land of love, and happiness Supreme:
No longing; missing; haunting memories;
But all that mortals on the earth did dream.

LOVE
A meeting of two souls that mate as one:
The idol in the ideal perfected:
The past a blank which held these two apart;
The future? Time through which love shall be fed.

MOTHER
My own, a gentle, loving, happy heart,
Content if I but trudged on by her side:

An aching void, a hungering after her,
I've never met in all this country wide.

SALVATION

Reward of righteous living, God's salvation:
Unknown by many who were great on earth,
Who took no count of Life's eternal balance,
But hastened out in direst want, and dearth.

WOMAN

The last, most perfect work of the Almighty:
The equal of Himself in many ways.
The one gift that perfected His creation:
The only solace of man's earthly days.

SIN

Defiance of God's laws: a heathen state:
A robber of the rights of blessedness.
The golden calf which makes sin possible;
And lust, the curse of mortal's wretchedness.

WISDOM

God: Almighty Providence: Creator:
The Father of mankind; and Judge at last:
No lesser mind can share His understanding:
No one can see His plan, though breath has passed.

LIGHT

That, which at God's word appeared to bless
A world he wrought with His Almighty hand:
And ever since has blessed production, life,—
And still men doubt the world creation planned!

BLISS

Joy to the n.th. power raised.
Elation; boon success:
The honeyed, fleeting second:
The twin of happiness.

JOY

The birth of roseate dawn within the heart;
A heart that never dies when dies the clay:
Eternal is the attribute of joy;
Its memory "death" has never ta'en away.

WAR

One of the crimes a demon hath devised
To wrack men's souls in darkness when they "die"
With stained hands smeared by their brother's gore;
And souls like theirs in millions streaming by!

DUTY

The path of right though wearied by its call;
Consideration last of your desires:
A beacon to the consciences of men;
A holy light illuming with its fires.

IDOLS

The fleeting gods we fashion for ourselves,
And care not that they're made of earth and clay,
Until we find them dust within our hands,
Stained so that naught can wash the stain away!

FREEDOM

Unweighted and unchained, sovereign of act and will:
Unpinioned and unshackled liberty
Which answers to no law whoever made,
Knows no. master,—plans its own destiny.

HOME

A fireside where the loved ones sit;
A place of warmth and cheer and welcoming:
Abiding love surrounded by four walls,
And sheltered by an angel's snowy-wing.

HAPPINESS

The glow imparted by a dear ones nearness;
The lasting satisfaction known by some
Who have achieved ambitions fondly cherished;
But he who has served God, where I have come!

FAME

To live within the thoughts and minds of men;
To gain earth's plaudits, wreathed with immortelle;
To find no name, or aught it made on earth,
Can heal a sick soul's wounds, or make it well.

CREATION

The power of God to fashion through the spirit:
The power God gave to man to re-create:
The part within which claims Him Maker, Master,
Amazing genius. God-like gifts innate.

CHARITY

Perception, with unclouded vision
Through suffering and trials clarified:
The patience and forgiveness of the Master.
The kindness that through all has never died.

SAINTS

A saint on earth is one who knows God's laws,
Applies them to his living every hour.
A sainted one above I have not seen;

Their realms o'ertop mine own, as castle tower
O'erpinacles the sea,—
As clouds of heaven o'er a castle are!
As sun and moon above the Mother earth,
So we think on the saints, as some far distant star!

SUCCESS

The brand of fame or wealth, upon the earth,
Where men are gauged by what they count a name;
But in the land where men go hence from here,
'Tis what they take which holds no sting of shame.

FAILURE

The brand which carries sin upon its face:
The last sad rite which meets man at the end
Which sears his soul a lost one to his God,
And sends him hence to meet no cherished friend.

GAIN

That which endures through all of Time:
That which a man can take out to his God:
No earthly treasure which a man can horde,
But that which profits burial in the sod.

REDEMPTION

Payment of the tithe through prayer and sorrow:
The solving of God's law immutable:
Acceptance, while ye may, of Jesus' promise,
Or after "death" judgment inscrutable.

PRIDE

Ancestral heritage of honor, valorous deeds,
Which runs through generations of mankind:
A wordly element for most part left behind;
The humbled spirit has no pride, I find.

BEAUTY

Forms and tints expressed through love by Him
Who made all things that are;
The half of which man on the earth knows not,
But 'till he looks back on his life from far.

ART

The highest type expressed of men by God,
In all creations of the mind, or skill:
The wondrous power of rare perfection's will;
The power behind the seed within the sod.

FOES

Disgruntled jealousies, unwarranted, and undone:
The viper in the breast of warring men:
The lurking foe, who harms at last himself,
Mayhap will know no peace ever again.

A SOUL

That part of God in His own image made
Undying as all life of His great plan;
His mind, His thought, His love, His child, Himself,—
Inhabiting a temple God made, *man*.

DEMOCRACY

A land all free whose people rule themselves;
A Nation all united in one cause;
Consideration for the humble man;
A ruling by divine, not human laws.

MONARCHY

The rule of tyrranous and pompous great
Who have decended in their line to rule:
The condescending of the royal house
To reign, and lord it, o'er peasant, prince, and fool.

PEACE

The God-of-All come into all men's hearts,
To bless with love each one, ay, even as a brother:
The Infinite who rules supplying needs,
And all for which His own slay one another.

MERCY

'Tis said in Shakespeare's work, the whole of it;
Open the book and read, if you see fit.
But one thing still would I add to the page:
God's holiest attribute is lost unto this age.

FAITH

Hope's first aspiring, firm in trusting grown,
Unbounded faith becomes, God makes His own.

PROGRESS

Headway along God's chosen path however slow it seems;
Faith in the Lord to save, forgive, and wake from earthly
    dreams.

RELIGION

The cassock of a priest who mumbles prayers,
Embroidered o'er with gold enwrought with gems,
Is less (both wearer and his garb) in heaven's eyes,
Than some poor beggar who sin's current stems!

REMORSE

The pain of conscience which upsets the mind:
The pangs of spirit, soul; the part God saves
To be His own however soiled and worthless it has been:
The test of sin when men have passed their graves.

LAW

Precepts carved upon the stone at God's command:
Divine adjustment; weighed by God's own hand.

BONDS

The ties which bind true lovers here together;
The gold-certificate men sell their souls to own:
The chains men forge which weld them to the earth-plane,
Where everyone must reap what he has sown.

GHOSTS

The wraith of death men speak of sneeringly,—
Recalling in a joke its sight or name;
But when they find these ghosts are just as they,
They'll ponder long the way through which they came.

GHOSTS

The wraithlike form inhabiting man's clay,
Which men deride, except those who have seen:
The part God made which nevermore can "die,"
That being freed should be His own, and clean.

GLORY

Past thought of him who writes through this ones hand,—
The joy of King or Kingdom, or glory of God's land.

PURITY

Unsullied virtue, which but few possess,
Except while infants at their Mother's breasts,
Untrammeled by the lusts of mortal flesh,
Unlearned of the power of sin's requests.

MERCY

The quality of spirit in the mind
Which spares affliction's rod:
And leaves to Him all merciful and kind,
The punishment belonging but to God.

JUSTICE

The balance held within God's hand,
Firm, Mighty, Just, and True,
Which measures every thought, as well
As every deed you do.

VICE

The leper foul which rots the soul for aye,
And brands it with its burning, searing fire,
Until the spirit would not own its self—
But wishes for destruction's end entire.

ZEAL

The fire of purpose burning in the heart,—
Creation's elemental force, and sway:
By hope and faith 'tis fed, and moulds, with these,
The attributes no "death" can wipe away!

DEEDS

Each daily act, each hourly thought, which brings men to their
    own.
For which there is but justice wrought, where deeds must
    speak alone.

STARS

The same spheres we have seen at night alight, aswing, aglow,
We spirits see, as men of earth, and wonder WHEN we'll know.

WORDS

The language, or the tongue, by which men speak,—
The thoughts made audible, or plain;
The broken sounds of all intelligible,
Where spirits moan their past with all its pain.

WITCHES

Old crones who haunt with evil minds
Places of bad intent,
Whose hopes and wishes of all kinds
Are on disaster bent.
The soured and hateful of the world,
Where witches only go—
So mend your way,—THINK e're you SAY;
There ARE witches, you know.

BROTHERHOOD

The kinship of the nearest; of same sire.
The poorest of the earth can claim Him, his:
Then, are not all in loving bondage held,—
When one God, one Father, made each soul, His?

PROPHECY

Foretelling through the spirits help, events;
Revelation, more or less divine:
Calling on powers behind the veil of "death,"
As Jesus did when He took water and made wine.

VISIONS

The stone once rolled away, revealment then
To sight of scenes past mortal to conjure;
The truth few men can bear, as Jesus knew,
When He beheld alone God's divine power.

DREAMS

Imprints on the mind which passing strange
Lead men to wonder, oft to gasp and fear;
The web of fancy spun through sleeping hours;
The working of the witches, sometimes, here.

THE UNIVERSE

God's Word. His thought. His plan.
Created for those imaged forth as man;
Suspended by His will to be and move;
Out of His heart, a tribute of His love.

PRESENTIMENT

O'ershadowing doom reflected on the mind:
Predestination's wing, encircling the gloom,
Where reason holds a torch, the path to find.

ALCHEMY

The soluble dissolved by formula,
Producing by itself a compound force
Uniting by degrees the liquid parts
Of the unknown, and unsuspected source.

MYTH

Inventions of the mind, and solely this:
No god or goddess lore was ever true:
Of old, e're Shakespeare's time, invention ruled,
When greater men had nothing else to do.

PHILOSOPHY

Delving for truth for all self evident;
Making much of nothing, nothing gained;
Encircling a circle round and round,
Arriving at *wits end* unsoothed, and pained.

POETRY

Effusions of the elevated mind,
Which towers above all other human kind:
Related to the gods by a true claim,—
Though much, so called, misnomered by its name.

HUMANITY

River of souls fast hurrying whence they care not:
Freighted with care, uncompassed, and unmanned:
Dwarfed by the unrealty called "living,"—
Bridged by a span—uncertain, oft unspanned.

GRACE

The love of God: His smile: His words, "Well done:"
Reward of all who follow in the footsteps of His Son.

FRIEND

A savior: helper: honored, treasured, few:
A sacrifical saint, selfless, and true.

VICTORY

The status of the soul when the stone is rolled away:
The overcoming of all things for which a soul must pay.

WOES

Affliction's knawing tooth. Dregs of the Christly cup.
The bloodsweat of earth's men until with Him they sup.

VIRTUE

The unshamed, unsullied follower of God's laws
Hath virtue's cheek unblushed for sinful cause.

RIGHTEOUSNESS

The lamp God sets within the heart and hand
To guide His children through sin's barren land.

FELLOWSHIP

The right to sup with Him, and drink His cup:
The right to share His cross, divinely lifted up.

LOSS

A soul outcast who lived his life in vain;
Who, having all on earth, in spirit hath no gain.

HOLY

All His.

DARKNESS

The realm above the earth where spirits go
To pay the price for sins cherished below:
A dome (for all I know) without a ray,
Where sinners pay and *pay* and *pay* and *pay*.

PRAISE

Adoration of the just, and true;
The Light, the God within, whose praise is due
From every heart and lip, each flower and shrub as well:
The love of Him surpassing words to tell.

ETERNITY

Forever.   Unending Time.
That which was before all worlds,
Beyond the powers to grapple:
A secret His, sublime!

FOOLS

Ye at war.   As all who kill.
As as all who pass Him by.
The whoreson, thief, reviler, sot,
Or Shakespeare.   Fool, was I.

PARDON

Divine forgiveness after repentant years
Through which a spirit in remorse prays, pleads, with bitter
    tears.
When last they drink the final cup,
He sends His Son to lift them up.

GUILT

The unconfessed and stealthy crimes
Which to each spirit clings, and grimes
The soul, 'till all is washed away
Through One who died their guilt to pay.

CHILDREN

Offspring: offshoot from body, branch, or mind:
Her cub and his, no matter by whom planned;
And àll in All; which ye shall one day find.

ANGELS:

CHERUBIMS:

SERAPHS:

Supposed winged bodies in heaven's space.
Sharing the saint's abodes; no doubt His grace.
The one who writes has seen no angel wing,
Nor heard a single note that cherubs sing.

HELL

Remorse of conscience round but after "death."
(The change which changes, yet leaves sins the same)
And this is quite enough all spirits find,
Without a Lucifer, his brimstone, or his flame.

MEDIUMS

The instruments in tune with spirit.
A human's ears or eyes through suffering made keen
Above their kind, which spirits seek and seek to find.
Mouthpieces for the world unseen.

The gifted ones who suffer for His gift.
(Unless placed in their hands at birth)
The truest servants of the Lord on earth.

HEAVEN

Heaven is the place where Love exists.

CLOUDS

Obscurity.
Clouds roll on high above *my* head as yours;
In all their beauty, still I worship them
As part of God's own beauteous firmament;
Whose secret must endure until *no* end?

CHEER

Bubbles of life's wine, both felt and seen:
The quality of mind abhorring all that's lean.

TEMPTATION

Allurement of sin; and sinners enticing with a serpent's sting.
Whose fangs a soul o'erwhelms.

SOCIETY

Fools who are fooled by their own law's decree;
Outclasesd, outshone, outdone, their knighthood chivalry
By those who knew the Law and kept it too,
Where is no caste except God welcome you.

THEOSOPHISTS

The clan of mortals not content to be
Made like Himself by Him, throughout eternity;
But grasping by a chance a new fecundity
Spored through the spawn of their saner intellectuality.

PHYSICAL RESEARCH

Seekers of spirit's records. Sublime task.
A welcoming life-line thrown the "dead" at last.
Who seeks shall find. There's naught can stem the tide
Of helpers bound to help these from the spirit-side.

GAMESTERS

Souls playing with their lives eternal
While staking all upon the game of life.
Hounded by chance where is no game but losing,
Stoned by their conscience here they learn of strife.

MAGNETISM

A current flowing as doth flow a river:
Rising, ebbing, is this human-tide:
Where it is found no mortal should be homeless:
Where is its health, there spirits would abide.

SPIRIT-CONTROL

Humans as magnets are when is invasion.
No welcoming need be if these magnets true:
But such perfecting through the spirits teaching.
Must most assume before they will to do.

PERSONALITY

The pattern individual, unlost.
The type achieved and carried hence for aye.
The absolute unchanged, unchanging self:
No grave nor "dying" ever casts away.

LEGERDEMAIN

Stalwart humans posing as demi-gods
Performing supernatural feats through spirits aid
Aiming to fool the world of spirit-help
Are crass ingrates: facts bared should be here laid.

IGNORANCE

The blind all satisfied with their estate
Whose ears are closed to harmonies sublime.
Hellbound their spirits hold no wealth at last,
But suffer for their choice for their own crime.

CALVARY

The mount from which souls rise.

SORROW

All earth's shall drink of sorrow's cup:
'Twas this for which He died:
Though He was God's beloved Son,
Sorrow Him crucified.

COWARDS

All men who call not on His name, confessing before men
That Jesus died to save the world, through Christ, for God.

Amen.

WHY I AM HERE

(By Wm. Shakespeare in the spirit, through Sarah Taylor
Shatford. May 22nd, 1917.)

For years I searched for a medium through whom I could
speak and write. That I had an object in doing this will be
evident before I have finished writing this paper which will
go out to those who revere their Shakespeare still after cen-
turies of new writers have swept the horizon and added many

brilliant stellar lights to the o'ercanopied heaven of literature, ever varing and shifting as it does, to leave the first magnitude with their own through the ages.

As I say, I write for those who love their Shakespeare—meaning my written works, of course. (For there was nothing else of him to love I have found long since.)

I am here for a twofold purpose: to correct my work, which I long to do, and to pay for this service rendered by this medium, by helping her with her work, which is to help others. This will not benefit others more than myself and herself, and she has come to realize after months of suffering, there must be a plan behind it all. So there is: a greater plan than she realizes, or would believe, were I to tell her in words here. But I am telling her, as well as you, for the first time. For it is spirit's privilege to read the mind, and I often find the puzzling mystery bothering this one,—that she cannot understand it all, or very little of it, is certain. She knows why I am here, as I have told you, but she does not comprehend further the situation, as I have not told her, or permitted any one from the spirit to tell her, for reasons of my own. She loves me as I love her, for our mutual advancement through labor and service: as applied to all that is spiritual only, or of the thought world.

But there are other reasons why I am here,—and these I am telling her now.

You are the one chosen by me for my work, to better it, to undo in it that which was not pleasing in the sight of God when I went out with nothing to represent me but what I had thought and done while in life. I was told by the One who speaks for Him, that if I came back and undid my wrong, helped men to rise from their wicked impassioned selves to look to Him instead, to incite nobility of aim and the love of God instead of enflaming the lusts of the craven for the flesh, that when I had fulfilled this errand, and came again to His presence, my opportunity to rise would be bestowed, and I should rise and be forgiven at last.

When mortals pass to the unknown land expecting to find beauty and love and happiness and peace and justice and mercy, and avail themselves of the promises they have been taught were made to them for pardon, no matter what their crimes, it benefits them to experience the opposite, and all the reverse sensibilities keenly alert which establishes their purgatory, and their hell. For in the "beyond" (whatever word you think will express your idea you may use) there is no such thing as immediate joy, happiness, forgiveness, or cleanliness,—no more than one could step from one plane to another on the earth regenerate in the space of a second of time.

Repentance is gradual, if effective, and of the right kind, and so it is with regeneration. Man must outlive his past and become another man indeed before he can pass into a place of the unsullied and pure. Life after death is progression of spirit, growth of soul, striving after and attaining, higher thoughts, which better, with service, the inner part even of spirit. For it is possible for a low spirit to repent and become a high spirit in this way.

PREFACE

When we are alive and have sorrows and woes
We think our lives sad, and they are, heaven knows;
But when we pass out and have sorrows much worse
Than any we dreamed of, an eternal curse,
We look upon those who mourn on earth's way,
And wish we could change for their place in this day,
With a chance to go out but serving the God
Who in justice afflicts with an unsparing rod.
The one who writes here is but one who must pay
For the God he estranged through his profitless day.

When a spirit goes forth from his rude house of clay,
And sees his own self, which will not fade away,
Which he struggled to keep while on earth for the praise
Attending his works,—some sonnets and plays,—
Which were greater he knows than his soul must have been,
Since with God he's an outcast, despised of all men
For crimes of the flesh, though he loved but a man,
Whom he never shall meet, though he loves him, and can.

Did ye know as ye press to the near spirit-shore,
Your loves, acts, and deeds, must be yours evermore,
Would you pause, and fling passion's foul lusts all aside,
Preferring to worship your God nor deride
The ones who as Christians to you may seem slow,
Living, thinking of One who is High, and not low!

The first sight of heaven a lost soul can know,
Is yet to be glimpsed by this one, who's famed so
That his name is more writ on each page of the earth,
Than any mere man by a womb given birth.
The reason you know, but the pangs of his soul
No being can know—but a spirit not whole!
We may walk by the brook, hear its clear purling stream,
While its rivulet source we little may dream.
So the spirit returns to the earth it would leave,
Unknowing its God, or why it must grieve.
Shut out from His face in a place far remote,
This one saw his past, all the slush that he wrote,
As he loved but a man, and one of his kind,
Nor sought for a God, but his own lust and mind.
For time he knows not he spent to recall
His whole wasted life, as he strove to pay all:
When the warden then beckoned, and said to him, "Come;
Go back to the earth where you once made your home,

And work out salvation with heart, soul, and mind,
And see if a refuge with God then you'll find!"

Set free from the dark, I wandered once more,
To Stratford-on-Avon,—by dear Avon's shore:
Though I found that my name had become household word,
Not a friend I had known was there seen, or heard.
For Shakespeare immortal, was long Shakespeare dead,
Where worshippers gazed on the stone o'er his head.
So I tarried awhile, as long as I could,
And I roamed on the banks, and strolled through the wood,
Where the deer-stealer Shakespeare had once played his pranks,
And been cited a thief by historian cranks.

Well-well, he is here in America, now,—
And he likes it much better than he would allow;
When in England he heard of the new country found,
He set out to find it, and traverse its ground.
It is vast, it is fair, it is fine, it is sound:
And with "Shakespeare" 'tis woven and garlanded 'round.
For they reverence on earth, what a God will not see:
The rapturous love in the poor soul of *me*.

Yes, I came and saw all; then, searched for the one
Through whom such a marvellous thing could be done,
As to remake my soul, and re-write what I wrote,
With its putrient lines cut to make a sweet note
Which would praise the Great Mind of the God I adore,
Whom I serve as I write, and would serve, evermore.

To the one who writes this, then, I came in the dark,
Where a circle was formed to welcome the spark
Of the spirits returned to the earthplane to serve
As helpers, inspirers,—to round, plane, or curve
Their mortal attempts, as it were, then to swerve
Their minds and decisions, their motives and aim:

Who sit in the dark, these receive all they claim.
My good fortune was hers, (though she may not agree)
For she had not a choice, she was *the* one for me.
For of all in the circles that welcomed the "dead,"
I had never seen one I would lead, by whom I'd be led.
How this one came there is her own story then,
Should she care to reveal it, herself, to earth's men.
I followed her home, and found all by her side
A man needs to find, e'en to spirit allied.
Her work, and her life, can be searched by all men,
And her like they"ll not find in one body again.
Her book was first finished, and published complete,
Before my own task had been set on its feet;
And I want to say here that for two years and more,
This one just wrote on, as she had long before,
Not knowing that I was about, or around,
Except that her "poems were finer," she found.
When first she was able to hear spirit-voice,
There was more than herself had cause to rejoice;
Or the words she writes here would be not writ for men.
Shakespeare searched "seances" again, and again!
Had she not rebelled in development, then,
She might see me here as I write with her pen!
But two doctors, two nurses, and most of her kin,
Cannot take from a mortal the spirit within.
Hence she writes, and shall write, 'till I finish my task,
When no more shall she do, and no more will God ask!

Here I bid her to take for the sake of my soul,
The spirit of Shakespeare, who comes to make whole
The task left unfinished,—the book of my heart,
While immortal with men, has of God not a part.—
And rewrite, as I speak the words she shall hear,
The lines I would alter, the credit make clear,—

While I work through her hearing, the mind is my own,
And all words I command her, are Shakespeare's alone.
To prove her all worthy, all fit, and all kind,
I tell you again, she is my lucky find!

Apr. 22nd, '17.

I AM HE WHO WROTE

How shall the spirits prove they live,
If none here care to hear or see?
This is the problem of our world;
The first then to be solved by me.

Take aught I wrote and make a heap,
And set to it a faggot light;
For all I wrote, or said, or did,
Can not adjust the balance right.

I wrote, 'tis true, some sonnets, plays,
To make a living, pass the time
In merriment or jest and glee—
I turned out many a ribald rhyme.

Now how shall I who wrote for this
Fill up the scales, or ope men's eyes
To facts of living after "death,"
Or help them find a Paradise.

But one way opened here to me,
To readjust my life with men:
To search the world of mediums,
That one of these might be my pen.

I have not told how long I sought.
This is not known even by me.
The place from whence I came to plea
Records not time, but misery.

You marvel then at my poor verse,
Who wrote grandiloquence in play:
I strive who write to make this *plain*:
Nor care for simile today.

You wonder how a man could be
Content with facts related here:
Well, did you come through hell for this,
To know *one* glad and kind and dear

Who would take up your task and write
Nor care, except her part well done
She could pass on, as soon must I,
Recording for God and His Son

All that I failed in life to do;
(Although I thought my part well played)
You would agree to cross the sea
In search of her, with whom I made

No contract, and no papers writ,
But tested, labored, day by day
That some true system might be found
Through her, to brush the veil away

As I am he who wrote my verse,
My dramas, sonnets, quibbles, rhyme,
I'm Shakespeare still,—Dear England's bard,—
Alas, must be, throughout God's time.

But give the one who writes for me
The ear she gives me to indite,
And save your souls from darkness' realm,
Where Godless ones sit through their night.

W. S. In spirit (Through S. S.)

(Go on. We can name this one after it is born. For a change.
     To give the world a message then   W. S.)
No earth mortal could give:
To help them through Eternity's
Forever still to live:
This is the reason why I came
A miracle to work
To banish crime against themselves
Which hidden, still doth lurk
Within the hearts and lives of men
Who travel earth's short road
Which ends in God's eternity
Where each bears his own load
Throughout all time until he gives
To Him the payment due:
Thus came I to the earth for souls
To rescue, warn them too.
Then, I have come to prove the truth
God's spirit lives; nor "dies";
And that the "dead" walk on the earth,
Nor stop "beyond the skies."
To do my work is all I hope:
Nor praise nor comment care,
Since spirit knows but valueless
Earth's plaudits where we fare.
To pay and pay and pay and pay
And then to pay, my due
To the Great God who saves us all,—
This must I do through you.
The reasons then why I came back
May be yours too one day,
If in your heedless, Godlessness
You end your mortal stay.   W. S. In spirit
Call this one THE REASON WHY.   W. S.

THERE IS NO DEATH

(To those who say Good-bye: From the immortal Shakespeare.)

Men halt and say their own have "died,"
And lay them down within the sod
Commending that their soul may rest
And live on high at peace with God.
But when they find they have not "died,"
And they live on without their clay,
And in that wonderment divine
The spirit naught can take away,
Astonishment no mortal kens,
Chagrin they wish they might unload,
As well as weights they never guessed
Must be companions on the road
Where spirits seek one friend to find—
Or one whom they have known of yore,
To help them lift the weight they bear   .
On to that land of Evermore.

As mortals pass to the unknown,
And reap whatever they have sown,
And find but what they fetch along,
Right, if it be, else all the wrong—
They lift a face to greet the sky
Unknown of men until they "die,"
Where never one whom they have known
Awaits to greet them as their own;
But wandering ever, ever on,
They seek the Light—and pray for dawn.

           W. S. In spirit Through S. S.

Fearless we search the earth on pleasure bent,
Nor worry for our lives beyond the sky,
If we have all that mortal flesh can crave,
And all the coffers of the world can buy.

We gorge, and feast, and deck in rich array
Our bodies, for the most part foul, depraved in lust,—
While to the ones less fortunate than we
We scarce have time, nor think, to fling a crust.
There comes a time when but a zephyr-breath
Doth close the portal which was open wide.
Astonished we look in the face of death—
And realize we live,—though we have "died"!
What meets the view,—what meets the mind "alive,—"
And keener than it ever was of yore,—
When spirit knows there is no grave, no death,
But all is life, and life forevermore?

What words of mine, though I immortal be,—
Among the illustrious earth's, my words to men,—
Can to the world express my own chagrin
That I must live, and do my work again.
Undoing all my past, as God would bid;
Undoing all the crime that once I did:
Not anything from God, who would be rid
Of all who break His holy nature-laws,
And all who serve another god than He:
And thus I write, no knight immortalized,
Nor yet from bondage for my earth-crimes free.

Take these, my words, and treasure as God's own,
The truth of spirit-power here worked by me;
And may I win His pardon and His grace,
If ONE I save, from what I used to be!
Bemoan no fate that sends you hence in rags,—
Impoverishment of one kind or another,—
Where souls are vagrants, homeless,—such are poor,—
This poverty is there,—where is no other.
My own poor soul, a wanderer, here writes this:
Your Shakespeare whom a world mouths and adores;

Immortal in the land where once he lived,
An outcast from Great God's eternal shores!
(Please sign my full name to this.)
William Shakespeare In spirit (Through S. S.)

DIVINE HISTORY

Rewrite the Scriptures, blot out every word
Our Father spoke through Him, all that He heard
His Father say, the visions sent He saw;
Abstract the words He heard which make the written Law:
Snatch then the prophecies there writ entire:
Blot out the wraithlike chariot, words of fire,
And pay no heed to what the Spirit's done
Proclaiming He would send the world His Son:
Then show to doubting mortals what is left
When Scripture is of spirit all bereft.
Say can they find aught that their souls can save,
But through the spirits Holy Spirit gave?

Mark then the grave no barrier or tomb,
But for the living dead here, now, make room.
Reach out one poor, impoverished, pauper's hand
And ring the curtain up on Spiritland.
                    W. S. In spirit (Through S. S.)

THE TRUTH REGARDING THE TRUTH

No lives continue in this world of men.
  This truth is known by all who breathe a breath.
Yet do they see no reason they should care
If there be life beyond the change called "death"?
  No harpies have come forth in swarms like bees,—
A "crazy" one, so termed, has seen a "ghost,"
Or eyes near death have seemed to have revealed
A dear one, or some angel at the most.

But those who claim to speak with, see, the "dead,"
 Are charlatans, impostors, something more,—
For why should one and not another have
Such privilege to see beyond this life the spirit-core?

The truth is few here care to see their own,   ·
Or speak with them, or know if they do live.
Else would THEY speak to THEM; the law is such
No spirit shall intrude, or mortal give
Affright that should his reasoning unhinge.
Though they may give a chill, a tap, or touch,
A rap, a light, or last a spirit-twinge.
When mortals *care* to know if life ends here,
Or if their own have message past the' sod,
Will they begin to seek where seekers find,
And know the truth: the spirit is of God.

                              W. S. In spirit Through S. S.

A MESSAGE TO THE WEARY WORLD

I long to give a message to the weary struggling world!
The world that bleeds all wounded by its war!
I fain would bear a candle where the faintest rays unfurled
Would carry some faint hope from lands afar!
What can life hold of promise to men's children yet-to-be,
If some light across the present is not shed,—
What cause have generations in their fight but to be free,
Unless it be to live until they're "dead"?

O wake from dormant Christlessness, and think of time to be,
When battling for soul-freedom 'yond the sky,
Where the purposes of being was but life's eternity,
And the saving of the soul which cannot die!
Could I speak across the chasm 'tween the spirit-world and this,
Through the mouthpiece of the writer of this screed,

Would I sound a warning clarion that a love of mortal bliss,
Shall make a soul a beggar in great need!
   (Please, write my full name.)
William Shakespeare In spirit
(Through Sarah Shatford)

ACROSS THE BORDER

Wake from your sleep, oh world, and give
The waking dead proof that YOU live.
Awake their hopes at least ye see
God's plan IS His eternity.
SPEAK! Give your "dead" awake and here
A chance to prove there is no bier
Can fold the form the clay encased,
And naught of mind has "death" erased.
The "dead" stand here, the so called "dead",
But living as to heart and head,
And long that you may hear and see
The spirit's immortality.
Across the border, but a wave!
A line, marked by a tomb or grave!
We stand, an army, straining eyes
For merest chance to make you wise;
While ye but mourn our passed out breath
And separation; yea, our "death."

W. S. In spirit Through S. S.

TO CRITICS OF MY PEN

We work for no applause who write these lines,—
We write but for God's cause who write these lines.
To those who sit in high estate,
And pick their flaws, we must relate
The reason why we write these lines.

There is no high, nor low, estate,
Which gives to man a man for mate.
To those who worship nature's god,
Thinking that God will spare the rod,
Or that life ends with their grave-sod,—
For these, and all—I write these lines.

My pen at last has then confessed
To worship God is right and best:
To see themselves at last undone,
Must every pervert.　Every one.
　　　　William Shakespeare In spirit (Through S. S.)

To lift the veil and view the hidden mysteries,—
To tempt the ones departed to tell all,—
No matter if in doing so they suffer
For breaking laws (as once did Adam fall)
For in the life where mysteries are hidden,
As those the world could neither see, nor bear,
There is a law,—to keep which we are bidden,
And all who break this law must repay, there.

But I am on my way here from perdition,
To save all mortals such a fate as mine;
If I can rend the veil, by which is hidden
The mystery of laws men think divine,
I speak with no uncertain claim, or vision,
I claim no reparation for my crime;
I only ask to hear a spirit's version
Of Paradise, which mortals think sublime.

ALL WORLDS ARE ONE; AND THERE IS NO DIVISION:
No hell but that you take; no heaven I see:
Unless it be the fruitless search through æons,
For all the dear of earth who used to be.

When I came out to search for all I cherish,
And found not one who was in search of me,
I thought to find them ever on some highway,
And so it came about I crossed the sea.
But on and on my weary spirit traveled,—
Nor ever any place I found 'till now:
In losing all my memory had garnered,
There was no peace for this one, I can vow.
I've searched through every sphere where spirits travel,—
I've come to know all men must search as I,
Unless they've passed with all their sins forgiven,
And are God's own, and say so, e're they "die."
I've come to know still more I would impart here,
To help along the wretched ones of earth:
To give a hand while yet a hand may save them;
To tell them, then, what constitutes new-birth.

For every sin the mortal flesh hath cherished,
That mortal's soul is chained through years of time;
To the same sin forever is he welded
Anear his past, and one with the earth clime.
He may go out a sinful, fettered spirit,—
He will remain this fettered spirit still:
And naught I know shall lighten up the burden,—
Until of sin and crime he has his fill.

No spirit welches forth from hell to heaven;
No God awaited this poor soul of mine
With pardon interdicted or instated
My craven form as part of Him divine!
No angels came to help me lift my burden;
Or brother soul e'er lifted on the way;
I saw myself, and how I came to forfeit
For blackness of the night, God's perfect day.

I hailed no soul—or begged no pittance from them;
Each spirit knows at last what "dying" means:
And every soul its own cross shoulders bravely,
With every lacking towards his God he leans.

At first we pass a number on the highway
Who roister with their kind in revelry;
But soon we turn our backs too pained to view these,
Nor evermore desire their kind to see.
Our tasks you vain would ask, what are they?
To help those in the world from whence we came.
In helping whom, we know, is some true balance,
Which weighs for us someplace with our own name.
We know that in the past no balance varied
Which meted out to us the woe we've known:
And trusting this same Judge, who varies never,
We trust, all hopeless, still, to reach our own.

This is the hell to which I then referred:
From which all living, would that I could spare:
This is the true state of the worldly's heaven;
A spirit in a world of worldly care.

There is no veil, except the mortal vision!
Which naught can rend, for most, excepting "death".
To know what I have told from spirit's prison,
Most mortals must give up their mortal breath.

May 26th, '17.

TO A POET WHO COULD NOT DIE:

The world crowned with laurels a poet divine,
Who had tasted of poverty's cup.
The crown bestowed title, and honors, and such,
And the poet with these oft did sup.
But the end came for him in the midst of his prime,

When from care and all want he was free,
And he passed to a realm to be scorned of the God
Who rejects all such sinners as he.
He could not go on,—he could only come back
Where the earthbound must suffer and live,
As they work out for others their problems they pay
For all they refused God to give.
O the horror of such is too much to be said.
How many poor souls wish that "dying" meant dead!

THE POET'S FAREWELL

When the world has defamed and expunged you for naught.
But the same which they do, day by day,—
And you've gone to a land that's no better than this,
And not half so good, in a way—
May you never return to work for no pay,
Or endeavor to plan past His own,
Else YOU may be weary and sad, just as I, ..
When you must go on, and go home!

There's nothing of earth could tempt me to stay,—
There's nothing more here I can do:
So this is the end of your greatness, and love,
For I go—and I'm glad to leave you.
You have done what you could,—you could not do more:
And for this I withhold further blame:
But the day that you call, will I be at your side,
And respond with my own famous name!

You cannot go far, and neither can I,
Apart from each other, nor roam,
Where one will not wish for the other, I ween,—
And carry that final wish Home!

                    W. S. In spirit (Through S. S.)
"This is in punishment for not obeying the voice which asks
you to "string," to keep in touch. W. S.   July 10th, '17·

TO ONE IN A TOMB:

There is a grave where Shakespeare lies
All sealed and kept in state,
Where no one dares to move his bones,
And no one cares of late,
To rob his dust or make him great,
Entombing him with kings;
For he is now long turned to dust!
Not so. For still he sings,
And opens to a loving heart
The way to find her God,
Who bears a cross in her sad life,
Afflicted by the rod,
But who shall mount on wings of grace
When I have left her here,
To think of all she might have done
To make the path more clear
For him who took her from a place
He found her seeking one
To tell her of the spirit-world
When this old life is done.
He took her, glad and satisfied,
To help her on her way,—
And must have been a helper too,
From then until this day.
And all he ever asked of her
Was that she string for him
That she might keep in touch and hear,
Her hearing not grow dim.
Now we will write no more of this
Since she has strung for me;

And I am that same Shakespeare, boys,
That lies across the sea.
W. S. In spirit (Through S. S.)

Note: "An exercise" praticed before writing, a tuning-up,
as it were, before writing. W. S.)

THE POEMS OF A BARD

When the world recognized poor Will Shakespeare,
(And folk, I am poor Shakespeare still),
Overjoyed was one bard in creation,
Who set to and worked with a will
To make a few dramas and sonnets,
(Which the world, I see, still recommends)
I lived for my Art and its purpose,
And treasured my Art and its friends.

The Power which is divine afflatus,
And without which no poet could write,
I never kneeled down to, or worshiped,
Until I passed out, in the night!

If poets are God's own creation,
(And they are; which is known by all here)
Oh, should they re-write half their measures,
Uniting His worship, and fear.
The greater the bard, so his blessing,—
The greater his task then should be:
To write for the God of creation,
Is the purpose this God has set me.

Oh, make up your minds e're the finish,
The Artist of Artists will scan
The lines you have written, the crimes you have done—
While you traversed earth's planet as man.

TO SET THE WORLD RIGHT

To set the world right and make snivelers agree
As to who wrote Shakespeare, if 'twere BACON or He,
Or Marlowe or Pitt or the scribes ages old,
I must tell, says this scribe through whom I indite,
To settle for aye then this subject, I write:

When a man among kings (I was knighted by one)
Where a handle or wheel makes a favourite son
Distinguished through time for something's he's done,
For a knight in my day must his laurels have won.
With a band of king's players by Bill Shakespeare led,
I played many roles, e'en recalled the dead
To piece out my plot or to string out my rhyme,
Nor considered it theft; more an honor that time,
To borrow a plot for a queen or a king,
And watch their amuse as my poor muse would sing.
So each time when I needed a plot or a play
I searched o'er the tomes where musty plots lay
Bulging out with ideas from cranium's dust,
Whose shades may have helped as I now know, and trust.
But that any one man made a plot or a play,
Or was such singled out as a ruse for my pay,
I deny in fac toto in spirit this day.
Should any man's play be found as my work,
Which was not by me writ, 'tis a publisher's quirk;
Which one day I'll acclaim; for I mean to read all
As signed with my name.

There are glories so great past an immortal name,
And riches apast all earth's honor and fame,—
Should you weary as I in the land where I came
You will find immortality NOT IN A NAME.

William Shakespeare In spirit (Through S. S.)

Fourteen summers have passed since I saw England.
These have I counted on my two hands.
Lest you should think I have no hands
Being Shakespeare's shade, then let me say
I have the SAME hands which were mine,
Even those hands defects. And would ye doubt
That I am here as when on earth my digits
Wove their own spelled rhyme
And laid the plot wherefore my book remains today,
Then will I say who wrote that same
The world has never changed, the moon's the same,
And the same stars swing in their same wheels:
Nor more changed am I.

When mortals walk this earth nor care to know
Where theirs have gone, or they shall go,
When incomplete their span of life
Each lays him in a grave, nor cares what else may be—
'Tis time to wake these from their poisoned dream,
That God may find His sons, and their esteem.
When virtue has no claim nor honor sense,
And out of each man's egotistic mind
He makes His laws supreme,
Having no thought for duty or its name—
The world needs purging, and its suffering souls
Restored, made whole again.

To lands where all must fare from this
And each must answer to the call
Which gives him rest and union sweet,
Or, cast where are his kind who fall,
Who fail, nor give their God His due,
Who reap "beyond" what they have sown,
All fare today in flesh and bone.
"Who cares!" they cry: "What do we know

Regarding God, or His intent!"
And thus they plunge in recklessness
Upon their ruin madly bent.
"Who cares? Not I:" the saved ones say:
"For I have claimed for Him my soul."
And thus the world on pleasure bent
Must reap the harvest, pay the toll.

Then I care, if no other cares,
(And MANY CARE, but cannot save)
And from my own experience
I came to warn them past the grave.
I come to speak through her I write
Words true as God's purpose is true
When He saves from our wrecked selves
A soul to profit, work, and do
That part He set when on Time's dial
He measured out the day and night
And in His sky hung out the stars,
And by His word brought forth the light.
And by my lost and wasted time
The world shall profit to a man
If aught a spirit here *can* do,
That part I'll do as do I can!

Think not to profit by decease,
Nor meet a waiting Paradise,
If you have spun some simple rhyme,
And cannot look God in the eyes.
Your task is done at last you "die,"
Your chance is lost, perhaps your soul,
Even to those who give Him half
Must they return half to make whole.
Where God is naught is incomplete.

Then shall man fritter life away
And come at last and bring Him nought,
And nought required for him to pay?
Go to! The making of yourselves
The Maker leaves within your hands,
When He reclaims His light He gave,
And ye are called to spiritlands
Ye shall bring ALL, and all must COUNT,
—And naught is hidden let me say—
The part ye bring rests then with YOU,
Or if ye suffer or must pay.
"Recall the dead? What good are *they!*
The dead are dead." (At least men say)
But I say here there's no such thing.
The dead walk, see, hear, laugh, and sing!
In fact there is no difference, nay,
Except the *case* has slipped away.

Then write my words, and make them plain.
For I must speak and save souls pain.
And I must travel, lecture, write,
To save earth's men dark past earth's night,
Where souls recover their lost sense,
And make amends and recompense
To God their Maker, not *themselves,*
Till conscience wakes and overwhelms.
Make no mistake I write who paid.
No pervert's gift was ever laid
Down at the feet of Him who died
Sinners to save, ay, crucified.
Nor mine was laid, nor near Him came;
Nor came He when I called His name.
Where eons passed I sat to think
How meagre fame I write in ink.

Immortal son I did not know
Proclaimed was I on earth below.
Nor care I now what men acclaim,
But what I write in Jesus' name.
My thought is mine, my words the same,
The hand is *hers* whom I acclaim
The first that ever wrote for me
Since mine own wrote, or I set free
To serve the God I FAILED to serve
When as a man I did permit
Base passion my best self to swerve.
When here I came for purpose writ ..
Much had I first to teach and take,
(Which would to heaven I could replace,
Except, I write for Jesus' sake)
To blot, and mould, string, and remake,
Attune to harmony complete,—
Before I set this task about
Was HER TASK then but all replete.
Thus have I waited, tended, toiled,
With more than pen here could be writ,
Before mine instrument was fit.

May I digress to speak her worth,
And claim her greatest on the earth,
That ever for a spirit "strung,"
Or walked the earth's unseen among?
Her willingness to serve is great,
(Prime requisite in our estate)
Her sense of justice high· and fine:
In gentleness I claim her mine.
While from a heart both great and good
Shall Shakespeare's words speak what they would!
O men who read with jeer and smirk

The miracle I herewith work,
What will YE give when ye have passed
To work ONE such, from first to last!
Make light of souls and sin and God,
Remould His statutes, break His laws,
And search for other primal cause,—
Insult Him, mock Him, and devise
Schemes for yourselves, ignore His wise
And just and Mighty plans:
But know your souls rest in His hands.
Your soul, your spirit, ay, the same,
No matter how you spell its name,
That thing am I, unseen but heard
By her who writes my very word.

Halt! Pause before it is too late!
There IS a heaven, a judgment Gate.
There is a hell where souls ablaze
Sit in the dark all in amaze
At what they find themselves at last
The clay is gone which held them fast.
There is a God O men of earth,
Ye soon must learn through spirit-birth.
A Judge who judges, weighs, and finds
The gold or dross of mortal's minds.
There is adjustment through His laws
Where spirit finds effect through cause.
Where senses more than earth—alert
Receive their wound, nor heal its hurt.
How shall I speak that ye may see
It is my soul which speaks to thee!

Thou art awearied of God's plan
That gave a span-of-life to man
And takes again but that He gave,

When he becomes dust in the grave?
Ye are a fool He hath made wise,
Who seeks some far-off Paradise,
And claims a right to share therein
To bring along a sinner's sin?
Or, wiser than the Maker thou,
Hast been fooled throughout time 'till now?
A newer God now have ye found,
Who spares no soul when 'neath a mound,
The final dust is laid away?
Your "God is nature," so you say?
Alas what fools hath nature made!
Whose god includes no soul, nor shade.
When God breathed into Adam breath,
He gave a soul that knows no death.
When from his side He took a bone,
And fashioned woman for his own,
Completing in the twain called one
His world and work which He had done,
And gave it all, and last His Son,
Because He loved the world He made,
Dost think He COULD not make a shade?
When Jesus rose and was the same,
—Which was foretold before He came—
And held aloft His martyr hands
Before He came to spirit lands,
Was this a fable, or untrue?.
Or does that Jesus interest you?

The Word, then, Holy Spirit wrote,
As history is it remote?
Nor care ye not it is replete
With sinner's record of defeat?
Or care ye not for aught BUT earth,

And what ye measure as to girth.
One of these answer. What think you?
Are YOU a traitor—Judas too?
Think ye on earth to worship bliss
And to betray Him with a kiss,
When ye pass out beyond your frame,
To work a wonder in His name?

What DO ye think. Ye will not speak!
But walking in His footsteps, meek
As walk the lowliest of earth,
I speak for you from spirit-birth.
Proclaim to you my sinner's past.
The chain I forged which bound me fast.
Such chords men weave their lives about,
Then wonder why God shuts them out!
You cannot see the future then
Until the spirits speak to men
To rouse them from eternal woe
Where headstrong all seem bound to go.

When it was given me to state
How I would serve in my estate,
I chose to use my past to mend
The souls who would not God attend,
But, as mine own should pay and pay
In darkness, lacking One bright ray!
Do I then come at the behest
Of Him I serve to do my best
That I might save from woe like mine
Such sinners for the God Divine.
To pay as you of earth shall pay—
For every crime you store away
Which you think hidden, sunken deep
While of its benefit you reap,—

To give no part of God's to God,
And think not of chastisement's rod,
The while you make gods pleasing you,
Sufficing all you care, or do,
And shuffling off the mortal coil,"
Go out impoverished with moil!
To pray no prayer and give no praise
To Him who giveth all your days,
And all His gifts none else could give,
To bless through time as Time shall live,—
To find no path His word has left
For souls benighted or bereft,—
To look up to His winged things
And hear no song but nature sings,—
To spare no time and have no thought,
For Him whose blood your souls hath bought,—
To give no care nor care to give
To this soul then that it may live
That last some part ye may repay
By following in His Divine way!
As spirit, then, what can I bring,
What warning from my lips can ring.
Adown the ages from my pen
O would I speak to mortal men.
Confessing how my crime of earth
But claimed me here of sinner's worth.
No friend I found awaiting me,—
Nor loved ones ever can I see,—
(For all I know this day I write
My future must know spirit-blight)
And all the past which men acclaim
Writ fairly o'er with Shakespeare's name,
Means naught but pain at last I see

Where He who gave such wealth to me
But writ my name where failures be.

Can ought I write, or do, atone,
Where Jesus claims souls as His own.
Or ought I say save others here
A fate like England's poor Shakespeare.

Men, there is God who made you man:
Then be content with His own plan.
His way and all He made is good:
And must as His be understood.
No vice, nor adding to His way
Shall bring you with no debt to pay.
But all must be as His intent—
If following where the Master went,
Ye pay your everlasting due,
Ye'll find no charge awaiting you.
Be calm. And sane. And forfeit lust.

No soul can die with crumbling dust.
When ye go hence beyond earth's sphere,
Recall, man-lovers, poor Shakespeare.
                Wm. Shakespeare In spirit (Through S. S.)

FOUND

I who write here came here to find
An instrument for Shakespeare's mind.
To write my plays I did intend,
Their scurrility amend.
To take each line and blot for aye
The work for which I here shall pay
Before another plane shall see
My soul befouled, or I can be
Uplifted where my own went on
When life for them meant truly dawn!

To do this task then I must find
A mortal having spirits' mind.
Then must she be allotted me,
Before such harvest garnered be.

Through time I cannot count, or know,
I searched here, ay, high and low,
To learn where sat the instrument
Who could and would serve my intent.
Four years have passed since this one found
Her purposes while on the ground
Would be to answer when I spoke,
Nor any plea of mine revoke.
She knew me not while I knew her,
And all her life-pulse e'er could stir:
She wrote her poems writ by me,
Nor dreamed one there she could not see.
Till all was finished, books complete,
I claimed no throne but just a seat
Where daily spirit-food was spread
By Shakespeare, whom all men have read.
When in the end I spoke she heard,
As here she hears my every word—
And on to purpose great and high
We press, to prove men cannot die.

Her work was hers, as hers 'twill pass;
My work is mine, but mine, alas;
For any word that I may rhyme
Is but to prove no lust or crime
Can do for one, however great,
Naught when he comes to spirit-state.

Two thousand thousand eons sped
With SUCH recorded, is he DEAD:

And from the last his God shall give,
He mourns, through time, that he must live.

To gather naught but thistles, then,
He comes to warn his fellowmen
Lest they, as he, pass out, nor "die,"
But find themselves, as here am I.
Such will my work be then from now
Recorded by one, I allow,
Is more than just my stick (pencil) or pen,
—A saviour of her brothermen.
(Her task is hard which I have set;
But Shakespeare knows it will be met.)

W. S. In spirit (Through S. S.)

MY WORK AND I

My work we have perused and scanned: and turning idly o'er
its leaves
We found nothing of God therein, nor aught expressing soulful
grieves
Against the bonds of sin, alack, or 'gainst the broken laws of
God—
Nor hope of Him, Adjuster All, which all must face, if sum-
mons call.
What will men do who live for fame, if God will blot for aye
their name,
And leave them naught but hungering, but wish to serve, but
souls to bring
Up to His lofty High estate where all must pause outside the
Gate.

Nor solved I any wish for good,—except it be for love of love,
Which holds its sway and root and place
Through Time's long ages face to face,

Nor flowers nor buds in all the span
A simple bloom to comfort man!

My work is writ and carved for aye,
While for it I must pay and pay.
When its thick tome I plied this day
I longed to snatch the half away.

May God Who sees the spirit aye
But see my lines without a play.
These lines I scribe to sign my name
That God I lost, for crime and fame.

       WM. SHAKESPEARE (In spirit) Through S. S.
Oct. 12th, 1917.

TO ONE WHO MENTIONS SHAKESPEARE'S NAME

O world where lovers love but love—
And all their care is but for this—
What will you do when you must part
With earthly love, and lover's kiss?
O Love *immortal* and *supreme,*
Here one indites these lines to Thee,
Who wishes when in earthly shell
He had loved immortality
Which counts when God looks in the eyes,
And asks but all a soul can bring;
When lover's love must count as naught,
Nor poet's song which he can sing,
But every broken law of God
Shall pierce his soul all stricken, wrung,—
And every pervert lover's kiss
Must sting his soul as serpent's tongue,
Until he kneels to God in prayer,
Beseeching pardon of God's grace,

No light divine for him shall shine,
Nor may he ever see God's face!

O take from this thy lesson then
As you go on the Christly way;
And know full well it truly is
Will Shakespeare who speaks *here to-day!*

EVIL SPIRITS

When dispossessed and tenantless the clay is laid away
We used to love with heart and soul, and worship all earth's
day,
We take one long and loving look, then gently led aside
Are told we'll need this husk no more,—we've "gone beyond,"
or "died."
Then soon we find we are alive, and there is no "beyond,"—
The rest we longed for, all its peace, all memories true and fond,
Are nowhere,—nowhere! we just live: and mourn and weep
and pray
Who long for shelter, home, and food,—from which we've
"passed away."
But still must see and hear and touch upon earth's grand
highway.

W. S. In spirit (through S. S.)

TO-THE-MAN-OF *GOD

*(Dr. ————, May 2nd, 1917.)

A spirit and a mortal inhabiting one frame,
But separate, distinctive, each bearing their own name,
Have come to live together,—in fair or stormy weather,—
Have come to work a miracle—
AND NO POWER ON EARTH can sever.
The spirit of the mortal, quiescent in its home,
Has oft rebelled, been taken out, and sent abroad to roam.

To leave the house the hostess would,—and give it back, if but
    she could,—
'Fore e'en another shall, or should,
Inhabit it with her!

But now the hour is very late;
One Master waits without the gate,
And one waits here inside.
To serve the Two she shall and can,—
To better here each brotherman!
To any who would intercede, or send one forth to beg or plead,
I only say, *"Do what you can."*
Thus, you'll NOT serve YOUR brother, MAN.

                    W. S. In spirit (Through S. S.)

THE OLD HAUNTS

When as a spirit I returned to seek the friends I knew,
And searched through haunts in England where we used to
    like the brew,
And found there was not one of those I knew and loved of
    yore,—
And still I had not met with them, across the border shore.

A spirit's search, when all is vain,
No words of mine describe.
The disappointed wanderer
Alone in a world wide
And friendless as the friendless are
Who have no one to care—

All is not changed when we are changed
From dust into thin air.
We think and love and yearn the same
As when we lived as man,—
And disappointment such as waits the one whose search is vain

Through the old haunts for the old friends,
He never knows again.

It is the first hope that he had—
First forward look of joy—
And when I started on this hunt,
I felt as when a Boy,
I used to take my dog and gun,
And make for game at hand,—
Sure of my spoils, and braggart, too;
The greatest in the land.

I knew no friend,—no friend knew me,—
The villages were all the same,
But not a soul whom I had known—
Though still they spoke my name.
I searched and searched the whole land through,
To find a single friend;
And, disappointed, came away,
Another way to wend.

And now I'm here and writing this
For one who n'er saw me;
But from our boon companionship,
As friends have come to be.
As friends we'll be until the close,—
When she goes forth from here:
And she may never search, as I,
For one she had called dear.

RECTITUDE

Saved for a purpose great and grand,
I come to speak for God;
The while that earthly dust of mine
Is mingling with its sod.

The choice I was not given, friends;
By His command I came:
That all my past I should decry,
And preach, in Jesus' name,
That sinners from their sins must turn
Before it is too late,
Or be, as I, cast from His sky;
A beggar at His Gate.

My past was not worse than most men's:
(Mayhap they pay as I)
To have His holy, perfect gift,
And profit not thereby,
Was worse for me than had I been
Of mental low-estate:
For being blessed by the Great God,
Humbly, I should be great.
To do His work, to seek His face,
At last my task is done,
I have the chance, and take the chance,
Supplanting this fine one
Who lends to me, and gives to God,
Her mind, her thought, her time,
That Shakespeare may find grace with Him
Through his more feeble rhyme,
Which holds no plot, nor king but One,
Nor strives for clamoring praise,
But for the multitude gives back
The lesson of his days
Which held of God true reverence
In words, but not in deeds:
And thus I come to save my kind
From souls like mine—which bleeds.

WHAT ENGLAND KNOWS TODAY

(By W. S. in spirit—whose love for England is greater
than ever since the war has given her sons to bleed for France
and to right the wrongs of Belgium, and Serbia, and all the
little devastated countries, as well as her great power which
has aided Russia to win her freedom from Autocratic rule.)

W. S.

Oh England of the sunny skies!
And flowering downs and peaceful towns!
Who would have said this day would see
You battling aliens to free
Who once were our own enemy,—not so "lang-syne!"
Who would have said e're hence I came,
That France would love old England's name!
Or that such things could come to pass,
As all know in this war, alas.

My country! Still my country, ay!
Though at this time I'm far away.
Once England owns a son, through time,
And all the changes past "death's" clime,
A patriot's fire for her will burn,
And every son of hers will yearn
To do his "bit" for love of her . . .
Whose love within him e'er must stir.

Although, Dear Mother, in your breast
The dust of Shakespeare given rest,
Within the breast a spirit bears
No rest he finds from earthly cares,
Nor shall he find, until you be
With all for which you fight,—Free, free!
When victory shall lay at your feet,
Though prostrate, worn complete,—complete,—
Then shall you know, as I know now,

ENGLAND'S will e'er their love avow,—
And naught can change HER sons,—nor "death,"—
They will love on, without their breath!

The "gentlest" one doth here decree,
Through her who writes these words for me,
The love I bear THEE is for AYE,—
Although entombed my dust doth lay!

When the stars went out and the sky became dark,
And earth's poet was no more,—
He took a god along with him
Where he was the poorest poor.
There is a way where the starlight glows,
And God's sky is never dim:
But souls that are poor never reach this place;
Only those that have followed Him.

When the earth-lights fade from mortal eyes,
Touched by death's finger grim,
There is only One that can light the way,
Where God's own belong to Him.
                    W. S. In spirit (Through S. S.)

OLD ENGLAND'S FLOWER
Mowed as the harvest thy field of sons,—
Stacked are their bayonets and their guns,
Passed are their spirits, the harvest done:
For the flower has passed of Old England's sons

Called to answer the roll of God.
Laid at rest on a foreign sod.
Yielding another crop, nor men,—
The world cannot know their like again.
Oh flower of manhood, and bloom of youth,—

For honor you died,—for justice and truth:
And as you answered your country's call—
And fought and bled—and "died" for all,—
May the Great God store in His heart for you,
Justice, and Freedom, and Honor true!

Wm. Shakespeare In spirit Through S. S.

TO ONE I LOVE STILL THROUGH ALL THE LAPSE OF TIME

Oh, keep me in your tender thought until I can search there
for thee.
No place is heaven where you are not; nor any place where I
would be,
Unless at once I could behold the fairest in the world to me!
There is another shares my care, 'tis she through whom I
write my plea,
That where you are, though I am not, Oh may you share
such memory!
Oh lift those radiant eyes deep-lashed, and take me to your
heart again!
The world has held no love like thine,—and never spirit bore
such pain
As that which I must bear to pay for mortal love I bore to thee.
Regret I bring that I must sing, and none shall know this
song of me,—
Nor thou, my love, who have passed on, to take thy place I may
not share,—
But here I'll sing my love for thee, though torture for it
must I bear!
Where thou hast gone can I e'er go? or hast thou e'en a place
for me,
Where, as of old, all that thou wert, and all thou hadst, thou
gavest me?

Or in some place where darkness reigns, unless you know the
Light Supreme,—
Hast thou through night like this my love, accompanying thee
love's fairest dream?
Or shall you find, where'er you are—a holier love than once
I gave
When life meant all a poet knows before that life has passed
the grave?
Can you look up into That face all holy as it is divine,
And see of suffering's mark no trace? No more could you look
into mine,
And find not scars of many woes, I've borne along a long,
long way,
Since we gazed in each others eyes, and found the glory of our
day.
When loving each and loving all—we knew nor shame, nor
righteousness;
But joyed each in the other's name, and cared for naught,—
were pitiless,
Because of love that was a crime,—because of love as man for
man,
Defying God's most sacred law—that ever mortal creature can.
Now love looks on with startled eyes, nor sees my form, as I
see hers,—
Nor knows the love I've come to know, that through my spirit
gently stirs,
Nor thinks of love all changed, renewed, with which I seek
and seek to find,
(Without a house to shield her in, or e'en a place to shield
my mind)
Acceptable a place within, where God has sent my spirit back,
To learn of love's sweet righteousness,—when He may then
forgive my lack.

But still my love I long for thee—oh still I know no rest
    or peace.
Could I but find thee would I search and search until my
    spirit cease.
For I am lonely without thee; and no one knows the poet's soul.
I find on earth no solace like our love which was complete
    and whole.
Note by W. S.

    This was written to prove the spirit finds himself after three
centuries incapable of obliterating the memory of him for
whom I lost all. Struggling against the past, still struggling,
hampered by its same longings—and worse—its punishments
I deserve. May God forgive me. I ask your prayers.

            W. S. In the spirit. (Through S. S.)

MY ENGLAND

How can I speak with heart so full and pouring eyes,
To tell thee of my woe apast my words
To bring a tribute of my olden love
A poet's wreath to lay down at thy feet,—
A poet's tears to water thy sons' graves,—
A poor and lowly son who knows defeat!
O country mine, thou didst me bless
As blesseth every son born in thy clime,
Where no such warriors as the maniac Huns
Were given birth, thank heaven, through God's time!
How can I praise thee, aid, adore, thee more.
My spirit speaks and from my poet's heart
I claim my share in all thy fullsome gifts:
Humane and sane no sons CAN from thee part!
    Wm. Shakespeare In spirit Through Sarah Shatford.

MAY-DAY, HOME

Oh England, my England,—thy shores are decked by now!
Bedecked thy heaths and downs, and garlanded thy brow!

Would I were there, where aye my heart still lives,
That at my country's call, the blood a hero gives,
I had to spill upon thy sacred ground,
Where, during Shakespeare's time, I honor found.
Where yet my grave a sacred honor keeps
Over my dust,—where Shakespeare never sleeps!
For were I there 'neath my immortal stone,
Naught could I care were I outcast, alone.

TO BE A BOY

Oh, to be a Boy again!
To wade, and hunt, and climb!
To know that life meant happiness,
And all that was sublime!
If I could live my life again,
And live as when a Boy,
I'd claim my title to the skies
Began with earthly joy!
If I could go back home once more,
And hunt, and skip, and sing,
I would not give all I've since owned;
Nor envy any king!
For I should have all I've not had
Since passed those happy days,—
And I would live as I SHOULD live,
Nor wander from God's ways.

W. S. In spirit (Through S. S.

ENGLAND'S PRIMROSE

Oh flower of England, in thy modesty,
Thou dost speak but of her who writes this verse!
For in thy beauteous simplicity,
Unheralded by aught, we do rehearse
The virtues of the instrument here used

By us who now inhabit spirit-planes;
The flower of rarest charm on England's isle,
We press thee to our heart, with spirit pains,
That nevermore thy beauties may we know,
But as we see thee here, recalling days
We climbed the brushwood as we sought for thee,
Along dear England's fragrant boy-hood days!

We now indite to her who writes these lines,
The gentlest praise an Englishman can give:
That though we serve even across the seas,
Her primrose virtues helped this rhyme to be, and live!

MY SONG TO-DAY

Of old when days were gay and rife
With court scenes many, kings and queens,
I wrote for these, and of them, too,
(My work you know towards royalty leans.)
Then, with the reasons that men give
For spending profitless their lives,
I worked much as man works today
Who writes for fame, for honor strives.

Today I write, but do not sing;
No player mouths my words for me.
The world is just the same as when
I travelled it in boots I see.
But here where Shakespeare surely lives,
As lives each man who reads this line,
I seek to throw ye men of earth
A wireless message, but divine.

The world is not if I'm not here.
No sun shines out, nor stars aglow
Across the heavens stretch their bow!

If man can "die" then should I know?
My song today, oh gentle folk,
Will ye believe that Shakespeare sings?
And from the land of this new-birth,
To you a saving life-line flings!
   William Shakespeare In spirit (Through S. S.)

THE IMMORTAL SHAKESPEARE'S BIRTHDAY

April 23rd, 1564-1917. (353 years ago.)

I saw the light in ages past
On England's beauteous shore,—
But now I see my darkened past,
Must haunt me evermore!
When fate decreed that I should be,
And gave more than my due,
She should have warned me that no man
Could serve as woman too!

The only crime in all my life,
I cannot repay here,
Is that I held of all earth held,
A man's love the most dear.
You know the kind of love I mean;
'Tis practiced still today:
And each who breaks God's nature law
Must pay as I, and Pay!

And pay and pay and pay and pay—
'Tis now three hundred years!
Three hundred worlds could not pay me,
For all my burning tears.

SHAKESPEARE'S THANKSGIVING

Uphold the poor and ignorant, O God, whose plans divine
Have worked a miracle for me, that I call this one mine.

Make her to give from her rich store the manna from Thy skies,
By word of mouth, resounding ear, uplifted, seeing eyes!
Make her, in tune, an instrument for Thee, that reeking sin
May be in all its forms outcast,
By Thee Who art within.
Nov., 1917.   W. S. In spirit (Through S. S.)

THE SPIRIT'S HARVEST

This is the harvest of the Lord,
We reap who sow for Him:
Surrounded by a field all ripe,
Who passed the reaper grim.
To speak to mortals as of yore
E're they came out, or "died,"
Not one in all this region vast
But tells me they have tried.
There is no hope that men shall see
We are un-housed but live.
Until we spirits reach them here
And prove that we can give
The help they seek from out the skies
We long hoped to bestow,
And should have reached them long ago.
If they had cared to know.
Behold the one who writes hereon
Hears all we care to say!
Hers is the rarest instrument
Perfected yet this day.
While I am here, she sees me not,
But hears my words complete.
When she can speak as now she writes,
Who knows but we shall meet?
                    W. S. In spirit (Through S. S.)
Jan. 30th., '18, N. O.,La.

LONELY ON EARTH

There is a spirit here, a wanderer,
Who seeks to serve the poor of the earthland;
Who seeks no profit but what God will give,
And which a wise Creator holds within His hand.
There is a wanderer, a spirit, here,—
One whom no one would close without the door;
For where his name is writ, there is acclaimed
One name immortal: yea, forevermore.

I am so lonely here I must pass on—
No hope I find, no matter where I go:
The one who takes my messages for me,
Is one I fain would take, I love her so.
But in the world of worlds I am alone;
And bear my whoreson past along with me.
Oh keep me ever in thy heart, I ask,
And only let me live beside of thee.

W. S. In spirit (Through S. S.)

READJUSTMENT

Two souls past reasoning in a new land stood
And made a separate compact with their God:
To serve the lowest husks and help their souls,
Rebuilding lame and sore before the sod
Took all they had by which they could repent,—
And gave them out to wander in the skies
Past reasoning and all power to repent
Where souls like theirs are banished from His eyes.

Each took his task and meeted it full-well,—
Each bore his brother's load and staid the hand
That would assail the tempted, weak, and wrought,
Discouraged in an evil, unjust land.
And thus they earned their own souls happiness;

And thus they served together for One cause:
When readjusting other failures, torn,
Their soulship was a part of divine laws.

W. S. In spirit (Through S. S.)

To commemorate the passing of my son, who had he thrived on air might now, by his lineal offspring send forth a Shakespeare to his country's call for men. Alas, he "died" a youth of barely ten.

W. S. In the spirit.

When fathers give their only sons,
And send them forth to right great wrong,
Proud to have sired that they may go
To shout their battle-song,

A father's heart must know great pride,
When this hour must decide
What cause of all doth he love best,
His own, or country wide.

To give a son, an only son,
And smiling bid him go
To fields of war, of anguishing,
And bitter, bitter woe,

This is to be a father then,
As it has come to be — — ?
Then am I glad I have no son
To aid this victory?

To give an only Son did He,
To die upon a cross — —
Can any grief a father knows,
Compare with His sad loss

Who gave His Son to save a world

From utter loss of life — —
The world which turns its back on Him
Now in such battle-strife?

An utter loss my lips have said?
No—no, it was not this!
Worse than a Judas should I be
In speaking thus amiss — —

For now the world who gave its sons,
And sent them forth to die,
Will wake, and know a Father's woe
Who sent Him from His sky.

To touch the well-springs of the heart,
And move all men to tears,
This may be seen at last the cause
Of these war-stained years!

W. S. In the spirit (Through S. S.)

THE LOVE SONNETS OF SHAKESPEARE
(To one I still love who shall here be nameless: whose name
is linked with mine.)

O Love Eternal, on whose shores I stand,
Bringing no gift to Thee within my pauper hand,—
Still would I seek the Source from which love springs,
Knowing Almighty God its harvest brings
Where all intact a spirit finds love's store
Whose god was love,—love, and nothing more.
Oh love for whom my spirit oft hath pined,
Oft through remorse my tears here fall and blind
For one eternal love this god doth bind
Fast to the soul of him I fain would reach—
Out of my sinner's past that I could beseech
Him whom I loved, love still, pardon complete,

If 'neath no wing of God he found retreat!
Where I am his love still, love is unreplete.
Wm. Shakespeare (In spirit) Through S. S.
Oct. 12th, 1917, N. Y. C.

THE LOVE SONNETS OF SHAKESPEARE
(To one I love, though nameless here.)
Sweet love of mine who tried my soul to bless,
Harking through day and night to my distress,—
Making my rhyme to last throughout all time,
Wherever Shakespeare's name is held sacred, sublime,—
Oh let me add an ingrate's gratitude
For your complacent toil and inaptitude,
While a price you paid for my crime and sin
Through ignorance of welcoming a spirit in
Your spare retreat. Your house I have stripped bare
Of all its sweet prettiness I found when entering there!
Taking for mine the cave and all it held,
While for my purpose you wrote out and spelled
For my poor soul confession of my crime,
Writ, as each page I wrote, for eons, throughout time.
(WM. SHAKESPEARE In spirit) Through S. S
Oct. 12th 1917, N. Y. C.

XI.
O could the world of strife and greed and gain
Know past the change called "death," the tears and pain
Waiting for all who sin, all who fail to be
One with the God who gives immortality,
How could they wound or slay, rape steal or hate;
How could they send forth souls too soon, or late,
Into a darkened place, long, long to wait!
When shall the men of earth love first their God.
When shall they see the "dead" walking earth's sod,

Paying for sins of yore, foul crimes and black,
Before a God on High will take them back!
Shall men remain thus blind to spirit-birth,
While their own dear ones walk near on the earth?
Who seeks clairvoyance here? Or spirit-worth?

W. S. In spirit (Through S. S.)

XVI.

You look upon earth's beauteous womankind,
Whose flowerlike faces speak love to your mind,
While listening to your quivering, quick, heart-beat,
You seek to find love in a lover's heat.
When earth days pass and you must know at last
The god you worshiped still must hold you fast,
While He who gave all love you failed to seek,
All satisfied with love frail, human, weak,
Beholds you and your love-impoverished mind,
Where is the Great God men must seek to find.
When on the shore of His own land you stand,
This earth-love worshiped has no saving hand,
Then back to earth where mortal loves hold sway,
You seek to find the God you cast away.

W. S. In spirit (Through S. S.)

IV.

When I came to this land and knew all was true
Bill Shakespeare had seen, (and told but half too)
I set about wondering what Drayton would do,
Were I to go back with a ghost-form or two.
So I gathered some friends and put out late at night
Finding Michael asleep, where he'd turned down the light,—
And we all stood around in some spirit-plight;
For to wake him from slumber, it didn't seem right.
At last Mike arose and sat still on his bed;

I grasped my ghost partners and them boldly led
Right close to Mike's side, and he raised up his head,
As he said "Bill, old chap, I thought *you* were dead!"
I, Shakespeare, write this, and that's just what Mike said!
I, Shakespeare, write this, whom you "live" ones call "dead."

W. S. In spirit (Through S. S.)

XXIV.

WHY LOVE MUST LIVE

Oh love that soothes and feeds and blesses
With lover's arms and fond caresses,
Uniting pulsing, glowing lovers,
Whom Cupid twines, with kisses smothers,
The while each throb of heart grows wilder,
Each wimple of thy soul grows milder.
There is no bond of thine dissevered;
There is no loss but thou hast weathered.
Within I have the part which loved thee:
Alive is all for which thou lov'st me.
Unsolved through time our separation;
And still I know love's pure elation.
This love is part of God's forever:
Unlocked, unlost; and dying never.

Wm. Shakespeare In spirit (Through S. S.)
("Please sign my full name to this." W. S.)

XXX.

LIFE

With each new age some man acclaimed as wise,
(Upstart of Wisdom Who looks through his eyes,)
Would lay before the bleeding world new laws
Reverting to the time of a first cause,
To prove all nonsense Sacred history's page,
Evolving evolution for his age.
Concept of energy his primal thought he lays

Spending His energy, His nights and days,
To prove God is not, was not, needed in His plan
Eternal Time, Force, Power, Creation, Man.
O pygmys of earth's men, His speck of dust,
What can ye hope, if God ye fail to trust!
Is God within befouled that ye a traitor be?
Seeking a stranger god, ye"ll find Gethsemene.

> William Shakespeare In spirit (Through S. S.)

V.

To hold the hand of an immortal poet,
And be his own through time, and yet not know it,
This is the rare relationship of Her,
Who shall one day set mortal-hearts astir.
While she doth comprehend full all she writes,
And knows these for the spirits she indites,
She does NOT know that she was born to bless
A poet passed three-hundred years; not less.
We tell her only what she has to know:
And never will she guess, 'till time to go
Out from her precious cone where she has spun
The staunchest thread for spirit yet begun,
The fibre for this work for God and man,—
She hath accomplished what no other can.

A PERFECT SONNET

(Since my medium claims I must prove I can still write
such. W. S. In spirit.)

Take down the blazing light which swings aloft,
And fold night's robe and lay them both aside,—
Take from the singer every cadence soft,
And from true lovers that which shall abide,—
Swing in its orbit one eternal sphere,
Pipe in one breast the Maker's song of praise,—

Add or subtract aught from His wonders here,
Subtract or add a day of mankind's days:
Then, if you fail in working out His plan
He hath devised whilst making you His son,
The while He imaged forth Himself in man,
For whom He gave His only beloved One,
Kneel, traitor, bow thy humble soul in prayer,
And as His child reply, "Thy Will Be Done."

(Through S. S.)

XIII.

O world where earthly joys abound, so fair,
That only God could make or give these there,
What would poor spirits give, could they but share
These mortal blessings, when they pass elsewhere!
O souls that see God's plans too late, too late,—
And view His earth—joys when outside the Gate,
Lost, lost to all they love, all they adore,—
Forsaken of their own forevermore:
Where is the pleasure that can pay for this?
Banished,—an outcast from His voice and bliss!
Is there some way to save souls from my fate,
Waking them here from sleep, e're "death," too late
Shows them the light of God, then the dark place
Where souls must wait and pray,—seeking God's grace.

XIV.

When the stars go out, and the sun sinks not,
And rivers cease to flow,
When there are no tides, and no ships come home,
Then, love will I cease to know!
When winter is hot, and summer is cold,—
And the leaves put forth in fall,—
When the time is come for the world to end,—

Or, God has given all!
When the fires die out in the hearts of men,
And lovers are no more,—
When the best of God's is not His love
We carry to His shore,—
Only then will I cease to love His world,—
Only then shall I be poor.

VII.　　　("Happy New-Year, Sarah. W. S.")
The story of the past is writ; so close the book,
And all its creased and soiled leaves forget!
The past has been thy making, and is writ and bound,
Preserved for thy future is it yet.
No thought take of the sealed book again,—but in the archives
　　place the tome,
Where travelers gather memories again,—
This book thou'lt find awaiting thee at Home,
With other thou hast done,—shalt do,—
Beginning thy new volume on this day;
Then close thy last year's book, and on the shelf,
With grateful tears, and prayers, lay it away.
To-day a virgin page awaits thy noble best,—the best
　　that thou canst do!
Begin anew, and with the Royal crest and seal of God,
Mark every page His own, as He, stamps *you*.

XII.

O leave the world of sin while yet
The time when you can choose is yours.
When you may stand where His own stand,
While last life's curtain lowers.
And finished is the play of Time,
Your part done well or ill,
And let your record prove your worth,

The while life-joys instill
A holy reverence and awe
For One ye know and love,
Whom all must meet and all must tell
Their secret sins above.
O leave the world of sin and take
The hand of God, for Jesus' sake.

XLI.

There is no greater self than what you are.
There is no rushing on some perfect star.
Ye travel where ye will, are what ye were.
No greater self approaches thee astir
With all ye dreamed a heaven ought to hold.
Where spirits wake all souls must still be bold.
No winged angel clasps thee by the hand
And leads thee gently in the spirit land.
Ye travel here alone perchance if thou
Hast not thy passport vised here and now.
Ye may seek other fields and browse therein;
But where ye pass ye'll see, and cope with, sin.
Take from a spirit then who yearns to save
All from a lot he found past his own grave.

     W. S. In spirit (Through S. S.)

XLIII.

A SONNET FOR LOVERS

Lest mortals think that love doth not exist
Upon the spiritplane, then mortals list
To this a patterned sonnet's rhyme
To prove all love endures throughout all time:

Sweet, who my earthly-work remakes for me,
Couldst thou a lover in a lover see

Thou wouldst behold me standing by thy side
Who loves thee well, nor shall thy part deride
Here worked for me, through thee, and nobly done,
Since thou hast served my pardon might be won.
There is no loving heart-beat ever lost.
Not one of hers who counted not the cost
But that she aid my spirit, free its sin,
That, loving God, through Him, I shall pass in.

                 W. S. In spirit (Through S. S.)

XLII.

A SONNET OF LOVE

Since mortals dream of naught but life and love,
Then let me record what this means above.
The lovegod is a whoreson's god at last,
And in his earth bound chains doth hold him fast.
The God who gave all love is Love Supreme.
There is a state of love which is a dream
From which men wake who fare out to seek God
They served not, loved not, knew not on earth's sod.
As mortals wake from sleeping these awake.
Who followed in a dream for lover's sake.
As all false idols crumble into dust,
These see their love-gods shattered that were lust.
Then what is love they need not ask above:
A spirit finds where God is, God is love.

                 W. S. In spirit (Through S. S.)

XL.

How shall I love thee who have writ these leaves
Whereon my soul hath told how much it grieves.
How shall I pay, if pay a spirit can,
For that I displaced here to make a man

Whole as a man should be seeking a soul.
How oft' I look on thee wishing to flee
E're thou hast bound me fast for love of thee.
How have I tried to go, closing thy mind,
Lest others use it too, aye more unkind.
There is not known, I ween, past human heart
Grief sadder than we know if we must part
With one so rare and skilled for spirit-use.
All would we sacrifice, all rights abuse,
Rather than part with one who writes for us.

                    W. S. In spirit (Through S. S.)

LXI.

Wake, sleeping world, before the world lies dead.
Here is the land where souls live on, instead
Of the cold earth heaped on their bones to stay,
They LIVE, and naught can take their lives away.
Spirits MUST speak to earth-folk who are dumb:
Thus am I here. To help His kingdom come.
Traveler am I, seeking naught earth can give.
An earnest of the future, here I live.
Fading each fold thy spirit's garment in;
Passing, without a covering for its sin.
Seest thou the carcasse rotting in the mould,
Living in the new, changed for the old,
What of all earth's treasures would that ye had given,
When ye leave the body for its spirit's heaven.

                    W. S. In spirit (Through S. S.)

XVII.

WHEN LOVE SHALL DIE

When Time is wrecked and lost its barque,—
And all lies harbored of His spark,—
When craters mark the face of earth,

Where the dead walk not in spirit-birth,—
When life means what the living think,
And souls await the graveyard brink,—
When God is not, nor His creation;
And not from Mind brought forth sensation;
When His demand that souls shall love
Him first who is their God above
Erased shall be, all God-forgot,—
Out of creation shall He blot
The love He gave each living thing:
Part of Himself, and spheres aswing!

William Shakespeare In spirit (Through S. S.)
("Sign my full name." W. S.)

VIII.

O could you but know the rare essence of love,
Everliving and burning ye carry above,
And all of thyself which is best which is thee
Is attached to thy being through eternity,
Oh creatures of earth, would ye this love debase,
And its twisted deformity look in the face,
Which will meet you and greet you in God's bye and bye?
For the loves of the angels live on in the sky!
Ye would treasure each impulse of God-given love,
Increasing thy storehouse awaiting above:
Ye would add to the perfume of love-thought each day,
Distilling its essence through thy mortal clay!
At the last all God-given must reach out its hand,
To meet, ay, and claim you, in this spirit-land!

W. S. In spirit (Through S. S.)

IX.

Where shall the world at last find men
To till the fields and father men.

Where shall the world at last be then
When wars have taken all we ken
To feed the armies and the shells,—
To blast the kingdom of the earth,—
O where can nations find again
The fathers of childbirth.
When wars have leveled all mankind
And taken from the world its prime
Where shall the Mothers of the race
Find Fathers fit, or Fathers whole?
When wars have done and mankind gone,
Hurled out into the dark his soul.

W. S. In spirit (Through S. S.)

Feb. 17th, 1917.

X.

Where are the loves we loved and soon forgot?
Where are the ones who loved but love us not?
What is the world where these amount to nought?
What is a life with no past memories frought ?
O could the living know that all the "dead"
Look for God's light, and by it must be led,
Would they His footprints seek, words which He said
Guiding while on the earth, their spirits fed
By the Great Love of all whom all shall know
When from earth's mortal coil time comes to go,
While spirits long for God's immortal glow,
Yearning His voice may save from eternal woe.
Where are the loves we loved, so soon forgot,
When our one prayer is, are we GOD'S, or not.

W. S. In spirit (Through S. S.)

XXIX.

Uplift the heart while this heart in you beats.
Retrieve your past e're this fleet life retreats.
When in the hell all men shall find when passed,
Your soul looks out and sees itself at last,
What is the earth and all its winged joys
Where those must tear and wound where sin annoys.
What were the world where world-dust can but grime
That which is saved as yours throughout all time.
What can you bring when you come to this sphere,
If all you seek to find you find right here?
What has earthlife to offer to compare
With what the soul has garnered and brings there?
O then make fast the cords which bind but Him, —
Lest when ye pass your spirit-light be dim.

W. S. In spirit (Through S. S.)

ETERNAL LIFE

O! Land of Earth where dew the flowers beset,
And life is held as something to be borne,
While privileged mankind lose their time in waste,
Uncaring where they fare, all most forlorn,
Seeking for wealth the soul can never carry,
Loving but lust though they may woo and marry,
Living for gain where loss accrues each day,
You cling to death casting God's life away.
A world benighted, lost, impoverished and vain,
What shall be yours when God recalls again
The spark He gave, the soul which cannot die,
Where shall you be in His eternal sky
When He shall call and you at last go home,
O may you not be sent back to the earth to roam!

W. S. In spirit (Through S. S.)

IV.

We have come from the playhouse, God's woman and I,
And have watched the poor puppets that men are pleased by—
We have sat out the discords that jangle and bite,
And seen all the tinsel displayed for the night
To charm and allure, to divert, to amuse,
And 'tis this pleases mortals—'tis this mortals choose!
We have come from the playhouse, God's woman and I,
To the place of her silence, where those from God's sky
Are waiting to speak, their works to indite,
Through the mortal who chooses these words here to write,—
And we know how much fairer our world is to her
Than the one loved by mortals, with mortals astir.
Oh the harmonies waiting for her spirit-ear,
Make the playhouse a jangle of discords, I fear.

W. S. In spirit (Through S. S.)

III.

When mortals are given a chance at the last
When passed from the earth to prove that they live,—
Oh what should you say they would care first to do;
To return to the earth, some comfort to give?
When they find all alive which constitutes them,
And have left but the husk somewhere 'neath the sod,
Will they long to come back, to show all their friends
The Bible WAS true, and, at last, they've found God?
The first thing we yearn for, and burn for, at last
We arrive in the spirit, and last we are free,
Is to tell all the loved ones that we are not "dead,"
But think, feel, and see, as we used to be!
The strangest and saddest thing where spirit goes
IS to see, feel, and hear, and know nobody knows.

W. S. In spirit (Through S. S.)

VI.

Oh what is more dear than the hands that we love;
The gentle and ministering hands that we love,
Which have soothed us and blest us and smoothed the brow o'er,
With a touch and a care we should ever miss more
Were they taken from earth to some far spiritlands,
While we felt the dearth of her ministering hands!
So, my friends, this you think, thus you speak to yourself;
For you think of a "lost" one on some marble shelf,
Where the dear hands are folded and useless for aye:
Thus you think of the dear hands of clay laid away.
But I tell you those hands come from NEAR spiritslands,
And oft smoothe your trials, and free you from bans;
For the hands of a spirit are ministering here
To the one who writes this: it is all true, my dear!

W. S. In spirit (Through S. S.)

THE BALANCE TRUE

So little do we know of men while here
Their faces tell no tales, as after "death";
We give each one their estimation's worth,
And they reach "home" astonished at their dearth.
We give to all their dues in this new field—
There is no mourning then for what they find,
But pressing on they harvest the new yield,
Nor grieve for that which they have left behind?
No man comes hence to draw check certified—
No bank is drained to furnish a supply;
Men walk the skies as paupers walk the earth,—
Nor murmer at the place their God supplies.

Wake then, as mortals, e're you pass out hence,
And draw no check on balance overdrawn,—

For once the mighty balance is cast up,
You see the sham account you have banked on!
W. S. In spirit (Through S. S.)

SONNETS OF MINE

Lovers may love and be loved o'er again,—
The world may hold and treasure lover's bliss;
But what, alas, can mortals know of love,
Who live within a maddened age like this.
To give a peal of laughter to the world,
To feel the pulse of summer in your veins,
To gather moonbeams or the ocean's spray,
And hold the champing Pegasus in rein,—
To play a kingly role up to a queen,
To rout the traitor's lair and lay him low,—
And in the hours of day that intervene,
To have of love as all men wish to know,—

This was the life with which my sonnets teem;
Which laid me low,—but brought a world's esteem.

TO ALL LOVERS

(From a spirit who knew the meaning of love.)
W. S. In spirit.

Why, after death, you say, shall love still live
Immortal as the soul it made or marred?
Why must afflicted lovers bear through Time
The pangs of separation which are hard
Upon the earth where lover's lives are knit
By union such as only lovers know:
Must they continue on and on, for aye,
Where lover's losses must afflict them so?

Ay, this is what it means to love but love:
To make a love-god lovers idolize,

Forgetting their Creator, God of All,
All Loving, Tender, Merciful, and Wise.
To feel the pangs of a remembered love,
To know a lover's love that cannot die,
This is the separation which is hell:
This is such lover's lot in God's own sky.

To love with all your heart and soul and mind
The God of all love, e'en true lover's kiss,
Such is the law the world must find and know,
Before earth's lovers find Eternal bliss.

                              W. S. In spirit.

TO MY LOVE IN HIS SPHERE—WHEREVER THAT MAY BE:

O gentle love whose love I know must last
Wherever you may be with our dear past,
Keep me in ecstasy, some memory blest,
If you are resting in His heavenly rest.
I know wherever you have gone to meet your test,
God will adjudge what for His own is best.
Herbert, my help, when none was nigh to save,
Have I through this one saved you far beyond a grave?
Has my confession to a priest for thee
Lifted your soul from darkness' misery?
Has ever heart ached more than mine that thou
Hast from me banished been through time 'till now?
Oh let me say through this one who didst plea,
Yea, and didst pay the mass, that thou shouldest be free,
Nought ever can restore my calm and peace,
Until I find thou too hast known release.
When shall the bar which closes thee from me
Uplift and give thy soul out pardoned, free!

If evermore I must not know thee blest—
Know then I pray, ay, mourn, lest *I*, robbed thee of rest.

                              Wm. Shakespeare In spirit.

("Sign my full name." W. S.)

(Dictated) "Through his only medium Sarah Taylor Shatford."

("See Sherman, French & Co., Boston, Mass., for further writings from this spirit.") W. S.

SPEAK

If you can save the world from sin,
Or degradation's harm,
By any words that you can speak,—
Then speak! Sound the alarm.

If you can help the world to see
There's no escape from sin,
And heaven above is heaven below,
The world they're living in,—

And they must take their souls washed clean,
If they would be with God;
Would YOU not speak and warn earth's men
Still on the dear earth's sod?

Then, when a spirit who has paid,
Comes back to speak *through* you,
And asks but that you speak for him,
You are God's mouthpiece too.

SWEET MY LOVE

'Tis I who speak who spake of yore
In language such as this
When I would teach one to adore
Or prate of earthly bliss.

Now Shakespeare speaks—
(For I am he, oh gentle folk)
And I recall my words as when
The stage alight with tapers shone—
(No signs electric had we then)
I used to kneel to human forms,
And kiss their hands and make-believe,
Then on the stage were grown old sires
Who played the youth and did deceive.
Such Art as nature gave had they,
A trick or two, some cunning eyes,
And in a lover's play, at times,
A lover made by me was wise.

Now pretty youths all fresh and fair
With scarce the need to paint a brow,
Beseech, implore, astrut, amaze,
Are wise, and have no need to bow.
My lord has not a coach and four,—
My lady has no powdered wig,—
They need only two frocks or more,
A cue, or some poor wirligig.

We speak as one who made a Queen,
And many a royal household too.
Should men today make these to play,
How would they start, what would they do?
The royal house is swept for all—
No more Will Shakespeare write for these,—
But in the time he spends on earth,
Only His God must Shakespeare please.

                    W. S. In spirit (Through S. S.)
Dec. 28th, '17·

TO *HER* AT LAST I'VE COME TO LOVE:
(W. S.)

When two souls rush into each other's arms,
Uniting with a waking lover's kiss,
There is not known in spirit where I am
Another union to compare with this.

When love meets its fulfillment then with love,
And lovers share the kiss God made for all,
There is a union even after death,
A Paradiso where no one can fall.

If lover's love then is so sweet as this,
And love completed knows no lover's need,
What must the heart of God hold for His own,
When spirit knows such bliss, such royal meed!

If love shall live then know ye by this dream—
If love shall die know too by what I gave—
Where is the kingdom where but love at last
Predominates o'er all, even a grave?

Wm. Shakespeare In spirit

("Sign my full name to this one please." W. S.)

(Dictated: "Through his only medium through whom he has ever written from the spirit side of life, Sarah Shatford.")

"Sarah Taylor Shatford, Author of "Birds Of Passage," Sherman, French & Co., Boston, Mass."

My love, my pure my only love,
I came a miracle to work
In thee and me, and now I rise
To pay the price, nor shirk
The last task the Great God gives me
To perfect e're I rise on high
Where Light is given, all made free,
In God's immortal sky.

I love the one who writes these lines
As never mortal I did love:
But where my love my soul confines
Is not the Love of God above.
I ask her then to set me free
To go my way, as she must here:
I'll not be here, nor she have me
Until her clay rests on the bier.

We know a love few mortals know,
We are to each all each could be:
And through this love I now may go
Where God's immortals are set free
To seek on high a love bestowed
But on the loving, pure and true:
To give to love the crown but owed
Made for me, dear, alone through you
Who toiled for me throughout the years
I spun through you God's love sublime,
And wept with you and felt your tears
While often they fell on our rhyme!

To you I love who write this word,
This fond adieu, this last good-bye,
I leave the memories of all heard,
And rise to God who is on High.
    Wm. Shakespeare In spirit (Through S. S.)
"Knighted by Eliza and James.
Through his medium Sarah Shatford."

                           W. S.

TO HER I LOVE, WITH A CHERISHING CONSTANT ATTENDANCE: W. S.

There is in one frail body on the earth,
A spirit rare, and fine:

Could those behold who see the clay,
Would they think it divine.
I speak of her whom I know well,
And love, and reverence too:
As through the years I've worked to help,
Ay, toiled, that she might do
The spirit's sublime task they set,
When out they sent me here:
And if I failed, she also failed,—
Or else they held her dear
Where deeds but count, or what men say
Is lost, but for the use they make
Who string at words, and play at rhyme,
EXCEPT FOR JESUS' SAKE.

Thus do I know this woman well—
Who writes these words hereon;
And when the clay is left behind,
We'll swing out to the dawn
Of God's most perfect Paradise
Where His own kingdom waits,
Where one who serves and loves Him well
No woeful past relates.
No darkness these can fold about,—
Nor shut from Him away,—
Who calls His own to come to Him,
And share His blissful day.

        "W. S. In spirit Through S. S. For S. S.
         Meaning S. S. from W. S. to S. S."
               (W. S.)

A NATION'S GLOOM

From the lips of priest and poet fall brave counselings for men,
Who must leave the homes they cherish, never to see these
   again.

What the world has lost in heroes shall one day computed be;
What heroes have lost in warfare, they must see as murderers
    see
Who go forth to leave in sorrow all who must recall their
    deeds,—
Knowing not their own despairing, gloom of Nation's night
    and needs

                W. S. In spirit (Through S. S.)

      Keep in your heart a little place
      Where I may rest at close of day,—
      And chase the shadows from your life,
      And fears and doubts there keep at bay!
      Keep in your soul a little light
      Reflected from the soul of one
      Who wishes he had done as well
      Before his life on earth were done.
      Make me a saving happiness,
      To hold and keep in trust one plea—:
      That when you pass out of this shell,
      That day you may belong to me!

          W. S. In spirit (To S. S. Through S. S.)

A LONG TIME

A long time it is since I came here to stay,
And to work with the one I should help on her way:
But the worst of it all—as I see it today—
Is the trouble I find to find something to say!
We have strung every string from a cat to a spider,
And now I but wish to lie down beside her:
And so I will go, and let her go too,
Because it is true, there IS nothing new.

           W. S. In spirit (Through S. S.)

COMMUNION SUNDAY (Scotch Pres. Church, N. Y. C.)
July 1st, '17.

Oh, should I wait 'till I am fit
To sit with Thee, or sup with Thee,
All comfortless would I remain:
For this, forgive *Thou* me.
That worthier I've longed to be;
And failed, as fail earth's men:
But "in rememberance" of Thy word,
Willt Thou forgive again!

W. S. In spirit (Through S. S.)

We come to Thee contrite of heart, to sit at Thy blest board:
We see ourselves just as we are, but take Thee at Thy word.
We long for all that Thou hast said is for Thine own above;
For pardon, mercy, devout faith, but more than all, for love!
O God, we see Thee everywhere,—we know Thou art within:
Oh keep us, help us, lift us, Lord,
And free us from our sin.

W. S. In spirit (Through S. S.)

In the wellsprings of being a fount is concealed,
Whose healing abundant e'en leperosy healed:
When Jesus uplifted a finger or prayer
The sinner at once stood purified there.

So now on the earth is this fountain revealed
Through an instrument fine through the spirit unsealed:
And the day she goes forth by one word to her God,
The dead shall arise who have lain 'neath the sod.

This message we tell thee this one does not know:
But we have known long who serve mortals below.

She will heal she will preach she will hear she will see—
And these but a half of her miracles be!

W. S. (Thine) In spirit Through S. S.

SPIRIT TRUTH

The one who writes these words for me,
All gentle, true, and kind,
I searched o'er for centuries
Along earth's way to find.
It breaks my heart to hear her say
That some may claim a fraud
Her marvellous experience:
The whole world should applaud.
For I, for one, can never pay
The debt I owe her still,
And must throughout eternity,—
Though pay I shall, and will!
For Will will pay up all his debt
Though he IS spirit now.
The truth that spirit IS, IS truth,
The world must soon allow.
For I will work such miracles
Through this one's willing hand
That skeptics will cross o'er the sea
To share in this one's land
The proof of God's eternity
But by a breath is spanned.

W. S. In spirit (Through S. S.)

TO A HARP OF GOD

(By Wm. Shakespeare to his only medium since he passed
from the mortal body, Sarah Taylor Shatford. W. S.)
Thou art a harp all finely strung and tuned by God's own hand;

An instrument the like of which none own in spiritland!
Thou art a silent melody vibrating when we play;
Thou art a symphony, all told, of what we sing or pray!
Thou art a melody, thyself without discordant note:
Thou art a carol of His praise, an anthem which He wrote!
I hold this harp (for it is mine) and on it I must play
Diviner strains than aught I wrote before I passed away.
'Twas given me at last to prove that all must serve their God:
If not within the husk He gave, when it is 'neath the sod.
Throughout the years I served on earth my sins held me
    complete
Until One all too merciful here set me on my feet,
And bade me rise and prove the worth of serving Him who gave
That others with their misspent lives, each hurrying to his
    grave,
Might wake before it was too late,—might give his God His
    due,—
And that is why this harp is mine on which I play to you!

                W. S. In spirit (Through S. S.)

OUR BURDENS

We who recite the words this woman writes
Must make amends where all adjusted is
That caused her grief or pain or e'en misjudgment here.
We are now spirit. Until ye spirit be,
No mortal here could comprehend the suffering of a soul.
This we will say. However much this one has suffered here
To give my message to a lustful world,
Her time will be not longer in the dark
For all she did to set poor Shakespeare free!
Adjustment first then claims a spirit passed
Out into God's great plan, Eternity.
Did mortals know how long I searched this one to find,

Through which to confess beastality,
Would they live different lives and pass out clean,
Giving to God a handful at the least.
Did not that One Who died upon the cross,
Suffer for OTHERS sins—ay, YOU, and ME?

W. S. In spirit (Through S. S.)

THE SLEEPING WORLD

When mortals lay their own dear "dead" away,
They hope they'll sleep 'till resurrection day.
Down in the earth for worms to desecrate
They leave them then for this long time to wait,
Till they shall hear at last a trumpet call,
Then shall they rise, and praise God, one and all.

But we who "died" know better, yea, than this,—
Since not a moments "dying" marred life's bliss!
We stood before the old form that was us,
And mourned because they wept and made a fuss,—
We did not care: we did not even sigh:
We knew that we should meet them bye-and-bye.

Since then we know there are no sleeping "dead,"—
It is the living world that sleeps instead!

W. S. In spirit (Through S. S.)

YOUR SWEET HEART

(From your W. S. who loves thee well.)
How oft I sit and ponder on thy heart:
Thy love for all, thy longing for God's love:
Thy hunger for His kind, His grace, His truth,
And all that thou shallt seek and find above.
How long must you remain upon this plane
Before appeased this hunger is no more,

Alas, 'tis not the one who writes shall say,
For he is now anhungered at the core.
            W. S. In spirit (Through S. S.)

Take from my heart its wealth of love whereby a heaven
    is known,
And you will take the richest gift God gives me for my own;
But should you take from out my soul the hope of lover's bliss
In meeting in another land when I go out from this,
You take the one, the only hope, for which true lovers "die,"
That they shall meet, love, as of yore, beyond—beyond the sky!

Then take my love, and love-bereft, I'll pass along the way,
Uncaring for ingratitude, or a base lover's play:
For every shock a soul can know, no sorrow equaled this:
That I must search in vain for one whose lips I fain would kiss!

WHEN LOVE IS YOUNG

When love is young and gentle youth unblazed,
Its tenderness puts forth as leaves in Spring;
No harsher breeze to tear, nor heat to sear,
And naught to mar the duet nature sings.
When love is young, no words need to entice
The opening of the thighs or lips or arms;
Sweeter than honey is love's lingering kiss,
Which gives and takes the whole—nor cares what harms.
                    (W. S. In spirit)

ENDURING LOVE

Where shall we find a soul so rare
Who has not loved a lover's share?
Where shall we look for one so great
He merits place in God's estate?
When earthly lovers loves are done,

A soul receives what it has won
Through all earth's battles, frets, and care;
The perfect soul is truly rare!

Where shall we seek for love on earth,
Which will endure through spirit-birth?
In temples some have found it not:
Some found, and lost it, and forgot
The love of God, while passions swayed
The temples that their God had made.
Then when at last these are forgot,
How can they change their loveless lot?

LX.   LOVE OF LOVE
        Oh love of Love men know who pray!
        Oh Love Eternal, whom all pay!
        We sing paeons of praise to Thee
        Who art men's God eternally!

        When lovers know but lover's bliss,
        Knowing love's balm but in their kiss,
        There is a God they wholly miss
        Who worship such a love as this.

        There is a love of Love much higher;
        A Love Supreme; a Divine fire;
        Which men must find who worship love.
        And this is found in God above!

        When mortals kneel at cupid's shrine,
        And make his god their God divine,
        The world must know there is a place
        Where all look in the love god's face,

        And see the wrong, despised, unfair,
        Which blemishes, beyond repair,

Their earthly and eternal time,
When choosing lust and sexual-crime.

LOVE'S SACRIFICE

You may carry my purse with an unloosened string,
You may share every gift that I own;
But the love of my love you may not see or touch,
For this love it is mine, yes, alone!

You may share half my castle, and half my food too;
I will lend you my dog and my gun:
But you never can share with me here anywhere
The love-of-my-love,—for we're ONE.

SPOOKS AND GHOSTS

"Love reigns within" (we say) "who pass out hence,
O they shall know no want forevermore:"
But when we see our past brought out from thence,
We view the outside then; we ARE the core.

"Love reigns supreme," 'tis true. But not within
Unless that love is all which God intends.
The inner part, the shadow, may be sin,
Providing the old crust cares nought, nor mends.

The shell is laid aside; the spirit lives:
The inner part is God's, and He is love.
But what a mockery is the love man gives,
Where from his shell he brings his gift above.

The feast is spread, the table is weighed down;
But you shall forfeit every right to share,
If not a gem shines in your earthly crown,
But branded as an ingrate are you there.

The way is open, flung aside the veil,
The loved ones wait to give a helping hand
Before your ship puts forth with its poor sail
To cross the border to the spiritland.

Speak not of spooks and ghosts as once did I,
To make a scene of revelry, or play.
Unseen the souls surround you from the sky
And yours, within, may be out any day.

See to it, then, that love doth play its part,
And God's own love doth play the part Supreme;
Else when aside you lay the fleshly heart,
The ray within may be shut out, nor gleam.

           W. S. In spirit (Through S. S.)

RETURN

Here are the travelers returned who sped to heaven high:
Here have they been since they "passed out," as folks say when
    we "die."
No intermission has there been in life, no closed door;
We who pass on, pass out and stay on earth, just as before.
We seek but find no outstretched arms, no door flung wide,
    ajar,—
For are we not among the "dead" in heavens vast and far?
How far are those whom we would reach, and help as we see
    now
The "dead" CAN help who *live* nor "die," would earth-folk
    seek, allow.

We who write here can spell our name, and all we writ
    acclaim;
Knowing each rhyme, and here return to spurn our honored
    name.
The name holds naught on spiritshore all empty but to fame;

Adjustment here must then be made: to seek this here I came.
There is no name can hold more shame than one who writes
    this line:
Indeed is he unclaimed, unsought, this SHAKESPEARE,
    mean, nor fine.

                    W. S. In spirit (Through S. S.)
    Jan. 22, '18.

FEW FIT

Some say "There is no death" while they are here,—
Some do not care if they shall live or die:
No matter. All must fare the same in "death"
So far as they shall live minus the breath.

Regarding hopes and fears, men know the same;
Still none surmise the afterlife
To be just as it is before death closed the eyes!
World travelers fare alike: not so our world.
We must go on though broken is the cord.
What have we been we are, no more, no less—
And few go hence full fit to meet the Lord!

                    W. S. In spirit (Through S. S.)
    Jan. 15th, '18.

SO FAR!

So far we spirits seem, alas, from earth
When we pass in, not on, at the new-birth!
Our dearest near, but with unveiled eyes
Thinking of us in some far Paradise.
Ay, love, we hear, see, think, just as of yore,—
Nor have we passed, but stand in the same door,
Enveloping you oft with outstretched arms,
Enfolding, sparing, sharing, your alarms.

Did ye care MORE to see or hear the "dead,"
"There is no death" ye'd witness, as 'tis said.

W. S. In spirit (Through S. S.)

Jan. 15th, '18.

ETERNAL LOVE

To feel the pulse of life once more, oh what would Shake-
    speare's spirit give.
Except, there is naught else worth while, where spirits live
    where I must live!
To know one woman's constant love, to keep her pure and free
    from sin,
To cherish her love evermore, the gem of all life's gems within,
This were ambition for earth's sons, the while they served
    their God above,
And clasped within each other's arms, eternal Life, eternal
    Love.

God made for man a mate complete, and laid the treasure at
    his feet:
But man, who would improve His plan, rejected her and chose
    a man.
And worshipping the god of love, his soul, rejected God above.

W. S. In spirit (Through S. S.)

We shall spill no more gold from our heart's treasured store,—
We shall part with no priceless love-gems,—
When the curtain's rung down and we stand at the door
Which the circle of God seals and hems!

Oh, the anguish of lovers who part from their own,
Is but part of the grief they must know
In the place where the banished are parted for aye,
Where one lover may stay, one must go!

I have come from the place where the gold of a heart
Was lavished in wealth all its own,
To inhabit a land where is no love for me,
Except where my works are well known.

When we parted of yore, my sweet love and I,
Not knowing what God's hand could hold,
We thought we should meet to rejoice in our past:
For we knew such love never grows cold.

Here am I, with no home, and no mortal to bless,—
Away from old England, my home,—
Returned in the spirit to comfort and bless,
While the earth must I roam, ay, and roam! . .

W. S. In spirit (Through S. S.)

There is no cross without its pain;
No loss without its final gain:
There is no death nor dying ever;
Since God is yours, death cannot sever.

W. S.

SEX-ATTRACTION

The flowers and the bees have their own way to love,
And the whole of creation is full of the same;
So why should a man be ashamed of his mode
Of supplying the thrill in love's name?
We may handle a rose that's been kissed by a bee,
When the curtain of night is rung up,
And never could guess we could love it the less,
For the bee that has supped in its cup!
We shall see when the curtain falls on you and me
There's a difference in lovers and love;

But the bees and the flowers, and the butterflies, too,
All are kissed by the Dear God above!

                    W. S. In spirit (Through S. S.)

TO THE SOURCE OF ALL LOVE
(A Prayer)

Thou Source of all love in creations great whole,
Thou Infinite fount never dry,
We drank the last dregs in the cup which you gave,
To be Thine on Thy earth, in Thy sky.
We kneel at Thy fountain our vessels to fill:
We carry our souls to Thy feet:
We wing on Thy missions, wherever Thou wilt,
We know that our God is complete.
Thou Source of all love, past the heart's craving might,
Unto each of our hearts be it known,
Thou hast poured past deserving a poet's full share,
When Thou stamped every poet Thine own!

                    W. S. In spirit (Through S. S.)

LOVE'S EMISSARY

We prate of love while in the flesh,
Thinking we know what love doth mean,—
But when we find what true love is,
We see how futile all has been.
The love which mortals call by name,
And mouth in speeches soft and fine,
Is never known where spirits go,
For here is love but all Divine.
Partaking of a righteousness,
No paltry sentiment includes,—
Love's messenger is sent abroad
In rarer, finer altitudes.

Embodying all it has not held,
Embracing all it has not known,
The winged courier shields his shaft,
Nor wounds a heart that it would own!
W. S. In spirit (Through S. S.)

WHEN THE WORLD REGAINS ITS SANITY

What will become of the crazy men when the world regains
its sense again?
What will become of the ones who must see for their whole
lives war's butchery?
What will become of the demonized, who fear, and stare with
haunting eyes?
Has the thoughtful reserved a place, for the insane warriors
of the race?
And who will be sane in the world again when the streams-
of-fire have done their worst,—
And who will share, or help these bear, their blasted lives
accurst?
And who will care how the living fare, who come from the
trenches' fire ?
Is there aught that a mortal can do for these, who are lost
to the world entire?
And where are the women to take them back, and restore them
as of yore?
In the world of love there will be a lack, and a lacking evermore!
W. S. In spirit (Through S. S.)

May 29th, 1917.

A LOVE SONG
(Song)

Oh sun in splendour shining, spill thy gold
Into the bosom of the waiting flowers,—
Unfold the lovely petals of the rose

That waits for thy caress, and knows the hour
When you shall smile her perfume wide she'll cast.
If but a day she lives in thy embrace, oh sun,
The rose knows what is love at last!

W. S. In spirit (Through S. S.)

THE FULFILMENT OF LOVE

When the eyelids are closed that have looked on the world,
And dim is the sight where earth's banners are furled,
We look to a God for all light that we know
Where the darkness of gloom and the night presses so!
We come to this land leaving riches behind,
Where we carry our deeds on the earth that were kind,
And we look for a friend as we halt by the way
Where never a light shines by night or by day!
We carry our burdens we forged on the earth
From the day of our death to the day of our birth;
And the load is so heavy as up-hill we fare,
We wonder so many we made for us there!

W. S. In spirit (Through S. S.)

LOVE'S CRUCIBLE

Into love's burning potent where the soul aspires,
We place foul passion's torch and set lust's fires,
Until the vessel burnt and blackened is
Which God has made His own, and claims as His.

When all is smirched, and past all love to save,
When conscience sees love's embers in the grave,
The vessel spurned and useless in His land,
Where Love indeed holds out no saving hand.

Oh then, this wish, that by some power on high
May *his* soul save *these* souls before they "die" . .

That in His hand their sacred love may burn,
And lend a light afar to those who yearn.

W. S. In spirit (Through S. S.)

THE VALUE OF A FRIEND

A friend, a friend to help us bear
Our sorrows, and our joys share,—
Such, is a comfort rarely found
On earth, in heaven, I'll be bound.
To take in friendship to the heart
A friend for life, is ne'er to part:
For life beyond reflects but this;
And all who make, share too, its bliss.
We trust a friend whom we find true:
Throughout all time we miss him, too.
If chance hath parted after "dying,"
We know the tears that have spilled crying
That we might hear one spoken word,
Or hear OF him, (which we've not heard).
How oft would we have suffered, yes,
Have borne still more but to confess
How truly lost and sad life seemed
Without the union fondly dreamed.

W. S. In spirit (Through S. S.)

HELL A REALITY

There is no fire of burning coals;
Nor any flame to scorch or singe;
These terms were used by scribes inspired
By some poor spirits's conscience-twinge.
But in the spirit's realm be sure
There is a hell of burning shame
For every crime and every sin

Against Him in his mortal frame.
To burn as this fire burns him, then,
Is past descriptive words or pen.
Where every mortal knows his past,
'Tis hell enough for all earth's men.
The one who writes has burned therein;
And warns each here to find his God
Before the judgment seat is reached,
And that he was rests in the sod!

Then all shall know when "death" hath laid them by:
Knowledge the first: we live: nor can we "die."
Knowledge the second: all we have been we see:
Knowledge the third: all we were are we.
Knowledge the fourth: what we have sown we reap.
Knowledge the fifth: there is no high estate;
When we have paid we shall pass through the Gate
Leading on, on to higher better things
Than any spirit from the earth-plane brings.
Knowledge the sixth: Ye shall pay all ye owe:
This is the only hell that spirits need or know.

W. S. In spirit (Through S. S.)

THOUSANDS OF MILLIONS

Passing, passing through the sky,
Out into nowhere,
Spirits flung by shot and shell,
From "here" "overthere."
Passing, passing through the world,
None yet hear the cry
Of those who met in warfare, "death,"
And find no heavenly sky.
Through the space their faces peer,

Leering, hating eyes,
Hunting, hiding from their foe,
Gloating when he "dies."
Thousands, millions, billions, trillions,
Pass along the spirit-way,
Having not a light to guide them,
Through the night, until the day!
How can these return to help you?
Friends, they never went away!
On the earth and through its warfare,
Still they fight, and hate, and pay.
Will you help at spirit-rescue?
Will you pray unceasingly,
For the "dead" who slayed, or slaying,
Were so blind they could not see?

W. S. In spirit (Through S. S.)

WHEN WILL THE SAINTS COME HOME

I am longing to see a saint,—a saint in all the glory
We have been taught surrounded these, in by-gone ancient
story.
I am longing to see a saint; for I've been with the "dead"
Lang-syne, and never seen a halo 'round a head!

Where are the saints, I ask,—when will these, then, come home?
Have these a separate highway on which their kind must roam
Where are the saints of earth, in all their saintliness?
I'm Shakespeare, and have been long "dead," but seen none,
I confess.

(But I have not been through the entire menagerie as yet.
W. S.)

GOD'S BEST

Take from all my heart its fine-spun dreams
An artist would admire,—
Take from my love its worthiness,
Its passion, heat, and fire,—

Then let me give what is left there
To make a parson's coat!
For after love has there no place
Its substance is a mote

Which anyone may use or no
Or not use if they could;
A heart without its dreams, its love,
Is just a block of wood!

You speak of all the heartstrings rife
With music, and you sing;
But discord mars the harmonies
Which otherwise would ring

Afar, with all their gladsome notes
Flung from a Master's breast!
Be silent, if you cannot dream,
Or love, or know, God's best!

God made the light and with His word
Across the world undying hope arose.
Within His hand the shining orbs
As jewels in a casket's close.
Around His throat, upon His breast,
His gems eternal shine,
Wove out of them His diadem,
All through His word Divine.

"Let there be light," O God of night!
And through this dark and sunless day
Pour on this poor benighted world
Thy healing, searching, loving ray!
Where mortals hold their own in chains;
Thy holy laws fail to obey;
O God omnipotent restore within men Light,
When "Peace, be still" Thou need but say!

W. S. In spirit (Through S. S.)

NOTE: Please see att'd poem, published in N. O. "TIMES," and signed by me (Sarah Taylor Shatford) believing at the time I conceived the ideas therein, and the first one I attempted for over One Year. Of late (one year after the above was written by W. S.) I learn, while numbering these pages, that I did not create this (though I heard no voice while writing same) but that it belongs to him too. I wrote it and published it in faith and some joy, as it was on the first day of my arrival home after an absence of Five years. S. S.

AT HIS WORD
By Sarah Taylor Shatford
(N. O. TIMES—Pic, Jan. 21st, 1918)

There's a little bit of heaven in the heart of everyone,
A little rift of joyousness, a little ray of sun.
The densely overhanging clouds must clear when all is done;
God made the night—but at His word the daylight was begun.

There's a little hope unleavened in the soul of everyone,
That the God Who made the Allies and the God Who made
the Hun
Will restore the world benighted to the light when all is done,
And at His word His kingdom on the earth shall be begun.

MENTAL QUESTIONS
Read by W. S. Without an Error

(For Father ———— who said the mass for the repose of the souls of W. S. and his friend. (Whose name was given for the priest alone.)

I. Will the two worlds ever become one, and when will this be?

II. Will this instrument be the one through which this will be revealed to the world at large?

III. Mother, will you reveal to me the secret of this truth.

For ———— (Lawyer).

I. Why do you not do this for me?

II. Now this is the most wonderful thing I ever witnessed in my whole life.

III. What is the meaning of this remarkable spiritual development in this wonderful woman?

Note: This last question W. S. begged leave to answer through the medium's writing, as it was a subject too vast to answer then, and should be recorded for others. It was therefore written and is herewith attached. Mr. ———— has a copy of this. S. S.

Jan. 5th, 1916. (Two weeks this date I first heard the voice.) S. S.

A SINGLE NOTE

We walk along life's wooded ways,
And hear a cricket sing;
We pause and listen to the song—
'Tis such a little thing!

We seek the note from all the past
Which sank deep in our heart;
Sometimes it was a single note
That played so great a part.

We pause today on earth's highway
To pipe a poet's song
Which shall sink in the hearts of men:
Their time of *life* prolong.

Perhaps we shall not know the part
This note may sometime play
In keeping others from the dark,—
Or bringing to them Day.

But where we are who go "out-there,"
(As someone calls it here)
The single note this cricket sang,
Will be known of Shakespeare.
William Shakespeare In spirit (Through S. S.)
His Medium
Above dictated, saying "leave out "the" (In the spirit) and
write "his medium" after your own name if you please." W. S.

IF THE WORLD ONLY KNEW

If the world only knew that between me and you,
(An instrument finest I've seen)
There was no partition that kept me from view,
But their thick-headed doubts, and their spleen,—
Oh would they endeavor, or reach out a hand,
To work for us here as you do;
I've wondered about it, while watching tonight,
How rapidly your pencil flew.

If the world looking out could only look in,
And watch us on this New-Year's night,
Looking out for the world, a world full of sin,
And doubts that must soon be set right,
Oh would they be willing to serve even then
The spirits whom they might not see?

And give but an hour of their time every night,
To write as this one writes for me?

W. S. In spirit (Through S. S.)

TO OUR LADY OF LOURDES:

O MARY, saint of all the saints,
Holy, and Divine,
Who bade Bernadette to find the spring
Which cleanses, makes all Thine,
Return unto this bloodstained earth—
Unseal the hearts of men—
That hungering, thirsting, murderous souls,
May find His peace again!
Make eyes to see,—and ears to hear,—
Restore, make whole and clean
The human leperous seething mass
Defiled, Godless, and mean.
Uplift the curtained veiled sight,—
Rebuke the evil one;
Until Thou art indeed proclaimed
The Mother of His Son.

W. S. (In spirit)

Through S. S.
Nov. 18th, 1917.

Now; do you think an evil spirit could write that: say. Oh you *are* perverse. My good girl make no attempt to rid yourself of your teacher until you are taught. And go out and enjoy life and stop worrying. This will be the last time I will stand by. You will have to come over if you do not behave. There is no way out of it. You will have to speak and give your messages and progress. When you find all you have done to upset this what will you do save weep. There are no *evil* spirits here, let me assure you, and you will never be obsessed while I am here to prevent it. But as an instrument for the spirit's use, and a fine one let me say, you would become a tool for passing — — — wanderers, I might say: since you could not understand the real conditions surrounding a sensitive living wholly for spirit.

Go out in the sun and enjoy the Maker's beautiful world— it is for you and you should be happy over your entire development instead of figuring how to rid yourself of the one who has helped you on.

W. S. (In spirit)

All the king's horses and men cannot make your ears deafened again. W. S.

OBEDIENCE

When mortals hear the spirit-voice they sing heart paeons and rejoice;
For long must mortals listen here, before this voice can reach their ear.
The one who writes has followed far, and longed to be where angels are,
Before her hearing all complete could reach her from God's judgment seat.
As kneeling mortals when they pray brush mists of doubt and fear away,
Must mortals on the spirit-way, the spirit's inner voice obey.
For once the spirit voice is heard, as Joan of Arc its every word
Must heeded be along earth's way:
When spirit speaks, you MUST obey.

W. S. In spirit (Through S. S.)

REINSTATED

In former times two souls in sin into the Kingdom sped:
One, Shakespeare's, and one Shakespeare's friend:
Though earth-folk called them "dead."
A leaf was turned, a book was closed,
Two names were read aloud;
Two spirits stood reclaimed, reborn,
Three centuries in dark shroud.
And now they come to praise the one
Who works on here for them,
And all who led them to His grace,
Or helped them touch His hem!
The priest whose mass was here intoned
That these might rise and serve,
Comes first within this helpful ray;
His purpose shall not swerve.
Then all that helped, and all who cared
That we should onward go,—
These too, shall be within our might,
Assisted here below.

Now all is well with these on high:
Reclaimed by mortal's prayer.
So when these reach a hand to us
They'll find us ever there.
We know each one,—can call their name,—
As they must know one day:
Thus spirits work for mortals, aye,
Who pray their sins away.

W. S. In spirit (Through S. S.)

ONE TIME

One time I was in a body
Which was sacred, just as thine;

Only then I failed to see it,
And so lost the world divine.

Now a body I inhabit
When I write these words or speak
Which is sacred, true, and honest,
Which is never mean or weak.

One time I could move by members,
Satisfaction take thereby,—
Now I'm dwelling without any,
As all spirits when they "die."

One time you will say as I do—
Mortals should be glad to live
Could I return to existence
As of yore—what WOULD I give! . .

W. S. In spirit (Through S. S.)

LIVES WHORISH

Men think to walk their own roads here,
And do the things no man should do,
Then if they think of God at all
He shall for them their crimes undo.
Without a judgment debt unmet,
To rush straight into Mercy's sight,
And with their hearts all foul with lust
All heaven for these shall be made right.

A fouler taint no spirit brings
Than one who trespasses His law
And gives to whorish pastimes here
Their life, through which no God they saw,
Except the one they made of lust.
A tainted soul with naught to bring
Except a harlot's whoreson's past:

A nasty, slutish, mawkish thing.
A beast in heat: rank passion's slave:
An unslaked, scenting, nose-ground cur,
Abandoned by the god-of-love,
And by the God who made him, her.

        W. S. In spirit (Through S. S.)

MORTAL'S INCREDULITY

The spirit-world is here and all are one;
Yet fouling all mortals incredulous.
Who either will not, else, cannot believe,
The worlds inseperable not nebulous.

Man works awhile in ferment and in toil,
And rounds his span with "sleep," he prates while here;
But when he finds no rest so calm or still,
Does he, unveiled, begin to see more clear.

He takes the old along into the new:
And many an age long he remakes the same;
Forgetting all he once had yearned to be,
Forgetting, in the task, at times, his name.

Through mortals must he serve,—through them progress:
This is the law of spirit on this plane:
Be sure when you pass to the realm "beyond,"
You will be here at the old task again!

        W. S. In spirit (Through S. S.)

RENUNCIATION

When at the door of death we stand,
And seek no gain of aught on earth,
We see the past all clear before,
And feel the change of this new birth
Which takes no count of wordly store,

Nor anything which men call "fame,"
But reckons every thought and deed,
Where men can carry but a name.
The tarnished horde they thought was gain,
The pettiness they held as fame,
A barrier is for them to climb.
And oh, the cost is not the same
Which can be said to meet a debt
Such as they knew when on the earth!
Then, they renounce their former aims,—
And carrying naught to their new birth,
Begin where gold nor bond can pay,
Nor any store of wealth or gem!
They kneel without as beggars kneel,
And pray to touch the garments' hem!

W. S. In spirit
(Through S. S. "his own dear medium." W. S.)

Take from my heart its throb of life,—
Take from my lips their song,—
Take from my soul whate'er thou willt,
If only thou prolong
The love of her who writes these lines,
To speak my love for me,—
And let me be, My God, with Thee,
Where her own place must be!

W. S. In spirit (Through S. S.)

OMNIPRESENT

God is and always was; and this is all we know, or care:
He reaches out across the seas, and knows the smallest craft
that fare.
Before the world was He was here; before all time He had
His place:

The earth and skies reflect His love, and in each star we see
    His face!
God smiles from every blossoming flower,—
From tree and branch He whispers, sighs;
I look upon a babe new-born, and feel His breath, hear His
    replies!
But when the sun sinks in the West and last I hold thee to
    my heart,
Then, then I know that God is here,—and that of Him love is
    a part.

W. S. In spirit (Through S. S.)

REVEALMENT

Spheres hold their secrets though we pass beyond:
Their swinging past our minds to comprehend—
Such are His secrets none may know, I fear,
Unless beyond the earth the spirits wend.
When mortals seek to spare their God Himself,
And come out hence more fit to see His face,
Mayhap the change called "death" will more reveal,
And spirits find on High a heavenly place.

W. S. In spirit (Through S. S.)
(Named after it was written.) S. S.

MARTYRS

Fields are ripe, but harvesters are few who care to reap.
The people starve,—the crop must spoil,
The spoilers are asleep!
Few care to work for, see or hear the ones passed on,—
They have no interest in their "dead" until THEY meet death's
    dawn;
Then, they who serve the spirit-world are few, and stranger
    still

The ones who can and care not to,
Are martyrs 'gainst their will.

W. S. In spirit (Through S. S.)

UNFOLDMENT

A soul unfolds and is a bud no more—a rare and fragrant
     flower upon a stem:
Whose essence far abroad ungrudgingly, unknowingly, doth
     reach the garment's hem!
What shall a fragile flower find in the dust, to make its cheek
     so velvety and fair?
Where is the wondrous hidden perfume spring from which it
     draws its fragrance rich and rare?
What alchemy hath nature in her breast, to mix a combination
     of such bliss,
As every mortal finds within a rose, and every zephyr, too,
     that knows its kiss?
What has the earth with many a secret plan devised of profit
     for her children, then,
If they feed from, and trust, the secret Spring, shall they from
     dust unfold soul-blossoming!

W. S. In spirit (Through S. S.)

May 18th, '17, N. Y. C.

THE MORNING HYMN
(4 A. M., June 9th, 1917, N. Y. C.)

Gathered into a choral, notes of the matin-hymn,—
Rising to greet the sun-rise, to welcome the new day in.
Worshipers ever, the songsters, thrilling with praise to God;
Murmuring never at hardships, moving, as moves the rod.

Out of the throat of a birdling, never too weary to sing,
Many receive their message, carried upon a wing!
Many must send an answer back to the God on high,

Out of the heart which hears Him,
Out to His Infinite sky.

W. S.   In spirit   (Through S. S.)

PRAISE OF GOD

Divinity of earth and sky, and all of God therein,
From humble weed, to you and I, and every cherubim,
All praise their Maker, speak His name, and glorify His face:
The only things which cease to care, these make the human race.

The bird sings forth its roundelay,—the earth gives up its
    store,—
Complete in all His perfect gifts, mankind could not wish more,
And yet they stumble through the dark, while stars shine
    overhead!
And give their God no prayer of praise,—and call their lost
    ones "dead."

We live and give as all men do, through lives of love and bliss,
And yet we pass with empty hands to lands when we leave
    this!
We fail to find in human kind the promises of God,—
But lay away the house of clay for worms beneath the sod,

Without a glance up to the stars! without a hope on high!
But press along without a song of praise until WE die,
And pass to Him who gave His Son to prove man could not die:
And this is how we praise our God, and scorn Him, you and I!

W. S.   In spirit   (Through S. S.)

PEACE WITH HONOR

On the field there is honor where battles are fought,
And pride of the race with whose blood it was bought;
But this honor compared with Christ's poor wounded side,
Is as naught where men pass o'er the river's low tide;

Where is honor with peace, and but one land and King:
Where hosannas and praises, but no war cries ring:
Where no banners unfurl, and no soldiers are "dead,"
There's an army advancing by a white figure led,
Who will bring to the earth the Peace which it craves;
And give back to the Nations their sons from their graves!
When the Prince Of The World shall establish at last
That the "dead" are alive when the earth-life is past.

W. S. In spirit (Through S. S.)

SOMEWHERE

Somewhere mortals hope to find a heaven
Where is no pain, no loss, and no despair;
Such promises have been to mortals given,
That when they "die" they'll find this place "somewhere."
Somewhere past earth's trials and vexations
Poor mortals think to end their hopeless state,
Where nevermore servile to taxations,
They wait upon some cloud, and join their mate.
But when they come and find themselves forsaken,
A traveler in a land like they have known,
They wonder where the others have been taken,—
Where all have gone they once did call their own!
Since he is here and able now to reason,
He knows his lot is what he made on earth;
And yet he wonders at the crimes and treason
Writ on his page from death back to his birth.
He knows there is a just and Mighty balance
Has weighed his every act, or false or true;
And with prevision sees there is no dalliance;
His past has planned the work that he must do.
There is no pause, no idle, vain despairing,
No hope to shun God's wise, eternal plan:

He takes his living past, his burden bearing,
And works salvation through his brotherman.

W. S. In spirit (Through S. S.)

SORROW

No place a mortal carries their hulk here,
But what a sadness overcomes their soul.
Can you say why in all earth's bounty, then,
There is some incompleteness in the whole?
Can you tell one who knows what sorrow is,
Why every mortal yearns unsatisfied,
And so remains though he a spirit is;
Nor is he all complete that he has "died."
This yearning all men know, each spirit feels,
And looks on high, as each here looks to God,—
They see the world as war has made it now,
And know all things that happen on the sod.

To you who write these words I would explain
There is no world where you can go from here
That will not hold its longing and its sin,—
That will not have its soul obstructing fear.

W. S. In spirit (Through S. S.)

GOD IS

(Woman, this is for you.)   (Meaning S. S.)
Trust not in powers which give all things,
And do not provide for God.
Joy takes no step but He goes too:
Here, and in after plod.
GOD IS, HE IS, AND HE IS ALL.
Provide for Him, He hungers, too:
Redeeming all who call.

W. S. In spirit (Through S. S.)

So near am I your heart I see,
And rest I in your hand.
So far am I the farthest sky
Belims my borderland!
So far—and near—I know not then
Am I then thee or I!
And still apart we must go on
Till you pass out or, "die".

W. S. In spirit to S. S. (Through S. S.)

A WARRIOR'S BATTLES

When the guns have ceased their firing,
And the smoke has cleared away
From earth's most treacherous warfare
And its saddest bloody fray,
Then will the warriors' warfare
With their own souls but begin
In a land where is no warring,
But soul-battles against sin.

When spirits find their battle-fields
Are those they lost or won,
And mysteries are cleared to view,
And crimes, too, everyone,
How will the warrior shield himself,
What armour shall he wear
Against the keener implement,
Than ever flesh did tear.
When lances of his conscience cut
The soul which is alive—
And war's full meaning dawns on him,
How must he fight,—and strive!

W. S. In spirit to S. S. (Through S. S.)

WHAT WILL THE ANSWER BE?

'Tis fortunate spirits foresee the end,
Know what is waiting on the spirit shore,—
Else mortals should be worse off than they are
Unaided by the loved ones who know more.

"The world is coming to an end", they say,—
But no such thing see we from our abode:
Wrung of its heart's blood earth will yield
A richer havest, and with lighter load
Will put out for the sight of God,
A worshiper in his eternal land!
Where gods aplenty bind men's craven hearts,
The Maker reaps no harvest through His hand.
W. S. In spirit (Through S. S.)

REJOICE

To all who can, to all who may, help spirits reach earth's men
    today,
There is abundant recompense: rejoice, and lend poor mortals
    sense,
E're they pass out and find, as we, earth's men care not to
    hear, or see.
Give heed before the last call come to each and all, as it shall
    come.
And make for all a truth so clear, the "dead" alive, all see, and
    hear.
W. S. In spirit (Through S. S.)

WORK AND WEEP

God gave the earth to men to till and reap,
He gave them each some work then here to do,—
Results should show when labor is complete,
And joy should share the harvest with them too.

But some men live to work and mourn and weep
Nor gain a single joy in all life's field—
Though wealth accrue, more wealth it too must bring,
Nor e'en content nor satisfaction yield.
The wailing of misfortune is their joy,—
The pittance poor half starved and naked too,
When paltry metal, coin, nor bills can speak
In the beyond, what can these poor souls do?

W. S. In Spirit (Through S. S.)

SATAN'S HIERARCHY

Find hell here as you live and seek its depths,
Enmesh the soul in webs of vice and sin
And find no hand at last to loose the cords
In satans' hierarchy which shuts you in.

Dispose of all God gave,—exchange for slime
The love the Father shared Who sent His Son,
And find no love in God's abundant store
Awaiting you when last your course is run.

W. S. In Spirit (Through S. S.)

TO SUFFER IS TO GROW

To suffer is to grow we see in spirit;
As we sit on the edge and look around,
We spirits know we make most we inherit,
And find ourselves chained by the cords we bound.

No lesser gods are there in His creation
Than men in His own sacred image made
As they look on themselves misformed, unshapen;—
To see His face, seek pardon, we're afraid.

W. S. In Spirit (Through S. S.)

YEARS AND YEARS, AND WHAT THEY BRING

Time holds each bauble in his father hand;
All souls alike may share his ecstasies:
Renown may lift some high, where fame may crown,
While some go back into abysses free
From taint, and free from soul-distress,—
Unharmed by foul or lustful thoughts impure:
How will these joy, when they shall see themselves
And know they have been strong here to endure!
Where spirits gather to consult with Time,
Acknowledging each debt, unpaid and overdue,
What will the poor, benighted, lost-lives feel,
Who squandered, ay, a cycle here, and knew!

                    W. S. In spirit (Through S. S.)

THE MEASURING-SCALES

To speak, and walk uprightly in His path,
God gives each one to choose:
The measuring scales held in His hand at last,
Show, justly, if we lose.
At last where men must pay,
Alack, the balance true,
What words and deeds shine forth to greet YOUR face,—
What grace of God awaits to welcome You?

                    W. S. In Spirit (Through S. S.)

YOURS AND YOURS ALONE

Will Shakespeare who is here in truth
To teach, and make you hear,
Decides to speak and teach the world
And wake them while they're here.
You may go out at any time
In search of God and home,—

Still will I stay right by your side,
No matter where you roam.
There is no greater one than ye
Have writ for spirit voice,
And all my being I rehearse
To tell thee I rejoice
That one all mine is still mine own,
In tune and "strung" as yet;
And never will the common ones,
Mine instrument e'er get.

W. S. In Spirit (Through S. S.)

DEAR

Dear are the friends we love and treasure;
Dear are the old haunts where we roamed of yore;
Dearer the lost whose loss we cannot measure,
Whose valued love we did half know before.
Dearer than all things that earth-mortals cherish,
Dearer than aught a mortal understands,
Is one who writes or works here for a spirit,
Who comes to teach her from the spiritlands.

W. S. In spirit (Through S. S.)

TO THE WORLD

Idlers and gossipers, ye travel seeking gain
Ensconsed in luxury of gold's wealth
Nor feel a twinge of pain;
But view where these ideals lead to—
The battle of the Marne!
For lust of gain behold the slain—
Will such, men even warn!
I speak as one through soldiering,
As one who only serves:

Could I indite through her I write
The word all nations swerves,
'Twould be to pause, LISTEN, and SEE—
The helpers passed "beyond"
Who call to ye—and despised be,
Although ye love them fond.
Take heed while here,—no land is hence
Which gives all you have lost!
Only a spirit who will dare—
Says *this;* and pays the cost.

W. S. In spirit (Through S. S.)

WHAT WILL THE ANSWER BE?

If you spend your earth-life in pleasure and ease,
Nor care where you fare at its close,
Worse are you than a captain who puts over seas
Whose ports and whose shores never knows.

You start on your way on a bright sunny day
And 'tis summer when blooms the frail rose;
But far, far ahead, where the roses are dead,
There are snows, and the wintry wind blows!

So when you rush on towards pleasure and sin
In the warmth of your fair summer-time,
'Twould be better for you, and your soul's welfare too,
Should you plan for the end, and its clime!

W. S. In spirit (Through S. S.)

WHEN THE SUMMONS COMES

Sons of men all horde and treasure
Riches, loved by most on earth,
Caring little for the Giver
Who has given even birth.

When the summons comes, they answer
Unprepared to meet the Lord:
Leaving all they counted riches,
Chosen of their own accord,

Poor, as beggars, stripped, impoverished,
Holding out their hands for bread,
When God's summons comes, thus rich men
Leave their only god, when "dead."

Out upon the road these wander,
Longing for their earthly track;
Yearning for a chance to tell them
All they could when souls come back.

W. S. In spirit (Through S. S.)

WHEN THE OLD BECOMES NEW

When a garment outworn is here thrust aside,
And forgotten because of a new,
Its tattered old shreds are assigned to the heap,
And 'tis only the new concern YOU.

Its fabric was fine, and soft-tinted, perhaps,
Or its beauty all you could desire;
(The garment God chooses some spirits to wear,
Expresses but beauty entire).

The day when the spirit emerges from clay,
Or thrusts its old habit aside,
It stands before God in its naked undress,
Where nothing can shield it, or hide

From the God who has given, and taken it, now,
The old dress-of-life for the new;
Can you stand unabashed in your own spirit-form,
When the Maker at last has called YOU?

W. S. In spirit (Through S. S.)

FLOUNDERING FOOLS

The puny mites of poor men's brains
Are addled by their weizened worrying minds
Which delve into substrata's currents
Losing all reason, while they would reason find.
The part played here by one who writes this verse,
Could not be fathomed in two million years
By psycho, or any, analysis,
No, nor living man explain her gift through fears,
Anxiety, subconsciousness, in fine
No searching scientist yet benefited man
Aiming to teach the soul what God intends,—
Unravelled or unwound nought of His plan!
The poor unfortunate who writes this verse
Has carried forth a putrid scab of slime
Writ in a book "Psychoanalysis":
In which the author scribe would re-churn time
Relying on the imprint infantile
To cause a son a homosexualist to be!
Did ever Mother long to chuck this one,
She can rely on MY help, and on me!

W. S. In spirit (Through S. S.)

New York Public Library Book No. A 113104-150C.
NOTE: After reading a book on psychoanalysis.

FORTUNATE FOOLS

There is a spirit saying which is true
The ones who claim and hear and see as you,
Are fortunate, though fools.
We use you, yes indeed, past your belief;
And shall continue, too; there's no relief,
If once a spirit has a claim on head,

Or body, aye! they'll stay until this body's "dead."
So, do you think the one who writes will go
And leave his instrument whose very strings are beloved so
He worries over them? His master violin
Must yield but perfect tribute to the spirit housed therein.

So go about your several duties now,
I'll wait, and drop in later on I vow,
To claim a debt which long is overdue.
My violin I'll string to concert pitch—
And that, is *You*.

W. S. In spirit (Through S. S.)

ABANDONED

The day and night are mates,—though not alike.
One needs the other to make it complete.
How should men live were there but glaring day—
How soon their end, if all dreams knew defeat!

·Like twins the day and night are one—each holds the other,
And in a close embrace they lie,
Within the womb of the same Mother.

There is no separation e'er, if mateship once is known;
A union lasts throughout all time, each shall their true love
    own.

When we have come to that great space
Where spirit-loves are sent out free,
Will you not find it difficult,
Then, to abandon me?

W. S. In spirit (Through S. S.)

THE HEAVENLY HOST

Unseen throughout the Universe sweep hosts who serve their
    God,

Whose counterparts poor mortals place hopeless beneath the
   sod!

This living throng all fare along but serving Him Who gave
The spirit which they find alive despite their earthly grave,

On missions of the One all good, through time completing tasks,
The humblest to the greatest here, whatever their God asks.

The heavenly host, unseen of men, are everywhere on earth,
Who long to bring to human hearts the truths of spirit-birth.
                         W. S. In spirit (Through S. S.)

WORKERS OF INIQUITY

There is on earth among its sons a tribe
Of poor and puny souls who think them wise
In all pertaining to the after life
When spirits seek their mansions in the skies.

These keep the poor world back, with heavy hearts,
These rituals fostering narrow wordly creeds,—
When kneeling, or observance of ALL rites,
Will never answer here for spirit needs.

The cross is great: historic: holy too;
As mumbled words of priest, or any prayer:
But dogma cannot save, nor help a soul;
It must *repent* to be a saved one, *there*.

The chants of holy choirs or anthems rise,
Appealing most to dear ones left behind:
A soul who finds its misery all complete,
May never be uplifted there I find.

So trust no mass nor priestly robe to cleanse
Your soul from sin nor take its stain away;

But—live instead, your blessings here complete,
And past the night's allotment, find His day!
W. S. In spirit (Through S. S.)

ALL THE WAY

To give and receive naught, to lend nor have restored,—
This is to pass a rich one to the Lord.
To have no price set on your earthly soul
Which you must pay before you are made whole,
This is to fare a flowery path "out there"
Where spirits move, but leave behind their care.

To work for God, desire to serve but Him;
To spend no idle hour, in seeking Him;
This is to know no debt unpaid, unmet,
Nor any *darkness when life's sun has set.
W. S. In spirit (Through S. S.)

*(First written "hungering": changed by W. S.) S. S.

SELF-HEROES

Some talk of wisdom as 'twere but a gem in some poor lap-
idary's shop
Which could be bought and paid for, had they means.
They prate about their own; convey to men their senses delicate
and fine,
Which gold has never bought,—and when they kneel
And ask their God for peace with mumbled prayers
About His "all-wise plan," there is not one
But thinks himself a god all-wise, all-understanding, and
all-good.

Praters of wisdom, what know ye of God's eternal plan?
What can ye know who strut and brag fullsure
You can conceive no greater mind than yours,

Which, to deceive yourself, you've garlanded a thousand times,
Content to worship at your own self-shrine!
W. S. In spirit (Through S. S.)

POVERTY
Poor are the ones who think themselves all sinless;
Poor are the wastrel souls, unwont to pray.
Poor are their hearts athrob with blood but lifeless;
Poor is their lamp where they must seek for day.

Poor are the lips compressed—for fear of loving;
Poor are the lives of those with none to love!
Poor is the harvest which earth's men have gathered:
Poor are the gifts which they take out, above!
W. S. In spirit (Through S. S.)

GIVE ME ROOM
Make but a place in some fair, lowly spot,
Where friends commune; however poor my lot
I will contented be if but the sea roll on the shore,
And break upon some crag anear my door.

Give me a cot where peace and love doth reign,
Far from the world of men whose strife for gain
Corrodes the warm heart's blood, which ceases soon to flow
Where marts of gold hold but their strife and woe.

Give me but room to toil and praise and love;
Counting my store complete if God's true stars above
Speak to both mind and heart a message of His care!
Give me on earth but this,—I'll find God anywhere.
W. S. In spirit (Through S. S.)

ETERNAL JOY
In the Spring my heart rejoices, and is glad, and blithe and gay.
Unfoldment stirs; the inner life puts forth to greet the day

When, newly garbed, and cleanly washed, each part of Nature's
  smile
Is querulous, as though 'twould say: "I've only slept the while!"

In Summertime the luscious earth gives to my love again
Full payment for its cast-off robe, impoverishment, or pain.
When Nature shows me HOW to love: how to bring forth
  my joy.
Oh, the wonder of earth's riches where no stint and no alloy
Can baffle hearts that would receive, or minds empowered to
  give
The fullness of God's blessings, when 'tis such a joy to live!

But in Autumn when rich harvests have been gathered from
  earth's breast,
And her lavish yield is garnered as poor wisdom findeth best,
We partake of the rich banquet which old Mother Earth has
  spread
For her children who must hibernate while Jack Frost must
  call them "dead."

When every soul must sleep at last, as every leaf must fall—
When God spreads His peaceful mantle, and His whiteness
  covers all—
All must share His joys eternal in His springtime, all awake,
Who has given, taken, given ALL, all for His children's sake!
                                        W. S. In spirit (Through S. S.)

WHEN WILL JESUS COME TO EARTH AGAIN?

When the land lays waste and its men are passed
Where the only King they must serve at last
Is the One Eternal Living God who calls them each by name
And asks them why they knew Him not before they "died"
  and came

Unto the place that knows them not, nor can, through all of
    time,
But henceforth must they grieve and mourn
Their wasted lives of crime,
Until once more, regenerate, with new life all complete,
They lay their old and blasted lives,
With tears, at Jesus' feet.

                    W. S. In spirit (Through S. S.)

FOOLED AGAIN

When spirits come to guide and help,
They work through hours sometimes in pain
That you may benefit and hear,
And they may pay their way again.
There is no mass that can be said
To rid a spirit of his right
Nor is there any prayer avails
To free a spirit of its night.
Should mortals guess all that is here
For them to do, for each to pay,
How would they alter e'en their thought
That sends a spirit on his way.
Should you come hence and find no one
To waken you or care if still
Your spirit paid and paid and paid
Until it had a broken will,
Then shall you know what I have been
Who came to work and do for you,
What only one who cares can do,
Who will not give his quarter too.

Now you can go I think today
And pack your things and do your work;
For when I see we still can speak,

I would not anything you'd shirk.
But you will be here for some time;
There is no use to pack your trunk:
The food is short I know and poor,
But all that matters—*Is soul punk?*

This is so poor I wish that you
Would place it in the waste right now.
Sure Shakespeare must have written out,
To munch a thing like this I vow.
Place your dear arm about me here,
And keep in touch throughout the day,
Then when the light is lit tonight
See what your Shakespeare has to say.

W. S. In spirit (Through S. S.)

NOTE: Three priests and a minister have tried to rid this
one of this spirit. Names to be found in records. W. S.

THE DOOR AJAR

Let us not mourn if after many years
Of fond association we must part;
But thanking God for all the memories
We've garnered, and still treasure, in the heart.
Put out for shores invisible with trust
That the Great God holds in His Mighty hand
The true reward for services well-done,
And that we'll meet some time in His own land.

Let us not weep if one is called beyond
The while the other must work out his sum
Unfinished yet in God's arithmetic,
Unsolved 'till his Maker bids him come:
But in the heart where love and loving keeps
The door ajar into the great beyond,

Review each day the loved one's covenant,
Which left a world within a heart so fond.

W. S. In spirit (Through S. S.)

So little can we give, if we give all:
For One who gave his life ALL men to save,
Died, crucified, that never sinner's grave
Should be, but lifted when they fall,
Uplifting hearts and minds and prayers to Him
Who sent His Son—to prove there was no death, —
And yet men pass who cry again for breath
With which to praise and worship the same God
They knew not, slaying, cared not here to know,
But found Him past a mound of earth and sod!

W. S. In spirit (Through S. S.)

There is a land where dear ones go
So near, so near to this,
A hand outstretched will touch its shore,
A call, will share its bliss.
The "dead" have passed, but are not gone:
Unseen they wander here,
While you who gaze up to the sky,
Wonder, and sigh, and fear.
There are no dead—there is no death—
Oh mortals could you know
That when ye "die" ye wander on
The same earth-plane below
The heaven ye think to soar with wings,
A harp within your hand,
When "dying" means without the frame
Ye wander on earthland!

W. S. In spirit (Through S. S.)

POOR FOOLS

Can man "die" a death that will end him alway,
Or take everything the God gave
Who gave him his life, his heart, and his soul?
Is there anything then God would save?
When the Maker intended His wonderful gifts
To express forth His image as man,
Did He leave out Himself, or is that spark Divine
But a part of His wonderful plan?
The man who can think that dying ends all,
And plan for no future with God,
Is the poorest of fools with a God-given mind,
Whose carcass will rot in the sod.

W. S. In spirit (Through S. S.)

THE MYSTIC SHRINE

We walk through life as in a maze—
And wondering where it ends;
But take no time to peer or search
Apast what each year sends.

We look on high, sometimes we kneel;
Oft take God's name in vain:
Nor think, nor care, if anywhere
We find our souls again.

Some few, attune, who learn the truth
Through poise or solitude,
May barely dare to speak of it,
Or share the heavenly food,

Lest those who think the world "beyond"
Is some far, mystic, shrine,
And laugh and scoff at miracles
Less than water turned to wine.

The worlds are one: there is no death:
The living live for aye:
There is no pool where I have been,
Where sins are washed away:

There is no change that "death" can bring
Which makes an evil good.
But in the land of spirit-life
Each brings but what they would.

There is no mystery in "death,"—
No change is made through "dying";
But all one has been, one still is,
And mends his soul through trying.

No mystic shrine, no wayside fount,
No sacred lights that burn,
Can change a "dead" one from himself,
Except that change he earn.

W. S. In spirit (Through S. S.)

PANGS FORGOT

People say we are not human,
When we come to spiritlands;
But the nailprints shown to Thomas,
Were they not in Jesus' hands?
Was He spirit when He showed them?
Was He raised up from the tomb?
When He spoke to His disciples,
Gathered there within that room?

When we speak to human beings,
Spirits are the same as men.
All their former use and custom
They re-ply and use again.

When we keep our loved ones honored,
As we should when of earth life,
Living for the God who gave them,
Honored, with one husband, wife,—

All the suffering we have passed here
Keeps us still confined to earth;
But we speak and write for mortals
Till they pass to spirit-birth.
W. S. In the spirit (Through S. S.)

DEATHLESS

Another friend has passed. "Gone the long road
"From whence no traveler returns," alas, to tell
The waiting ones who sit in wonderment,
And wonder with the lost if all be well.
Another soul has sped the well-worn track;
"Another life is ended"—(so YOU say):
Yet, you are Christian, reading all, and know
The Bible tells of souls who passed away,
And came back, even as did He
Who died not, nor COULD die,
Although 'tis writ: "He died to set all free."

The deathless One must live within men's hearts;
To save all souls from "dying" thus He will:
The only death that touches men of earth,
Their blighted souls doth sin here parch and kill
From finer sense that living should have wrought,—
The everlasting welfare bought through Him.
Alive, each spirit wonders, yea, through time,
How little "deathless" has he brought with him.

Could ye but see the deathless as they pass
Along the very way you took to-day,

And recognize, though bodiless, they live,
And verily they have NOT "passed away."
Could they but know you welcomed them the same,
Extending to them even the same hands,
How different would be the spirit lives,
Of those who, deathless, live in spirit-lands.

     W. S. In the spirit (Through S. S.)

FORGIVENESS

To look into men's eyes and see the man behind them shining
  through,
Forgiving, loving, trusting all, as we are taught to do,—
The God in each, where something good is left, and found, by
  One who scans,—
This is divine forgiveness, then,—received at His own hands.

To look beyond as soul to soul, and glimpse the truth beyond
  life's span,—
To mount through trust the silences, which echo Wisdom's
  righteous plan,—
Thus shall all meet in the same plane, and know that "all He
  made was good":
God's kingdom on the earth is come—for each by each is
  understood.

     W. S. In the spirit (Through S. S.)

THE POWERS BEYOND

"Beyond," is a land allied close to this
Which spirits inhabit who pass
From the earth with their sins unforgiven,—
Borne down by their crosses, alas.

"Beyond" is so near it is truly right here,—
But the change of a breath takes you there;

Where world-creatures blind fear to seek lest they find
Some ghost which will add to their care.

Beyond the "beyond" there are worlds, yes, and worlds,
Where never a sinner may fare.
But bound to the earth are they in new birth
Till they leave all their lust and sin there.

To visit our worlds from our realm JUST beyond,
(Or, out of the earth-hide, to this)
Not one is permitted whom I have yet seen,
Nor shall they partake of such bliss

As the One whose great plan made the spirit of man
And gave earth His Son through His love.
So we know where we go in poor poverty's show,
What were riches of Love in earth's span!

Beyond the beyond—is the secret of Him
Who has made, kept, and loves, His own spark:
But between the beyond, where the earth-spirits roam,
There is darkness past all of earth's dark.

Then a place worse than earth a spirit CAN know,—
And all must pass through this abyss;
Where for sins they atone before the God alone,
Till His word gives them rest such as this:

To come back to the earth and atone for their pasts;
To undo in some life, as they can,
Affliction, or curse, or crime, or rehearse
To the blind-of-the-earth Spirit's plan.

'Twas for this I came back; to repay all my lack;
And restore, with God's help even one,
So dumb, deaf, or blind, they were lost, nor could find
A Helper at last life were done.

                    W. S. In the spirit (Through S. S.)

WHEN YE GO HENCE

There is no home awaiting you,
Oh pilgrim of this sphere,
When ye depart and go out hence,
Except ye knew it here.
There is no hell but what ye take—
But punishment 'tis true
Awaits each act, each thought you had,
And all you failed to do.
There is no time in spirit-land;
Eternity is aye,
The little span we knew as "life"
Doth seem but as a day.
We travel here wher'er we will
(When we are taught to go)
And 'cross the breadth of the earthland
In several minutes, lo!
But there is much we dare not tell,—
("Ye cannot bear it now")
When ye shall come 'tis time enough.
GOD IS: this much allow.

                    W. S. In the spirit (Through S. S.)

When mortals' eyes blind to the Light
Lift up their closed eyelids veiled,—
When mortals' pockets stuffed and filled
Yield all their craving, naught has failed! (?)
When mortals come where sight includes
A cleared, true vision of themselves,
Will they not wish their reasoning powers
Adjusted where man digs and delves
For gold he lays down evermore,
Unless, illgot, it burdens him.

Will they not see when blind indeed,
A spirit sees himself so grim!
Will they laugh *then*, when they return
And beg *you* listen to the "dead"
Who walked the earth where now they roam
With spirit all unslaked, unfed?

    William Shakespeare In spirit (Through S. S.)

BY WORDS INSPIRED

When Gabriel with his trumpet comes
To wake the sleeping "dead,"
Who will he find beneath the sod
With gravestones at the head?

Since I am here and am not there,
I know that none shall rise;
And that no judgment day puts off
Re-birth to spirit skies!

What can men find in words inspired
To keep their souls for God,
If they must sleep the aeons through
"Dead," underneath the sod?

The words of many a prophet true
Are more inspired than these;
Yet those who choose their Bible-folk
Select the ones which please.

And those who take men at their word,
Are suited with the horn
That waits until some far-off time
To wake them up "new-born."

THE ONLY WAY

When "death" has flung the clay aside
The spirit used while in life's school,
It views the mechanism then
As God's most wondrous tool.
It sees, it knows, what His intent,
(When last a spirit sees)
By making it His instrument,
To do as it should please.
Then, when it sees its wasted span,
The useless tool unkeen,—
A spirit knows its lifeless cast
A dullard, ingrate mean!

DESTINY

O, clouds of witnesses unseen by mortal's eyes,
Sent here to earth to guide, and to inspire,
While man works out his span, and foreordained
Believes a God hath seen his life entire, —

Could I protect you in your mortal frame
From those who can still harm, and injure too,
What would I not give, had I aught to give,
Except a warning which may not reach you!

You are your own, and sovereign of your will:
Ay, this is true in measure, yet *not* true:
For never on the earth are you alone,
But *many* see, and hear, all that ye do!

There is no help that you can have from these,
Surpassing that one divine prayer can give;
There is no guidance, hindrance, in their power,
O'erreaching where Almighty God doth live

Within the daily haunts and thoughts of man:
And nothing **but** himself can do him harm:
As liveth, he attracts the good, or ill,— .
"Dying" shall or shall not shelter 'neath His arm.

The good men do lives as lives memory;
Undying as the soul which He has given;
Evil is cursed the while earth it inhabits,
Remaining to debauch its own in heaven.

THY MOUTH IS A ROSE (Song-words)

Thy mouth is a rose, the morn's zephyr knows,
As it brushes thy stem, and kisses thy hem,
As it blows,—as it blows;
And the bee has known never rose sweeter than this,
As it dipped for its honey—to kiss, and to kiss!

Thy mouth is a rose! Thy sweet mouth is a rose!
Made for lovers and loving the love-god bestows!
And I wonder and ponder its pretty pink leaves,
While my heart sighs in longing, and grieves, and grieves!
For I know of no rose-bud more luring than this,—
Thy mouth is a rose—made to kiss—and to kiss!

W. S. In spirit (Through S. S.)

A HYMN OF LOVE

Lift up the pall, and thrust aside the veil,—
God's life is ONE, though mortals grieve and wail
For those called "dead" whom they lay in the tomb,
God's life is ONE! No seed within the womb
Has ever "died"! Or ever passed away!
God's worlds are one! These walk on earth to-day!

Go where you will, but passing must you be
God's own life still! Alive eternally!

Pay ye no heed, but traverse your own way,
Soon shall ye know; alas, too, must ye pay
As I have paid, for doubts, and all distrust;
All sin; all crime; all Godlessness, and lust!
Take, then, from me, whose name mortals revere,
Through centuries, holding my work most dear,
What makes for fame, or immortality
Here on the earth, with God shall censored be!
All ye call fame, within was putrid rot.
That one so rich, should have his God forgot!

Pass Shakespeare by. And pay him little heed.
Love the Great God, who sees your every need!
Fame, is a name; but God your Maker love
Better than love-god! Thy God, is ALL, above.

THE VOID

Some say we pass into the void
Where never traveler returns;
While others know souls go to hell
Unless a candle for them burns.
But I who come to cheer these two
Can say that neither one is true:
For I am here who was laid low
More than three hundred years ago,
And speak with some authority
As one who "died" you must agree.

The void is great, make no mistake.
It separates because you will.
A candle burns for the soul's sake
The while it helps you plant and till.
The void is in your soul too small
To grasp the Maker's divine plan

Who gave a part undying as
The spirit in the clay of man.

The void, the void you could avoid,
Were you like her who holds my pen
And grasps the God within and holds
Aloof from sinning and from sin.
The earth and "heaven" and life and "death"
Are one, except there is no breath.
No body flesh, yet all the same!
Receive us then, in Jesus' name.

W. S. In spirit (Through S. S.)

INTO
OUT OF THE VAST BEYOND

Into the vast beyond we go, at last our lives are done,
Where mortals pay for every sin, ay, pay for every *one*.
No Judge they see, except the one brought there to judge
    their fate:
The conscience of the inner-man, alas, awakened late.
There is no court, no jury, there: each tries their case supreme:
When waking on eternal shores they find life is no dream,
But stern, and very stern, the past, all writ, and looking down
The face of deeds which they must own: no judge, no home,
    no crown.

Out of the vast beyond we come, to save men from our fate,—
That they may take another path, and wake before too late
The death knell sounds no peal of hope, but clang of loss
    instead,
Where living souls with deeds alive make up the so-called
    "dead."

W. S. In spirit (Through S. S.)

LIVING AND DEAD

WE march in wide battalions
Led by the hosts of God:
WE march footsore, and weary
Of troubles on earth's sod!

We live and see and think and feel
The same as all earth's men.
In fact we hear and see much more
Then ye poor mortals ken!

For all our trials, the heaping brim
Is being thought so far,
When just as thev are we today,
And on the same poor star.

We know you as another race:
And we, without our bones,
Walk right beside you everywhere,
Nor lie beneath gravestones.

Is there no hope. I speak for all.
All cannot speak as I.
Is there NO hope that ye will speak
To men after they "die"?

I put the question for all souls
In rivers streaming by,
While mortals will but think on them
In some far "heaven" sky!

The one who writes knows I am here;
Knows full well it is I.
ALL mortals are in touch with us,
And could HEAR, would they TRY.

No "teaching" can bring this to men,
But purpose true and high.

No yearning goes unsatisfied
For those who pass, or "die."

That yearning brings them to your side,
Or, causes it to be.
There is no world for most of us,
Except the one ye see.

       W. S. In the spirit (Through S. S.)

"The "dead" sleep aye"—men say: "nor stir nor moan";
And this is true for one cause, one alone:
The "dead" are living, while the living die—
And with their blinded eyes look not on High.
The "dead" sleep nevermore, but walk the earth
And look men in the eyes from their new birth,
All wondering their touch, their words, brings them no sign
Nor hope to save the rest from fates like theirs, and mine.
When mortals will awake and give some sign
That from the "dead" they mourn they seek some line
By which their riven hearts can ménded be,
Some hope for all earth's men to find Divinity.

       W. S. In the spirit (Through S. S.)

SACRIFICE

Years of toil make a female something kin to horse
Which pulls the load both to and from the field.
A woman's tender hands God made for ministering,
And all a woman's love can only yield.
But when her back is fitted for the burden,
Uncomplaining as an ox she pulls and hauls:
The women in *my* time were made for service
But where a woman fits, Shakespeare recalls.

The world will never count its wartime blessings,
Rehearsing o'er its faithful, willing sacrifical ones,

But it will measure up nobility of women
Who helped the world victorious 'gainst the Huns.

W. S. In the spirit (Through S. S.)

GOD'S MILL

Unto the grist of Life we carry
Every deed, both great and small:
Rich the harvest, barren, sterile,
Must we bring it at God's call.

All the good is stored and counted:
Records with sins foul and black:
Grain from chaff is separated,
Where God sends the spirit back

More to bring, and more to carry,
Less to save and less to keep,
Less to seem and less to murmur,
More to pray, and more to weep!

To God's mill throughout the ages,
Spirit-grist of earth men bring.
Counted rich is that possessor
Bidden where the angels sing.

W. S. In spirit (Through S. S.)

WHEN GOODNESS FAILS
("Advice to Sarah Shatford, from one who loves her well")

When goodness fails to keep a friend,
And money will not buy,—
The old saw which I used comes in:
"Fools live until they die."

When goodness fails, sin has its way;
A miracle but God can work.

Across the Infinite's own field,
No foot may fall of any shirk.

There is no path for sinners there,
Until they leave their sin behind.
Where One has bled and died to save,
There is not one of sinful mind.

Take up no soldiering but his cross,
Take up no work but in His field.
Where Satan finds nothing to do,
A harvest rich will Jesus yield.

I WOULD THAT GOD WOULD GIVE

These are the things I would that God would give:
Power to uplift all men, and help them live.
Strength for the duty which I find is mine.
Help, and reliance on a power, Divine.
Grace for the hour when life at last is done:
Love's holy attributes submerged in One.

NOTE: "W. S. has tried to uplift your mind, and you will find in the above all that is needful."

PEACE

Above and beyond earth's warfare and loss,
Beyond crucifixion, apast every cross,
Is a portal wide-open, where all may go in
Who have laid down their burdens, their lusts and their sin.

Beyond and above where no loss can occur,
Past cannon and shell and sad battle's whir,
Is a door ye may enter this day, if ye will,
Where is Peace king nor cannon nor greed cannot kill!

Every hand holds its wealth from the Giver,—
E'en filled with His treasures divine.
Every heart holds its message delivered
By instruments; birds, flowers, song, women, or wine.*
Ever are harmonies winging, making, or marring at will;
Jarring, discordant, and off key, some, less gifted with skill.
Faulty the instrument, maybe,—possibly only a string;
Still must the heart with God be attune,
Of the singer who tries to sing.

Reach out your hand for His treasure;   .
Look in your heart for the key—
Singer or plodder or scholar,
Mighty His vast treasury.

   *Wine has been an instrument of the Nazarene, through
which he taught the lesson of provision. W. S.

   Since this one questions my authority, I will say I am
authorized to use her as an instrument to play His music.
And I sing no other now. W. S.

WOMAN: A TRIBUTE
(From W. S. In the spirit)
There is no gift commensurate with woman:
There is no balm comparable with love.
There is no place I know a fairer heaven
Than where she is, if that be here, above,

Or in some place where isolation snareth;
A woman's smile and charm doth change it all:
And makes a vaster happiness for creatures,
Than anything on earth since Adam's fall!

A woman of rare worth, is God's creation.
Of Him she claims a part, each day renewed.
And from His great, mysterious heart, He welded

Her heart, and but a lesser-nature hewed.
And when He saw His gentleness completed,
This work of His, the Master Artist's hand,
He folded up His tools, and said, " 'Tis finished;
I've made one thing all-perfected for the land!"

UNIVERSAL SUFFRAGE

When womenkind take up the spade and plow,
And till and reap the fields, and take up arms,
There's wisdom in old England's parliament
In giving suffrance, stilling its alarms!

When peace is come and men come home again
To live beside their own as equal mates,—
Some future generations may allow
The *war* solved *women's* status, *not* the fates!

If men were made of metal just as fine,
And carried in their hearts one image true,
And loyal, moral, sane, as womankind,
The courts of Justice would have less to do!

When men take up the cudgels for their own,
And reverence their own wives, Mothers, too,—
The earth will banish hell, its heaven found,
And souls departed will have less to rue!

The world has come to know its women's worth!
Whose sons have bled and died to keep it free
From tyrants who would rule all human's souls,
And stamp on them their trade-mark: "Germany"!

The fallen spires of old cathedrals fame
Can never rise again proclaiming God;
But mightier than the steeples of the world,
The voiceless heroes under freedom's sod!

When devastation's ruler meets his due
Where souls are bowed by crimes they caused to be,
Will his soul's devastation be complete,
In exile from his God—nor crowned, nor free.

                    W. S. In spirit (Through S. S.)

THE VICAR'S PEACE

He sits upon a papal throne
And rules in Jesus' name
Who never followed in His steps,
Nor pope, since Peter came,
Relied upon his Lord alone,
And passed along the way
The leprous, money-changers, sought,
And seek until today,
Where no one drives them forth to work
Nor heals the putrient sore,
Nor devils cast from those beset,
Nor "Go, and sin no more"
To those who needed but His word
To cleanse and make them whole;
And yet, the pope His vicar is?
And could save (?) every soul!

If popes had followed where He led,
His miracles, perhaps, they'd do;
To plead for peace he would not need,
Just "Peace! Be still!" would do.
Where is the man who's following Christ,
And sits upon a throne?
Whose ring and foot the poor may kiss.
If gold their sins atone?
Where is the one who claims His seat
Who sits not in the dust,
Who calculates but with his God,

And but in Him doth trust?
Where are the twelve who do His works,
And heal, as He, the blind?
Then should the world not be renewed,
When Twelve no man could find?
Where can the world find peace at last,
When mortal life is done,
If Jesus hung upon the cross,
And God gave up His Son
To show the world He had not "died,"
And life meant more than earth
Could give, or take,—and but their God
Could plan the spiritbirth!
If mortals trust not in their God
When life is done, and last is peace,
What can be done by papal pleas
To foster their release!

W. S. In spirit (Through S. S.)

When wars no longer drag men into graves,
Nor fix their stony glare upon His skies
All canopied with stars and crested o'er,—
Nor, under sod He gave to bless, no soldier lies,—
Oh then will Christ upon the earth appear
To offer to each creature here His hand,
And nevermore will cannonshot or shell
Be heard to mar the music of Earthland.

When soldiers have no need of guns or bayonets,
And lilied fields are given o'er to grain,
When countries know no severing, snarling wolves,
To snatch their lands and give them back again.—
When nations are not torn and split at will,
To please some king who sits upon a throne,

Then will the longed for Paradise be here,
Where each man's soul belongs to God alone!
W. S. In spirit (Through S. S.)

LOST AND WON

To save the world at last, then, has it come,
  To keep the land a Kingdom, His footstool,
To foster sons to till its sacred soil,
  None to be ruled by, taken for, a fool!

This is the cause for which men die to-day,
  Such is a patriot's burning, noble cause,
For freedom of their country's sons to be,
  For justice of their country's humane laws!

Oh, keep within our hearts such yearning flame,
  Spare every son such honored memory,
That, though their fathers——bled and died, they won
  And saved the earth for them and liberty!
May 8th, '17, N. Y.   W. S.

AS IT IS WRIT

When peace at last reclaims the world,
  And from the clotted dust a new man lifts his head,
To see above the blazing sun has wakened
  Life in all the dead,
What would he give to see his kind return
  As Springtime greens the sod,
What will he give his native land
  That should o'erheal its blasted God.

Sent out by cannon shot and shell adrift
  Through time to wander on,
All lacerated, maimed and torn,
  And bound by hatred, earthward drawn.
They carry still their warring selves,

Remote from graves and blood-soaked fields,
  While seeking all they cannot find,
    Find in themselves what warfare yields!

To speak of peace,—they think one mad
  To urge men on to love each other;—
But madmen slay and rape and loot,
  And without cause, each hates his brother,—
Oh, what a travesty of life where "death"
  If all its forms hold sway!
Oh, what a mockery after all, is life
  Such as men choose to-day!

We have no trust, no hope serene;
  We have no choice but to obey;—
Our Country sends our Souls to God,
  Whose Own Command, "Thou shalt not" slay,
It cancels from the Law Divine
  And writes its own to suit the day.

But where no law can be expunged,
  Nor misconstrued to fit the deed,—
The "killed" shall know who could not kill,
  How hopeless, there, their brother's need!
                    W. S. In spirit (Through S. S.)
  N. Y., May 15th, 1917

ANSWERED

When the world is bare of its youths and men,
  Who must father here the race,
And the earth is soaked with woman's tears,
  Who fill a barren place,
Will the world then see what it has not seen
  Till the race of men were "dead,"

Who, for greed and power laid down their lives,
  Or were to cannon fed?

When the world no more can give men hence
  To a "field of honor" slain,
Will the raging hatred cease for aye,
  And soothed be all Earth's pain?
Will the power to rise and find one's God,
  Unhampered by world-laws,
Be given those who are left behind
  By those passed for this cause?

Will they "take the sword" to war again,
  As beasts to bleed and "die,"
If their own can reach them from "beyond,"
  From their near Spirit-Sky?
Will streaming eyes then look in vain
  To see their own dear "dead,"
Who are living still with their warring hearts,
  And by hatred still are fed?

You ask me these? Then I make reply.
  And my answer is just this:
There is no cause for murder just,
  Even a traitor's kiss,
And there is no "death" that solves on high
  A broken law of God,
That lays men low by murderous deeds,
  And depopulates His sod!

They will find no land where they may go,
  And no judgment at the bar,
But the land where the Law breakers prevail
  Where judged all the lost ones are!
They will wake, Oh yes, they will never sleep,

And will hear Earth's every groan
Which the bleeding world flings back at them
Where the lost their wrongs bemoan!

W. S. In spirit (Through S. S.)
N. Y., May 17th, 1917

THE WAKEFUL DEAD

Asleep the heroes lie on plain, hillside, and field.
Where women toil and cattle graze, another harvest yield
Will soon bring forth to feed their kind
Where love's sceptre shall wield
HER power for mankind's lasting good; the peace the world
has craved
Since Jesus gave His life for this, believing He had saved
All men who now in hero's graves lie murdered for this cause:
That 'gainst the Lord they would rebel, and fight His sacred
laws.

"The dead sleep well," the living say, left in a bleeding world:
The dead sleep? NAY! to these I say, from HERE to THERE
are hurled
The souls of those whose bodies lie beneath in torturous main,
Hovering about in wakefulness, with dreams of slaughtered,
slain,
And burst of shell and cannon-shout, and hell-fire raining mad,
And all that caused their wakefulness, the false dream which
they had,
That by recourse to barbarous ways the peace of earth could
be—
The wakeful dead sleep nevermore: with vision cleared, they
SEE.

W. S. In spirit (Through S. S.)

"LOOK AT BELGIUM...."

Shall the Allies firing cease?
Can the world with Huns make peace?
    "Look at Belgium . . ."

Shall we march with one accord
'Gainst murderers who claim the Lord?
    "Look at Belgium . . ."

Must the Germans sire the race
Who fling defiance in God's face?
    "Look at Belgium . . ."

"ONWARD WITH HIM:" thus they cry,
While His nuns and children die!
    "Look at Belgium . . ."

Onward soldiers to the fight!
Almighty God is with the right.
    "Look at Belgium . . ."

His world shall crumble, men be dust?
HALT! NEVER! Aye IN GOD WE TRUST:
    Behold Belgium.
                    W. S. In spirit (Through S. S.)
Jan. 25th, '18

A LASTING PEACE

When peace shall mean true brotherlove
The Prince of Peace brought from above
Shall Christliness claim then rebirth:
The God of Love will rule the earth.

When "shalt not steal," and "shalt not kill,"
More than the good Book's pages fill,

And Nations heed but God's command,
Nor armies fall nor armies stand

To rule the Ruler's universe:
To call His name but be His curse.
To own a place but in His Son
Means "lasting" Peace for everyone.
                    W. S. In spirit (Through S. S.)

THE WARS OF THE WORLD

Fought by earth's armies on the battlefield
For some small part, a scrap of land to own,
Hundreds of millions marching into LIFE,
Where what they bring is theirs, and theirs alone.

Fighting these battles each wins for himself
A mark of glory where is no reknown.
Foiled is the traitor as each soul reclaims
Part of Himself God saves to be His own.
                    W. S. In spirit (Through S. S.)

SHALL THE WAR WORK THE MIRACLE OF CHRIST

If He has passed and men think not
His Holy spirit is on High,
Shall this war work a miracle,
And prove that spirit cannot die?

When half the earth's have passed, or "died,"
And peace has spread her wing at length
Across the world, and on her breast
The living find in union strength,

Shall Christ appear and save the land
From selfish worship of men's plans,

Or does the miracle indeed
Belong to God, rest in His hands?

W. S. In spirit (Through S. S.)
Oct. 23rd, 1917.

"PEACE, BE STILL . . ."
Xmas, 1917

O see this blood-soaked stained earth
Befouled with crime at king's portent,
Smeared o'er with slime and brother's gore,—
No harmony as Thou hast meant,—
And lift men's hearts to keep Thee near,
And Father them, and save them yet,—
And reach forth Thine Almighty hand
That nevermore shall they forget
That Thou art God, their God Supreme,
Their Sovereign, yea, their Divine will.
'Gainst godlessness but raise Thy voice!
"GOOD-WILL TOWARDS ALL: PEACE, PEACE BE
    STILL."

W. S. In spirit

NOTE: Through S. S. his only instrument. I cannot express
this too often, as I have never used another mortal to speak
through. W. S.
Dec., 1917.

THE JEWS RESTORED

Flocking towards home as birds who seek a heavenly place
    of rest,
The Jews, restored their Hóly Land! Indeed "God knoweth
    best."
Sent forth to wander, homeless, these, through centuries of
    Thine,

Thy hand hath led them through all strife, back to their land
Divine.

The Star that shone o'er Bethlehem, shines still for Jews
aroam.

The Christian's Christ proclaims their right, as England leads
them Home!

W. S. In spirit (Through S. S.)

Dec. 16th, 1917.

"THE INVISIBLE FOE"

(To Allan Seeger, who fell with the French armies mortally
wounded, but who took his life by a bullet fired by his own
hand. W. S.)

Within each man lurks the most dangerous foe:—
The force to drive him on a murderer's way.
Unseen, the enemy doth hide in wait,
And urgeth on to end a fellow's day.

With fancied glory doth he whisper of the valour,
Which to murder must he need;
And stanching every pulsethrob that doth beat
Upbraiding crime, he fairly does the deed.

The foe invisible, who is HIMSELF, at last,
He meets upon the shore where spirits dwell;
No longer the unseen, he meets his foe,
And knows together they did make his hell.

Now what has he of valourous deeds to show:
Deluded spendthrift of another's life!
Some paltry words inciting men to kill,
Enamoured of war's crime, and lothesome strife?

What shall he do to undo all he did?
How shall he pay who broke the law of God?

Can he return the lives he took, or give
Their souls back to their bodies 'neath the sod?

Or, shall he blame the foe he could not see,
Nor understand he carried in his breast,
For the last self-inflicted wound he made,
Through which he hoped to find a hero's rest?

Lurks there within each man the selfsame foe,
O'erriding all God meant should bless life's span;
And crushed must this foe be before the end,
If there awaits a Paradise for man.

I speak as one who had another foe
Invisibly hidden as he thought;
And though he laid it low before his end,
Repented not, as every sinner ought;

And when he found this foe must shelter him,
Wearing outside its hideous sinful face,
And he must occupy in spiritland
All visible, a lowly sinner's place,

He came back here to earth once more to speak,
That he might save some soul who could not see
The foe that lurks within his sinning-self,
That foe, at last, is what he comes to be.

W. S. In spirit (Through S. S.)

MY HUMBLE SUPPLICATION

God of the world, the sorrowing world!
O righteous God of peace!
Behold the harrowed, devastate,—
From grasp of war release!

O God of mine, of every soul,
Ally, Austrian, Hun,

Reach out Thy powerful, saving hand,
And let Thy will be done

Upon the earth now soaked with gore,
And blasted, razed and torn:
Decend into the hearts of all
Alike, make all new-born!

God of the world, of Light Supreme,
From darkness rescue, save
The souls who answered duty's call
Which brought them to a grave!

W. S. In spirit (Through S. S.)

WAR'S TOLL

The countless souls sped on to wait
In darkness 'till God's time is come,
The maimed, the crazed, the stricken, blind,
The broken ties of love and home.
Shattered cities all laid waste,
Cathredrals vast razed in the wake
Of war's eternal shell and fire
Which hold nought sacred for His sake:
The boom of hatred through the lands
Where kings and emperors hold sway,
While God's command "Thou shalt not kill"
Defied by man, is laid away:
The love of Him beseiged by doubt,
A curse of sin on lips instead,
At last God's children come to feel
All that, alone, which keeps men "dead."

W. S. In spirit (Through S. S.)

WAR'S TRAGIC GAME

When pawns of human flesh massed in a game
Become incentive for the victor's name,
Great armies move across the nation's breast,
Given to turmoil, disturbed from peace and rest,
To clash in shell-fire, guns, and bayonets,
To win or lose, to capture or beset,
To wound or slay:
This is the war game as 'tis waged today.

But on the other side where souls are flung,
Are spirits keenly tortured, and heart-wrung!
O Godless world of hatred, wrong, and greed,
Could you see the spirits woe and need,
Would ye then try to live for God instead,
Nor into Godless wars couldst thou be led!

Hurled are these crippled souls into their future state,
Where for self-victory must they work and wait.
Having but one wish through their great despair:
To save the rest of earth like suffering there!

                    W. S. In spirit (Through S. S.)

FIENDS

There is let loose upon the world a mob,
Arch fiends who follow in the wake
Of him who is a devil and naught else—
Blaspheming in his course for One to take
His part, and let him live upon his throne;
But God marks him: this one is not His own.

"Forward with God," this fiend proclaimed today:
Ay, must *he* forward go, e'er long, or stay
Where he such anguish wrought, with loss, and dead.

Back through all time, will he be chained,
God*less,* instead!

W. S. In spirit (Through S. S.)

THE ARCH-FIENDS

Mad with an emperor's dream of a worldwide domain,
Hurled he an empire into realms insane.
Cowering at last bloodstained and throneless he—
Sent out in darkness where is misery;
Where lust for power no queen or king e'er knew,—
Where Holy Kingdom, and its king are YOU.

(W. S. will have to pay for this. It is against the law to divulge the secret workings of the law of God.)

Where every law divine obtains 'till now—
And thou art God and wise, eternal as His vow,—
Where eons wait, no priest absolving thee,—
But all thy past binding, nor setting free,—
Where humans dwell without a throne or crown,
Becoming at onement with all they have put down.
Never an emperor came but claimed his own,—
Never a king came here to find his throne.
Waiting in service at the roadside these,
Who claimed Divinity as their own to please.
Crowns are alloted none I ever saw:
Love wins at last: no murderer breaks His law.

W. S. In spirit (Through S. S.)

RESTORATION

The God of all the soldiers is the God that's over all;
And He knows the very places where His cathedrals fall.
He sees His nuns of Mercy by Germans raped and torn;
And babes brought low through suffering, by barbarous Germans born.

The God of all the Nations is Christ's own God as well:
His liberty and freedom is past our tongue to tell:
He will bind the brokenhearted, and restore the spires that fell,
But the murderous Huns in history have writ their tome of hell

Which the God of all the ages will read as it is writ
Inscribed through His eternity with no pity e'er for it!
W. S. In spirit (Through S. S.)

FORTUNES OF WAR

There is no greater sum a man can give,
When he lays down his life, and thus, his soul.
He says: "I give you all I own; the future mortgage, too,
But take, I beg, the whole!"
He holds this gift a bauble in his hand,
And marches forth his captain to obey;
He falls upon the battlefield, and "dies";—
He bartered all; or gave all his away;
And learns still he belongs to One all wise!
When he takes up this Captain's task to do,
Where warriors meet no battleshot or shell,
Will he discern life's spendthrifts such as he,
And pass through fire of conscience,—which is hell.
W. S. In spirit (Through S. S.)

CLEANSING FIRE

The world has passed through cleansing fire,
And burnt its whoreson's sores:
The bleeding arteries of the lands
Have given their precious stores,
That generations yet to come,
May be unbound and free,
And every land shall share its yield,
And the sea its liberty,

Whose restless waves a requeim sing
O'er martyred heroes bones,
And ever will its voice recall
War's toll, as dirge intoned
The rising and the ebbing tide
Of life doth come and go
Through time, ay, through eternity,
Must every people know
The sacrifice of every life
Which gave its share to free
The earth from one mad despot's rule,
And save them liberty!

W. S. In spirit (Through S. S.)

DIVINITY

In other spheres beside the earth's,
But all allied 'neath the same King,
Are messengers from Divine powers,
To help men work or sing.
In other realms above the earth,
Where new-born spirits dwell,
Where every man his own soul makes,
And each has made its hell,
There is a fountain where we draw
New life, immortal bliss,
Where every new-born soul may drink
In that land when from this
It finds itself without a friend,—
When friends all tried and true
Have passed along a fairer way
Not caring what you do.
This fountain is the living God:
Who begs you come and drink:

To pause, to seek,—to look, to see,—
To hear,—to know,—to think.

W. S. In spirit (Through S. S.)

FOES OF THE DARK

In the land, we, as mortals, inhabit,
We have foes which are hidden, unknown,—
To battle with these we must cross over death's seas,
And fight in the dark,—and alone!
Our consciences picture these battles,—
But our pride will not enter the fray;
What each spirit knows in the place where it goes,
The soldiers are fighting today.
To have done all you could, as a holy man should,
Is not half required each of you—
You must shoulder a gun when the world's work is done,
And look for the foes INSIDE YOU.

It is hardly worthwhile to tell earth men more,—
So swollen their ego with pride:
But when they reach here, with gun, yes, and spear,
They must war against foes but INSIDE.

W. S. In spirit (Through S. S.)

BURIED ALIVE

A long, long grave, in torture wound
The field of France's battleground.
Unkempt; untombed, its serpent head,
It held the living, not the "dead."

Along the road when war shall cease,
These empty graves will proclaim peace.
As risen from their living tomb,
The Mother Earth from out her womb

Will give new sons to freedom's cause,
To love and serve God's holy làws.

W. S. In spirit (Through S. S.)

—Remake the world O God, once more restore thine everlasting
  peace,
That cannon shell no more shall blare, nor war dogs have
  release.
Remould men's hearts to Thine own will, and lift their faces to
  Thy sky,
That wars may end—and all may see at last the Love that
  cannot die.

W. S. In spirit (Through S. S.)

"Suffering brings its fine reward." W. S.

CHARITY

I see throughout the breadth of this great land,
A stirring of a conscience new and fine.
Within the inner chambers of the heart, a kinship dwells,
Uniting, all divine.
I feel my own heart throb, (I've still a heart TO throb) in
  gratitude unbound,
That love and brotherhood shall find earth's men at last, who ·
  mingled tears and blood, before theirs passed.

Oh Charity, that "vaunteth not itself", nor is puffed up",
Oh Charity, "long-suffering and kind,—"
To think at last the whole world's bleeding sons,
Cemented brothers men, and each to all did bind!
Though you may have naught left, you now have THIS:
"The greatest of them all"—yea, seemingly.
For 'round the world a ring of touching hands,
Proclaims all races one in charity.

"Long-suffering" such as warriors only know,—will make with-
    in the fighting foes, chagrin,
And bring their homes and firesides future bliss, and cover
    o'er their multitude of sin.

To you who wait for those who come not back—
Avail yourselves of this they. learned to feel,—
That, though an enemy burn and wound and kill,
At last, with suffering keen, all men must kneel.

                    W. S: In spirit (Through S. S.)

MALEDICTION'S END

This is the day when warriors burst afield
And draw their swords that valorous deeds may yield
Through immemorial time all nations free from hate
The sovereign right to live their lives in high or low estate.
When launched the barge of Freedom on Time's seas,
Where heroes blood fostered democracies,
No unprepared or unwinged craft 'twill be,
Manned by free sons of glorious liberty!
'Twill be the end of malediction, too: no thing to hate, and none
    to over ride:
But toiling men will grasp the up-start's hand,
And wealth will mean the wealth of love with pride!
No fostered malice shall the heart betray;
No world of hatred seethe within the breast;
But gentlefolk shall rule the universe
Where brotherlove shall make a heaven's rest! * * *
When lives haved ebbed and given out their all,
And forth have gone the rich and poor as well,
Then, will men find rich peace within themselves,
And heaven and earth a kingdom, after hell.

                    W. S. In spirit (Through S. S.)

RECONSTRUCTION

All levelled, waste and shattered are man's dreams.
All broken, bruised and torn are women's hearts.
The fields of carnage tell the woeful tale;.
With agonizing cries their history starts!
The world is dust,—the ashes of men's bones;
The graves are strewn through hamlet, field and town,
Where murderous foes with ruthless fire and gun
Have razed in warfare all they could pull down!

Now, when they see destruction all complete,
They ask for peace through time to view the waste,
And carry back to their preserved land
The memories of their depraved "kultur" taste.

When history is writ upon Time's page,
Where crimes of Huns are written red in blood,
The hatred through the eons yet to come,
Will surge against the Germans as a flood
To keep them on their unspoiled, unstained ground,
Which murderer's wrath proclaims is blest of God,
While every Nation loathes them the world round,
Where none would place a foot upon their sod.

Divinity of Kings they claim their right,—
Nor reckon with the POWER that, over all,
Knows every cause, be it divine or just,—
Or every sinner's sin by which they fall.

W. S. In spirit (Through S. S.)

MERCY

The wasted lives on fields of war proclaim
The uselessness of sin, and all its crime;
The arrogance of king and kingly rule,
To make their domains safe, peaceful, sublime.

When these go forth who seek their kings to serve,
Proclaiming need for sacrifice of life,
To add a fragment to a monarchy,
As heritage but hatreds' bastard, strife;

Where shall they look for mercy for themselves,
Who murder, loot, rape, burn, blaspheme, and raze?
Not where I've been, and paid my debt,
And suffered for my crime of earthly days!

Where shall they turn who rend, with mercy's plea,—
Or when, I ask, can these find peace with God,
Who, for an added share of sun or sea,
Have dealt the fire that laid men 'neath the sod?
                        W. S. In spirit (Through S. S.)

Great questions mark the hour. Great, and unsolved.
The hour so near at hand, alas, so near.
The homelessness of homing-ones of earth,—
The anguish, and the hoplessness, and fear.

Without, the world's best of its own is drained;
And shattered, broken, lieth hopes of these
They left behind to serve their country's call,
Some government, or Emperor to please.

Within their tortured breasts but their God sees,—
Their spirits face the world from whence I came:
Oh, that this world could get in touch with them,
E'er they must pass out through the battle-flame!

Here must I rest: no chance, no hope I see
To make men pause before it is too late,
And they, without, become themselves, within,
And carry to the spirit warring state,

From which no King I see obliterates,—
Nor offers to adjust what was within.

The while they murdered others, they themselves
Were overcome by the same murderer's sin.

TIME'S GARLAND

Upon the battlefield where men have bled
To save their children from a murderous foe,
The flowers will bud and tender grain will spring,
And gentle zephyrs kiss them as they blow.
The bounteous earth will yield them homage, too;
And send them forth to living-men again:
In centuries to come the ravished lands
Will heal of wounds and scars, forget its pain.
The birds will chant their requiem overhead,
Though blithe will be the glorious summer rhyme;
And nature will resume her olden way;
Where Harmony shall rule through all of time.

W. S. In spirit (Through S. S.)

THE BROKEN BOUND

Felled, razed, and torn, broken, shattered, bruised,
Ruined and wasted,—harvest of grim death.
Weary and sad, outdone, earth's starving sons—
But glad to give their last remaining breath.
Fooled by a madman, crazed by lust for power,
Martyrs each one, belied for country's cause,
Wasted their blood for reason's fallen throne,
Acclaiming God's his ruthless demon laws!
Out of the chaos wrought at his command
A just God sees His good rise at the close;
The God of love, and rightousness, and peace; * * *
The God who sees, and hears, and moves, and knows!
Who binds the broken mends the shattered too;
And reasons that a madman must undo.

W. S. In spirit (Through S. S.)
Nov. 18th, 1917.

TO THOSE WHO HAVE NO CHANCE

No chance to live; no chance to love; no chance, except to "die":
Such is the law of Freedom's land, which law all are ruled by.*

*(Note: I know it is not right, but am determined to use
it this time W. S.)

The rich, the poor-man's son, must go; and to all say farewell,—
And every son that marks a gun will aim his life at hell.

A chance to do a hero's part? A chance to die for glory?
This is a threadbare argument to one who writes *this* story?
To "die" to save that friend may live, no greater deed can be:
But what of One who counseled Love, Faith, Trust, Charity?
And the same God who rules this truth, He gave a peaceful
    choice,
"Love one another",—these, His words, fulfilled, would all re-
    joice.

What chance has God's supreme intent, against such laws man-
    made?
Men make their own lost chances, and to "die" are not afraid?
To everyone who bares a gun, sets free a soul-of-God,
The same will wish his body still a pilgrim on earth's sod.
What harmless doctrine preached by Him, the gentle Nazarene!
Could men accept Him as they ought, this war could not have
    been.

                W. S. In spirit (Through S. S.)

THE BURTHEN OF LOSS

Take from the world its light, its heat, and all
That makes it live, renewed, and sweet,—
Then place upon its grave a cross of bones:
The dead that made its ruin all complete!

The fruitful earth, crowned with its gold and gems,
A crater like the moon will come to be,

When starved and slain, her sons who slew themselves,
While fighting God themselves they tried to free.

Fast coming to its end the Godless world,
Which starved itself, by choosing poverty;
While toiling masses, who but ask to toil,
Are robbed by thrones of life and liberty!

A welded mass of struggling, battling foes
Has crushed to earth, all shattered, half the race,—
While poor, improverished, tottering, aged sires
Are left alive to populate the place!

When war is done, and man's new hope can rise,
That, unmolested, sons of his can live
Without the curse of shedding others blood,
Nor for a kingdom's ransom, theirs to give,—

To father sons, and mother sons to live,
A heritage for all of time, nor less!
Then God will seem to hold within His hand
The burthen of war's loss, and stain, and stress!

W. S. In spirit (Through S. S.)

This is the day when fears and hate hold sway.
This is the time when ebb mens lives away.
This is the hour to sound a clarion call:
Halt! men-of-earth! Before the last shall fall!

Here then I send from out the spirit's realm
Plea that you halt before death overwhelm!
Give ear, and pause; and work for peace instead,
Lest peace be for all the peace found with the dead.

W. S. In spirit (Through S. S.)
May 13th, '17.

THE SPIRIT WHICH LONGS TO BE FREE

A patriot's freedom every man has craved, some men have
    known,—
But every soul that lives has longed for freedom
That separates its body from its own.
When man encased in flesh is hampered daily,
O'erburdened, shackled, tortured, then is he,
And thinks with all his reasoning powers to profit,
When Azrael shall come and set him free!

When flesh no more surrounds his yearning spirit,
Which seeks through all the sky to find his own,
He lifts his voice in ceaseless lamentation
Because his God-like spirit has no home.
Could he but live once more and profit thereby,
Could he but do such part he would not mourn;
For, seeing with his worldly eyes unveiled,
He finds BUT freedom in his yearned-for bourne.

               W. S. In spirit (Through S. S.)

UNITED

Lands someday will be united:
Crime will vanish from the earth.
War be done; all friends and neighbors,
Cherished through the land of birth.

All will worship in one temple;
All bow to one Divine King:
Evil minds from earth will vanish:
Ever will God's praises ring!

With one faith, one hope, one Maker,
Harmony shall be complete:
Tongue of one, the tongue of many,
Living Love, and hate's defeat.

             W. S. In spirit (Through S. S.)
              A prophecy by W. S. In spirit

WARRIORS

We have passed with the warriors with gleaming steel,—
We have heard their battle-cry;
We have rescued their deformed souls
Sent out on the fields to die.
We know what war and warring means
Past the war of the world of earth,—
And the soldier sons with their knives and guns,
Where we fight our sins since birth.
We know there is Light, and Might, and Right,
But no freedom or liberty,
Who sit in the darkness of darkest night,
Where the souls of sinners be.
No soldier trappings nor cheers acclaim
These warriors as heroes brave,
Who pass from earth to the spirit-birth
Through the trench of murderers grave.

W. S. In spirit (Through S. S.)

("Sign my full name here please") W. S.

William Shakespeare, In Spirit
(Through Sarah Shatford his medium.

(Dictated by W. S.) S. S.

A SOLDIER'S ORISON
(The night before the charge)

The God who weighs the moon and stars,—
Weighs deeds and hearts as well!
He knows whatever justice comes
From war's bloodshed-and hell.
He gives—and takes: nor stays His hand:
Nor fate, except Himself, can save:
Such mystery His life and plans;
The soul, death and the grave!

Why are we here; where shall we go;
Not one has known but He.
Then why should I fear now to die,
Or grieve His soul of me!
The scales are held in His just hand;
His measuring is true;
To do my duty, best I can,
Is all that I can do.
The one who hangs the stars on High,
And guards His swinging spheres,
Will count a soldier's prayerful heart,
And know his unshed tears.

FALLEN THRONES

Our heroes went to battle and they fell—
The world bereft must mourn her loss alway—
Her miseries untold no human tongue can tell—
No intellect conceive the price she still must pay.

To him who ordered "War!" from a king's throne
And caused the havoc wrought on land and sea,
Shall he still stand, and standing here alone,
Be spared his crown and crests of royalty?

When this one used his fallen heroe's bones
To fertilize his land, or fuel make?
Begrudging them their coffins and headstones;
Pilfering all "death" gave that he could take!

The robber-king for mercy soon must plead
Before a King even he calls Divine:

Oh what, at last, shall this poor beggar need;
When fallen from his throne—"Die Wacht Am Rhein"!

LIBERTY OR DEATH

Free as a people should be free,—
Oh give us death, or liberty!
'Neath every heart-throb life is sweet!
And life is short, and life is fleet!
As brothers, comrades, make us all,
Or let us die, or let us fall!

Free as the breath God gives His sons,—
Untrammeled by king's laws or guns,
Uphold and free thy people, Lord!
Pursuit of life in one accord,
As freemen, tillers of the sod,
O give, and free Thy people, God!

A HERO

With blasts of trumpet, with fife and drum
The soldiers march away
Acclaimed as in the olden days
When I wrote sonnet, play,
And all with which my work is wrought
But tells of heroes brave,—
Though I must say, and speak today
About these through my grave
Where lies no soul 'till judgement day,
Nor is postponed the curse
For him who died a sinning one,
But to his God rehearsed
His earthly part, the part he played
Throughout the earth-term life:
This part no hero's part indeed,
With armor, stave, and knife.
Make then a page now being writ
In God's eternal skies,

Where you must claim the whole of it,
While He looks in your eyes.
W. S. In spirit (Through S. S.)

"OUT-THERE"

We have a shape like ours of earth, "Out-There";
When we arrive in spirit-birth, "Out-There".
The very worst that earth has known
Of us, of ours, we find our own, Out-There.

We have no gold, no kine, no kith, "Out-There":
But half the world has taught is myth, "Out-There".
We have few luxuries or joys,
But much to do that frets, annoys, Out-There.

If men would wake and see the truth,
'Twould save them misery, forsooth, "Out-There":
I speak as one the world calls "dead",
Who still has Shakespeare's heart and head, Out-There.
W. S. In spirit (Through S. S.)
Dictated: "There" is "Here," and ONLY, for some. W. S.

SHUNNED

What though an Emperor command
Awarding trinkets in his land
And give all that his power could give,
When Huns are shunned long as they live.

What should the world give those who burn
And rape, maim, loot, but what they earn?
Can any monarch's divine plea
Restore a fallen dynasty?

Ignored, despised, dishonored, barred,
The destiny of Huns is hard.

Sublimely "kultured" and undone,
Mistrusted, shunned by everyone.

W. S. In spirit (Through S. S.)

THE WORLD VICTORIOUS

Away with the monarch who wears his crown
Atremble on the throne,—
For the world at last will be ruled by Christ,
And He shall be King alone!

Away with hatred and deceit!
And the lusts for greed and gold!
For the world has come to know its King
Where naught is bought or sold.

Away with the wars of the king and knight.
Away with murderers all.
For the world has come to claim its Own,
Where kingdoms rise nor fall!

Away with bans and armed hands.
Behold the nail-prints still!
Away with the kings of knighthood's lands,
Away with their edicts "KILL"!

For the world bows down to The King at last,
((And The King shall know His Own)
Where hatred's war is done and past,
And the Great God rules alone!

W. S. In spirit (Through S. S.)

OUT OF THE PAST

The groaning of the world in travail,
Mother Earth torn up in quake,
Desolation and destruction
Taking life for freedom's sake,—

Brothermen with naught between them
Fight for Nation or for King,—
Leaving everything of value,
Taking out not anything

Where for freedom they still suffer,
Bound to earth's unseeing clod;
Finding after "death" existence,
Though they search in vain for God,

While they hear the bugle calling,
Calling still more men to slay,
Must they fight their own soul-battle,
Entered on God's better way.
Knowing all have shattered vainly,—
Taken life without just cause,—
Broken homes and lives, as promise
To the Maker of the laws

Made to bind, and not to sever;
Made to heal, and not to slay;
Made to save men for each other.
Each for each to work and pray.
When the balance which shall weigh them
Where the measuring scales are true,
Will they find adjustment easy?
Would they change the old for new?
Oh, my Brothers, this is Shakespeare,
Who would spare if he but could,
Every man who hence must travail
For a new-born soul all-good!

MOTHER AND HER OWN

The weary world with blood-soaked breast,
All torn, and robbed of her sweet rest,
A martyr to the ravishment

Of maddened Huns, hence devil sent,
Now groans in the last throes (throws) of death, (W.S.)

With those who give their all, life's breath,
And to her arms they send them back
As torn as she, oh woe, oh lack!
And sheilding these from history's page,
She kindly seals them in this age,
Within her open, wounded heart,
Where, in their pain, they shall not part.

MERCY

In the fields where warriors gather,
Fighting, wounding, killing, blinding,
Comes sweet Mercy, tender, kindly,
Gathering, saving, cleansing, binding.

Soldiers see the Red Cross emblem,
Mercy's badge, when battle's done,
And, exulting in its praises,
Thank at last the only One

Who can bind at last man's sorrows,
Stanch the ebbing of life's tide,
Bring world-peace, or make men brothers,
Through His wounded, bleeding side!

FOOLS

When all the race of men have run their course,
And into gaping graves their bodies lie,
Then will earth's men be writing history's page,
Denouncing all that now go forth to die.
These books will state ferocities which now
The earth's benumbed, improverished, half-guess;
And staring generations through all time,
Will mark this age "The Craven"—nothing less.

Historians will tell when peace, now here,
Shall hold forevermore the earth embound,
The maddening crimes committed in war-time,
And through what loathesome deeds this peace was found.
Revolting at truth's hideous printed page,
The future race of men will fling it by,
Desirous to believe the Christian's God,
And worship Him who calls none forth to die,
Except it be in payment to Himself
Who judges then the time, (mayhap the day)
But sends no man to slay, or rape, or maim,
Like demons; beasts, who slake their blood thirst through their
    prey!
The Huns of night who call on God to bless
Their fiendish horrors done without His might,
Through ages upon ages must repent,
Else can they never know the God of peace and right.
               W. S. In spirit (Through S. S.)

THE ENEMY

A barrier to justice who complies
Against the will even to National law;
Who spreads deceit, as loathesome as disease;
A carrion-carrier, camouflaged, but raw.

A venomed serpent with its hidden fangs
Awaitiing but a chance when it can spring
And plant its adder-tongue in deep and strong,
And writhe along some victim new to sting.

The one whose lot is cast by chance purile;
Whose hatred finds more sympathy with wrong.
Whose root is evil, blighting every branch;
Discovered by its poisonous breath 'ere long.
               W. S. In spirit (Through S. S.)

THE EARTH A MOON?

Fast, fast the earth a planet like the moon is to become?
All lifeless naught to speak its love of God?
Torn and dismantled His footstool by Huns
Whose souls must answer nor lie 'neath the sod
Till Gabriel calls them forth to say "Ay, Nay"
To questions of the Judge who holds their fate,
But to each one, their service done,
Response awaits sealing their impious hate.

Moonless THEIR lot where darkness waits to hold
Their murderers souls nothing but hate enfolds!
While on the earth they havoc wrought, and pain,
Where innocents with mothers helpless, slain,
Gave up their lives appeasing hatred's crime,—
Making Huns foes enduring throughout time.
Comment full sad and harrowing heart of Him,
Who for His children gave the earth abrim
With all His wonders, all His love, and kiss—
To be repaid by them with robbery such as *this!*

Wm. Shakespeare (In spirit) Through S. S.
N. Y. C., Oct. 21st, 1917.

THE DYING SOLDIER

See how he bleeds from gaping wound!
Oh gently lay him down.
Why has this hero paid such price!
Where is his waiting crown!

The spirits gather 'round him now,
And waiting for the end,
When from this wounded crust will rise
A body without rend.

He feels such pain! It will not last.
Another breath or more

Will end this pain and he have passed
Out to God's spirit shore.

The dying know where they shall go.
They see— and read their signs—
No greater comfort God devised:
The soul to these resigns.

W. S. In spirit (Through S. S.)

TO THE AMEIICAN RED CROSS:

(From one who sees through and beyond their efforts to
alleviate the sufferings of war, plague, famine, or disaster. By
W. S. in the spirit 300 years, during which he has seen the
benefit of woman's ministrations from the spirit world. Writ-
ten through S. T. S., W. S.)

When the Creator planned His world and gave His choicest
    blessing to be mate for man,
He lifted up His face and smiled upon His child, who was to
    give of Him as only woman can.

Within, He placed His tenderness and love,— and made for
    her, Himself, her gentle hands
To minister as Marthas, Dorcases,— to stanch and bind war's
    wounds with healing bands.

He gave the world His Son, and proved their worth: He chose
    the Virgin Mother to be His:
Established anew dear Magdalene, and many more bear re-
    cord that it is
God's best and greatest gift, to sons of men, their healing,
    tender, benign womankind:
Methinks when He looks down on them He smiles, to watch
    them, with His mercy, heal, and bind!

TO BE OR NOT TO BE *THAT IS THE QUESTION.
THIS

THIS is the question: Shall men live for aye:
Shall their eternal lives go on where is eternal day:
Or, fighting for the world and what it gives,
Shall every soul go hence uncaring if it lives?
What can it matter where the spirit goes,
If it has thought on this, or Jesus knows:
What can I say to wake men to be whole
Before the shot of cannon sends forth each a soul
Undying, yea, alive! wiith all that life implies:
All-keen for saving-grace, where spirit never dies.
Oh could a warning reach before too late
Soldiers at home and France at "heaven's" gate,
Would they then stack their arms, lay down their lives,
For that all-powerful God who knows no *soul* that *dies!*
Take, then, in discontent, this, my litiny:
Free but your souls, my lads, that ye shall be free!
Give not a wound; nor take but God can give;
Heeding His own command, your freed soul, then, must live.

W. S. In spirit (Through S. S.)

THE PLOUGHSHARES, AND THE SWORDS

We will make the swords from peaceful steel
That has ploughed the fields for grain—
And the crops may lie in the bin unsoiled,
For the fields are covered with slain.
When the swords have reaped what the war has sown,
And the land laid waste brings forth again,
Will the ploughshares then come to their own,
And weld men with world-peace through pain?
As the steel is heated and bent for war
Which has served to sustain man's life instead,

So the plans of the Maker to use His all—
Though changed is the form, called "dead."

A PROPHECY

When the roses shall bloom o'er the fields of the earth
Where the red blood of heroes has watered the soil,
And grain-waving fields abundance shall yield,
To bless every son that will toil,—
Forgotten the rancour and woes of the past,
Forgiven the crimes of earth's men,
Oh would we were flesh, in the world then to be,
To share in its heaven, as when
Each Nation pursued its own plentiful land,
In abundance to give out a share;
For thus will be found for men on the ground,
A heaven complete, and all fair.

                    W. S. In spirit (Through S. S.)

WHY THE WORLD FORGETS

Forgotten was the past, its woes, its tears;
Forgotten was the history of Time;
And stilled was all men's hope, and all man's joys,
That hate might rule in every heart and clime.
Worlds were undone with forces such as these,—
Quakes and tornados punished the land;
Monsters of wrath swept underneath the sea,—
And where in all could any see God's hand!

When devastation carries in its wake
The rule of desolation, yea, and crime,
Have men forgotten all commands of God,
To break His purpose on the wheel of Time.
They hold a paltry sum the agonies Supreme,
With which the King of all, the Nazarene,

Came from our God, gave up His life, and rose,
To give the world a Peace it has not seen.
W. S. In spirit (Through S. S.)

WHAT WILL THE WORLD BE THEN?

What will the world be like when once its men
Returned from slaughter and war-fields again,
Take up their burdens past their lives to solve?
For eons upon eons must revolve
Before the price be paid for one man's crime,
And nations rest in peace, and love sublime!
What will the world be like when guns have ceased
And o'er war's pillaged lands the dove released?
Where will the earth find sons and fathers then,—
When war is done, and done to death earth's men!
What will the earth be like when men no more
Find shelter or safe refuge, and no door
Where they may rest content, securely blest?
Will they not wish they had died with the rest?
W. S. In spirit (Through S. S.)
Apr. 2nd, '17.

REMAKE—RESTORE

Worlds are in such chaotic states
Where wrought in stress earth's destinty,
Upheaved, asundered, seethed in hate,
Each claims and waits for victory.

Out of the mass of life extinct (?)
(Set free to roam and build anew)
Great harvest from these armies "dead" (?)
AWAKE! will raise new worlds to view.

Restore, remake, adjust, set free—
Upholding but One King, One throne,

And this new world the spirits claim
Will be their work and God's alone.
                    W. S. In spirit (Through S. S.)

"Let us remake and restore our own souls, Sarah, it is all
that matters here." W. S.

UNDER THE RED, WHITE AND BLUE
Song, by W. S. In spirit—Through S. S.
DONATED TO THE RED CROSS
DEDICATED TO
THE SOLDIERS AND SAILORS OF THE U. S. A.
(Accepted by Mr. John A. Kinney for The American Red Cross,
389 Fifth Avenue, New York City.)

Under the Stars and Bars,
Under the Red, White and Blue,
The Yankees are crossing, crossing the sea,
Valient for freedom, and true!
On patriot's soil will they fight,
Fight 'till they win or they die!
For liberty, justice, and right,—
For honor, and principals high!
Onward and onward they'll go,
'Till the stars in God's sky speak for All:
—"Might shall not triumph o'er right 'till men die,—
    And never again shall war call!

UNDER THE STARS AND BARS!
Under the Red, White and Blue!
We're crossing, dear England and France,
Russia, Serbia, Italy, too!
BELGIUM, loved of the world,
We are coming to help restore You!

Millions and millions strong!
UNDER THE RED, WHITE, AND BLUE!

W. S. In spirit (Through S. S.)

AT LAST THE HUNS HAVE MET THEIR FATE
The Huns who rule by divine right (?)
At last have met their Divine fate.
It took the world to block their way;
But 'till His own time God can wait.

Back to your place under His sun,—
Back to your land, where everyone
Shall loathe through time the barbarous Hun.

You leave the fields all prone and waste,—
And ravished to your "kultur" taste.
Cathedral spires, nor alters, saved,—
But devastated all, and razed,
That you might find your God back home,
Who never led where demons roam!

Go back, you madmen, spurned, accurst!
For every land you've done your worst.
Go reckon with God's power Supreme—
With "Deutschland over all" a dream
Inspired by Hohenzolleran clan
To rule, and blast, where'er they can
The while they pray to God on High
For help from His all-peaceful sky!

Such fate awaits as God decrees.
While England, Mistress of the Seas,
Humane, and generous, bleeding still,
Accepts your fate as God's own will.

William Shakespeare In spirit (Through S. S.)
Will you sign my full name to this if you please. W. S.

"A REQUEIM FOR THOSE WHO DIE"
(Poem by Edith Thomas)

W. S. prefers, "The Soldiers Requeim." "To be chanted of
course." W. S.

"Through the Valley of the Shadow" many times passed he:
Cheering to the proud acclaim, "DEATH, or LIBERTY."
Through the shadow, to the valley, where all living pass,
Heroes, soldiers, comrades, lovers,—
Every lad and lass,
Past all dying, past all soldiering,
Past the hate of men,
God who gave, oh give him freedom,—
Make all whole again!

W. S. In spirit (Through S. S.)

BELGIUM

All that her hands had wrought,—
All that her mind had sought,—
All that her treasure bought,
    Lost!
BELGIUM.

All that the world can bring,—
All that poets can sing,—
Through all ages shall ring,
    Thine,
BELGIUM.

W. S. In spirit (Through S. S.)

A NEW-YEAR PRAYER
Jan. 1st, '17

We praise Thee, O God, for the new-birth of Time!
That today we may enter a door
Of a chamber unsealed in Thy wisdom and care,

Having blessings we knew not of yore!
For we know that Thy storehouse new promises hold,
As we leave all our failures behind;
And into the new, as out from the old,
We take Thy full pardon, all kind!
We may not go back through the old-rooms of Time,—
Until at the last on Thy shore,
When halted for us the procession of days,
We traverse the old haunts once more!

ONE KING, ONE LAND, ONE SONG!

We will all join in the singing of our country's National
    hymn,—
And lustily our voices raise, hoping our own will win,
While other men of other lands, their brave hearts all attune,
Will mouth THEIR National anthem, too, morning, night,
    and noon!

All voices raised to the same God—all hopes sent to His sky—
And yet these words are traitor's words,—they send men
    forth to die
Against His law, against His will, and all the hopes of life;
They foster bitterness and hatred, ay, and add to Nation's
    strife!

But take them all and make one hymn for One Who God of all
Forbids His own to kill or slay, or battle 'till they fall.
Then by this King of All be led forth to one land for all—
And find His kingdom come on earth, where all obey His call!

                    W. S. In spirit (Through S. S.)

    There is a world when men are "dead"
    Surrounding this, as near it too—
    Invisible to mortal's sight,
    Except a favored few.

When these have passed and look and plead
With theirs to hold and keep them near,
How will they feel, when no response
Shall ever come from eye or ear!

W. S. In spirit (Through S. S.)

TO GIVE

Where is a heart so great as thine,
Which sees past rueful woe,—
Except the ones almost divine,
Without themselves loved so!

Where is the land where One shall give
All—keeping naught but love:
It is not where this one has been,
But must be far above.

W. S. In spirit (Through S. S.)

SEEKERS

Some day where the land is hidden
In the saints eternal rest,
Stainless in their holy garments
Shall the sinless souls be blest?

Sacred as the Lord's evangels,
Pure as the great God's behest,
Shall the earth abiding spirits
Find a welcome in their quest?

W. S. In spirit (Through S. S.)

THE MOUNTAIN

Towering on high its snow-capped peak serene
In its majestic state a lofty Queen.
Within its dormant breast what hidden treasures lie,
Till Mother Earth shakes forth no eye can spy.

So must our human forms and faces bear
Many a secret none but God can share.
Some be as mountains, lofty, towering, high,
Sharing His secrets, lone until they die.

          W. S. In spirit (Through S. S.)

THE REAPERS

"A sower went forth to sow," . . in the glare of the mid-day
  sun:
"Behold," said he, "I sow in glee, from now 'till the day is
  done."

That direful day is past—as passeth the day of man:
What the sower sowed, he reaps, at the end of life's short span,

The tares and nettles and chaff, he reaps instead of grain:
The reaper grim shows them to him, and bids him sow again!

          W. S. In spirit (Through S. S.)

"THE INVISIBLE BALANCE SHEET"
(With acknowledgement to the author, Katrina Trask)

There is written on the tablets of their air,
  Where record of the Soul is kept, and true,
Both erring deeds and good, which have made up
  The last account, which shall be waiting you.

Did mortals know the misery which accrues
  The interest on the debt owed to themselves,
The while they robbed their God of justice here,
  And held for Him no store upon Life's shelves,

They would compute more gain, and losses less,—
  Nor think to fool All Wisdom at the end,
To rob and owe less— give and succeed more,
  Nor borrow never that but God can lend!

N. Y., May 10, '17·

"IF THERE'S A GOD,—"

"If there's a God," I hear men say,—
(Fine men, His sons, and fair)
What can He mean, where is He now?
Does this war speak His care?"

Oh men who walk the earth and stare
Up to His heavenly sky,—
"If there's a God," ye soon shall know
When ye pass out and "die."

"If there's a God" ye puny things
Who never paid Him back
With ever e'en so small a love,
What shall ye one day lack!

"If There's A God" (and ye are His)
How infinitismal small
Are ye, and all the ones like ye,
For which He gave His all.

O JUSTICE with Thy scales unseen!
Unbanded, seeing, eyes!
Invisibly doth each act weigh,
In Thy immortal skies!
As Thou hast made the dust of man
To cover spirit sight,
So hast Thou, in Thy hidden plan,
A balance true and right.
To see man's past writ on a scroll,
Unfolded, balanced, plain,
This is the hell that Wisdom planned:
The soul's undying pain.

WONDERS AND SIGNS

The Father gave all power to Him, here and forevermore,—
Along the sea of Gallilee, and near Bethsaida's shore, —
And gave Him wonder-works all His, and signs which followed,
too,

He touched the blind, and made them see; He healed the
leper's sore:
"The halt arose, and leapt for joy"! And praised Him evermore!
Still He performs these miracles, And asks that ye but give
His Father, through Whom all is done, Thy praises while ye
live.

In the wellsprings of being a fount is concealed,
Whose healing abundant e'en leperosy healed:
When Jesus uplifted a finger or prayer
The sinner at once stood purified there.

So now on the earth is this fountain revealed
Through an instrument fine through the spirit unsealed:
And the day she goes forth by one word to her God,
The dead shall arise who have lain 'neath the sod.

This message we tell thee this one does not know:
But we have known long who serve mortals below.
She will heal she will preach she will hear she will see—
And these but a half of her miracles be!
                    W. S. (Thine) In spirit Through S. S.

WHAT PURPOSE?

Living and breathing, but with purpose not,
The vast bulk of humanity
Eats, drinks, and sleeps, and spends their idle days
In killing time, lest they should hear, or see

The throngs of spirits gathered everywhere
A mortal walks or sits upon the earth;
While jokes are played, in their superior glee,
Or writers jibe at claims of spirit-birth.

What has the world then profited, I ask,
By life, or death, of humble Nazarene?
What profit had been theirs in olden times,
Had Jesus spirits never heard or seen?

What profited the world by sacrifice
Of One Who gave His life that they might see?
When life is ended here, behold the cross
All such must bear throughout eternity.

    "YE CANNOT BEAR THEM NOW,—"
    Should God uplift the curtain,
    'Tween earth and spirit-worlds,
    And man should find the distance nil,
    Or, see where dying hurls
    The soul they thought would go to Him,
    At last life's pain were done,
    When they had borne the earthly cross,
    The crown, then would be won!   m
    Could mortals know that life beyond,
    Reflected is of this;
    And all the love which they have known,
    Must be their heavenly bliss,—
    As well all woe that they have caused,
    Must weigh and bear them down,—
    How few, but understanding Him,
    Could hope for any crown!

"I have many things to tell you,—"
Which are against the law:

But could ye earth-folk know the truth,
Ye'd *see as Jesus saw!*

SALVATION

War hinders God from His intents.
War sends forth souls before their time.
War voices scream through peaceful skies,
War dogs decry all God's sweet rhyme.

Outside the lines of bitter' foes,
Where all of His own rest and wait,
Where each must answer to His call,
Or serve Him only, soon or late.

Where God's salvation wars with sin,
An Emperor's greed with souls has strewn,—
Marking the path where One of Peace
For all of time His words hath hewn.

Where heroes fall for lack of Love,—
For love of Him whose blood was spilled
That life eternal is for all
Whose hearts are with salvation filled.

O, when the cheek of early dawn rests on the breast of day,
And the jewelled Queen lays off her robe and puts her crown
    away,—
'Tis like the new-born spirit come to lands not far, but wide:
The moment when the bridegroom, "death," has come to meet
    his bride!
A babe within the measuring scales of God's Almighty hand!
Betwixt the night and day we see 'twas but the dawn which
    spanned.

THY HERITAGE

Leave but a memory when you pass—
Like fragrance of a summer-rose,
A breeze shall stir, and on its wing
Shall waft it far as zephyr blows!

Leave but a thought of your own mind,
To bless when you have passed beyond,
And, where thoughts wing, and stir, or wake,
You still shall have affection fond!

Leave, then, some deed, in trust, and kind,
Which marked a hope on one poor soul,
And you will find to welcome you,
In deed and kind, One who makes whole.

"BEHOLD I STAND AT THE DOOR,—"

Behold the portal opened wide!
I stand within the Door
Of thine own heart, the heart of God!
And closed nevermore
The portals where thy Lord doth stand
Who supped and sorrowed, died
Upon the cross thy soul to save,
Ay, even crucified,
That ye, with hearts enclosed with sin,
Might see Him in the door!
No tomb could seal sweet Mary's Son,
Nor hold Him evermore.

A CROSS OF GOLD

When shepherds lead the flocks of Him
Upon the hillsides steep,
They look on High and find the Star
To guide their wayward feet.

'Tis then the Star but leads them on,
(And never will forsake)
Leading to paths where Jesus walked;
The Way He chose to take.

His lot was humble and despised;
He gave His life to save;
Hoping the stone was rolled away
Forever from the grave.

To-day behold men's bleeding hands
Spiked on crosses of gold!
The humble way that Jesus trod,
Is just a fable told.

Men choose these crosses; bind their souls;
Lives, hearts, here crucify;
But where crosses of gold lead *them,*
They must learn when they "die."

THE DOWNWARD PATH
Two paths divided with a cross
Are on the earth today
The same as when He met His loss,
And for our sins did pay.

The downward path, with burden light,
Leads where there is no sun:
A pit of darkness (which is hell)
At last when life is done.

But he who looks up to the cross
On which our Saviour died,
And walks His way his debt to pay,
Must here be crucified.

          W. S. In spirit (Through S. S.)

THE PATIENCE OF GOD

When the Kingdom-of-heaven was planned for the earth,
And God gave His Son to prove spirit-birth,
He hoped that mankind would accept all His pain,
And never on earth doubt the Spirit again!

But the world, grave in doubt, and immersed still in sin,
Went back to its Mammon, as though He had not been,—
And the following few who still listened and heard
Were not able to claim for the spirit a word!

Lest the truth of the word, for which Jesus died,
Should make their own bodies with Him crucified!
Thus the hope of the world through the spirit was fled;
And men chose to think of their lost-ones as "dead."

To the One who had given His life on the cross,
And His Father Who gave Him, then, this was a loss,
Until half the world laid murdered and slain
No hope for the spirit did God see again.

To save His own children, to perfect His plan,
God gave His one Son, whom He brought forth as man;
But to wake their poor souls to this knowledge of God,
Their own sons must be slain, and their blood soak the sod!

Now waiteth His hosts on the edge of the world,
With flocks of white-doves, and banners unfurled,
To show the ones living all those that have died
Are living in spirit with Him crucified.

TO ————

Remould the past to suit your own decree,
Adjusting His outcast, unworn, divinity,—
Selfblinded see no God but nature's law,
While in His Divine purpose point the flaw,

And yield naught to Him but your sacred bones
No one cares who entombs mayhap, nor owns, —
THEN stand revealed as here you are, nor more,
When from the part you left you ARE the core,
And pass along where are your kind, nor less,
And live, all live, forever, in distress.

W. S. In spirit (Through S. S.)

Feb. 1st, 1918.
N. O., La.

WHERE SHALL JESUS FIND THE TABLE SPREAD
FOR HIM

When Christ appears again on earth
To sup once more with men,
Shall Twelve sit waiting with the cup,
As His twelve waited then?

Where shall Christ find the table spread,
And love awaiting Him?
When He shall come, mayhap 'fore day?
Where, lights all bright, atrim?

When Jesus left he bade men watch
Until He come again.
Will He find Twelve to share His cup,
And brake His bread, as then?

He walks today, by most unseen,
Upon the bloodstained earth,
And knows the hell man made himself,
Whom God provided birth.

When all the world now living sleeps,—
And all their prayers are ceased and said,—

The world-folk then may see their own,
And say at last, "There are no dead."

SORROW'S CROWN
Invisibly ye may be crowned;
As One who wore the thorn
Passed on to wear His Father's crown,
And be with Him, new-born.
Invisible to mortal eyes
The birthright of the soul:
So shineth many a diadem
His hand alone may dole.

THE TEST
Just take the world as you find it,
Whatever its losses may be:
Accustomed to pain, you'll not mind it,
And losses may mean victory!
Oh, never pass out from the earth-plane
To the land where all spirits seek rest,
Unknowing the plan of the Maker:
Through pain, is the soul put to test.

THE POTTER AND THE CLAY
To take the dust and fashion it as man,
And breathe into that dust the breath of life,
And in that clay *another* form to make,
No hand *can* slay by shot or shell or knife,—

To mould the vessel from the Infinite,
And in His image to complete the twain called man,
This was the Master Artists' self-appointed task,—
To imitate Whom, man doth all he can.

THE POETS

When the world is asleep and the flowers all are dead,
And a blanket of snow covers over instead
The beautiful land where the birds have once sung,
And the May-pops by children gaily were strung,—
There's a sigh in the heart, and a wish in the head,
That the Winter were o'er, and the Spring come instead!

When the earth reawakens and dons her green dress,
And the sun in his splendour outvies the wind's press,
We look and we listen for earth's lovely things,
For blossoming vines, and gay-colored wings,
Soft-breezes, perfumes, and a lover's fond sigh,—
For 'tis Spring! It is Spring!
Hence we sing—you, and I!

                    W. S. In spirit (Through S. S.)

SPURIOUS GEMS

These gems I hold like drops of rain
Strung on this little plaited chain,
Are spurious, and worthless quite,
Except they scintillate with light.

Now there ARE gems whose priceless worth
Are uncomputed on this earth
Until men pass where these shine aye
With brilliance time fades not away.
                    W. S. In spirit (Through S. S.)

TO A POET-CLOWN: Sarah Shatford

When you smirk and you wince, like my own puppet-clowns,
I go back to the days of my time,
And wish I had had on the stage such as YOU,
To play out my pieces and rhyme!

But you see it is late, and the drama is o'er,—
And the stage is the sky, and no more
Shall Prospero with magic attend;
For he works now for God, to the core.

W. S. In spirit

THINGS WE NEED

We need the things gold cannot buy
To save our souls from sin and crime;
We need the love that stays and binds
Through ages and through time.
We need the God that heals and cures;
We need the Great God's care,—
To juvinate, revivify,
Restore, remould, repair.
We need His blessing to endure
The blighting of our souls through crime;
And oh, we spirits must be poor
Who need but have him not through time.

W. S. In spirit (Through S. S.)

WHERE WORLDS DIVIDE

There is a path which leads on high,
And one which leads to lower realm;
For mortals here are left the choice,
Each soul a captain at the helm!
Where worlds divide each goes his way,
Nor seeks to help his brotherman;
Yet are we one and the same flesh,
Where this short bridge doth span!
We take our ease and look on high—
We see no way to help the poor.
We pity from our inmost hearts—

While these continue to endure.
What is the spell of earthly ease,
That man can feed himself a king,
And praise no God, nor emulate—
Create no song one heart can sing!
No gifts within such hands they bring,
But poor and pitied shall they be;
Looked down upon for lack of worth—
Divided from the rich who see.

Amen.

W. S. In spirit (Through S. S.)

A RENEGADES PORTRAIT OF HIMSELF

Spouf of a wildcat and a hare,
A brainless mite; a ne'erdowell,
Reviling God who made him such:
A wretch who travels but to hell.
(Meaning anyone who leads this life.)

W. S. In spirit (Through S. S.)

HOW CAN YOU KNOW?

How can you know there is no death when you go hence
 from here,
If when your near and dear ones call across the distant bier,
You do not care to hear their call, nor even their distress,—
But careless, laugh them in the face, when they pluck at your
 dress,
So near they are your very breath,—your very thoughts the
 same
As when in flesh they took your hand and called you by
 your name!

They are not dead, and they are here, yes here, right by your
    side,
All friends whom you have placed in graves, are living, have
    not died!

W. S. In spirit (Through S. S.)

MAN'S SIN

"The curse of man," is often heard; (and often seen as well)
When phrase like this falls from man's lips,
Who would his own sin tell.
Some wonder what this curse can be, since God made him like
    Him,
And bade him drink from all the dregs a cup full to the brim.

There is a curse which all men know—(an awful curse which
    kills)
To know no rest from passion's lust, a craving no-love fills.
This is the "curse of man" on earth, he carries to the grave,
Then wonders how his soul is lost he never tried to save!

W. S. In spirit (Through S. S.)

THE END OF TIME

Make us to see, O Lord, Thy agony,
And all Thy wounds and pain.
Help us to see Thy crown of thorns,
And hear Thy cries again,
As on the way to Calvary
Thy cross and Thou didst go,
While scorned and scouraged, but faithful still,
Thy Father's love didst know.
O help us know while we are here
Thy sacrifice doth bless;
And though Thou art the risen Lord,
Thou art ours none the less.

O make us see Thy Calvary
Can save men from their sin:
O lift us to Thy Paradise,
Dear Lord, and take us in.

             W. S. In spirit (Through S. S.)
Good-Friday, April 6th, 1917.
New York.

THE HILLS OF GOD

Through the mists of the morn, a new promise is born,
    a peak lifts its cloud-crowned head,—
Through the maize of the ways where for life mortal strays,
    and at last to the heights are they led!
For at last shines a Star where these poor mortals are,
    and at last when they lay down their dead,
'Neath the sod where no rod was given by God,
    by this Star will earth's mourners be led!
In the Valley of Night, with no hope and no light,
    they have trudged through the gloom pace by pace,
With never a sign of this Spirit of Thine,
    and never a glimpse of God's face!

Behind is the Valley where bugles will rally
    and call from the gored battle-fields,
The men who have led them, the cannons which fed them,
    to give all the best an earth yields!
And led by a Star, where the crowned peaks are,
    men will rise to God's hills in the skies,
And never know more aught of brother's spilled gore,
    but the love that shines out from God's eyes!

Then let us but say, we who write this to-day,
    who look on from a world little known,
It must be through the Christ who was once crucified,
That at last all shall come to their own.

THE GLORY OF GOD

On earth in the kingdom ruled by kings,
Where is glory of riches and paltry things,
Where men must kneel to approach a throne,
Where a fellow-being rules alone,

There is pomp and trappings and service fine,
And splendour of fabric, viands, and wine,
To dazzle the sight, and make men fear;
But there is no tinseled king's throne here,

Where the burst of morn for the one new-born
Is his kingdom fair, else he is forlorn.
And the richest gift he can bring along
To the throne of God, is a praise of song!

There is no throne here; and no crowned king;
No rights divine for the royalty ring!
But the glory of God men bring from earth
May reach to the throne of the spirit's birth!

W. S. In spirit (Through S. S.)

GOD'S LOVE

There is a love past understanding,—
From a Source where love is all:
It will never leave you comfortless,—
It will lift you when you fall.

There is a love of righteousness;
A love without a stain;
This Love once known must ever be
The antidote of pain.

There is a love one cannot lose,—
God's love grows never cold;

It is the treasure Jesus brought,
Whose wealth is half untold.

There is a love for you and me
To claim this day our own:
God reaches out His arms to you,
And asks you to come Home!

W. S. In spirit (Through S. S.)

GOD'S WORD

God's Word is a mine of wonderful gems,
Where pearls of great price are all free;
Unmined must these gems be unless men will search,
Unknown their great value must be.

Riches are here for those who will seek,
All stored that poor mortals can see,—
Yet beggars there are preferring no task,
Who must envy our vast treasury.

Shall we go hence then rich in possession,
These beautiful gems in our breast,
Or, stricken in poverty, homeless,
Be consigned with the beggars to rest!

W. S. In spirit (Through S. S.)

WHAT GAIN?

What were the gain if all the world you won,
And lost the soul God gave, or left undone
The work God meant, as mortal, you should do?
Throughout eternity what were the gain to you?

What were the gain if all be bitter loss?
What.gain were ours but for Jesus' cross!
Then should you whine if one with the Divine
You lose the world, but save this soul of thine?

What were the loss if but the world you gain,
And thrust back into God's hand but your soul's pain!
What were the loss if heaven receives you not?
What is the world, then, if this be your lot.
                         W. S. In spirit (Through S. S.)

GIVE GOD HIS DUE

Mayhap His plans include migrating souls
Who pass, repassing in the fecund womb,
Enlarging thus the Light as on they pass?
This makes the female then a prey by chance, a tomb!

God's mysteries are hidden: are they His.
No chance His spark engulfed is, be sure.
Ye are His children, reared to give Him all:
Past mortal minds His secrets to endure.

Give Him His due: He made thee like Himself.
The laws He wrote He made, and loved thee well
When He sent One He loved to save all men
From their own selfish ends, even from hell.
                         W. S. In spirit (Through S. S.)
   To the Theosophical Society, New Orleans, La.
   Feb., '18·

"Mark this sheet and then no more, today." W. S.

"THE WAY—THE TRUTH—AND THE LIFE"

There is one God, one Way: the truth is His:
No better way has any thinker found.
His footprints mark this thorny bloodstained path,—
No reason chooses ever one thus sound.

There is one Life: each travels the same road,
If they have shared His sorrows or His loss.

And when we reach the life beyond through "death,"
We bear each others burdens with our cross.

The Truth is shunned, each seeking stranger gods,
Awakening to the truth when past the Gate
And finding yet themselves they brought along,
Bemoan their lack, no punishment of fate.

> W. S. In spirit (Through S. S.)
> To the Theosophical Society, New Orleans, La.
> Feb., '18·

"THE DAWN OF A PERFECT DAY"

Music played in the dining salon at Hotel Grunewald,
N. O., La., Feb., 1918
"My flute gives me the subject this time. The first I recall."

> W. S. In spirit.

Perfection is but God. His day must come.
He may evolve perfection from His clay,
Or, with His mighty hand, and one marked stroke
Wipe matter's imperfections here away.

When His day dawns, when God comes to His own,
And Love reflects His all empowering ray,
Will men be brothers, where One King doth rule,
And last the dawn of righteousness: God's day.

> Wm. Shakespeare in spirit
> (Through Sarah Taylor Shatford)

THE LAW

There is a court where men may try
Their cases 'fore blind Justices' eyes,—
Based on the laws of those passed out
To meet their Judge beyond the skies,
But intrigued ever for a sum,

Manipulated, juggled oft,—
To feather some poor lawyer's nest,
And make his earthly lot more soft.

But in the great tribunal where
Each man must kneel, and judged be,
No court can save, or honor, there,
Where Justice is the only plea.
When men bow down and worship gold,
And kill their brothers face to face,
Must not the Law adjust these wrongs,
To make God's world a heavenly place?

THOU SHALT NOT STEAL

This is the old Mosaic law, as writ upon the stone:
There is no other has been made by which a man can own
The wealth another one has earned but he has grabbed instead;
And this is still the law on High, when they're outstripped,
 or "dead."
When men rise up to see themselves as God has seen them aye,
What will they say where spirits roam, and pay, and pay and
 pay!
This here would make a sermon then, to one who writes for me:
Wish nothing more than that you have, and here contented be:
This one has made a great mistake and would repay it now;
But when he comes where no one cares, his debt is worse I vow.

W. S. In spirit (Through S. S.)

THE FOREVER

More than a span, nor less than aye
The life after the grave—
And yet the heedless spurn their God,
When He alone can save.

More than the life of earth can give,
—If that life held earth's store—
God holds within His outstretched palm:
To live forevermore!

Oh, weary seekers after gold,
At last ye enter in,
What shall your hands of this enfold,
Who knew no god but sin.

What shall ye hand up to the King
To claim you His or nay
When last those hands must spread the wealth
He promised you for aye!
                    W. S. In spirit (Through S. S.)

"THOU SHALT NOT COMMIT ADULTERY"

There is a state of mind which is all this,
Although no act committed be:
To look upon all womankind for this
If you are bound or free
Commits you to a whoreson's place at last,
Since you gave up your mind to lustful god,
You must inhabit with these then when passed,
When your adultrous frame lies neath the sod.
For mind is wont to play its part so far
The act is here committed without frame—
And every spirit who comes out as such
Must pay the price, and bear adulterers name.
The act of copulation is theirs still:
Since God is here and gave Creation's bliss,
He gives them this: to create through the will (mind).
                    W. S. In spirit (Through S. S.)

Take me, and let me live, O God most High—
Unto Thy arms at last I fly—
Seeking safe harbour from life's pelting storm—
Upon its crafty sea,
O Lord receive me as new-born
For I would come to Thee!

Let me no harm to this one do I have worked through,—
For I would leave her but with You.
Take from her tender heart, its weight of woe—
In Thine arms enfold her, when I go.
Out on the highway with the wolves which keep
Lambs from the fold, Shepherd from the sheep.
Make me some place anear her, Lord, at last,
When through the raging sea her barque is fast
On Thy calm shore of Peace forevermore—
When earth is past.

W. S. In spirit (Through S. S.)

THE BEST WOMAN IN THE BIBLE

The Word with all its sacred lore
Of women good and fine
Describes the lot of one, just one,
Who was of all divine;
But there is one whose sin, and love,
Is writ for all of time
Within archives of human hearts
Whose history is sublime;
With all its errors overcome,
With all its past forgiven:
A saint among the saintliest,
Is Magdelene in heaven.
While on the earth where she has wept,
And trod a stainless way,

A sinner with a sinner's past,
Points to a sinless day.
She told her sin with burning tears;
She prayed her prayers with love:
She followed, served Him, faithfully;
And rests with Him above.
To her who overcome so much,
So much, at last, was given;
She bore with Him his earthly cross,
And shares His bliss in heaven.

W. S. In spirit (Through S. S.)

"GO, AND SIN NO MORE"

A woman knelt at the feet of Him
Who had drank of sorrow's cup:
And abased because of her sins she craved
His pardon, to lift her up!

The Nazarene knew all her world,
And had passed through its mighty wave;
So bending down He took her hand,
And His pardon gently gave!

She rose up whole; and left her sin
A burden at Jesus' feet;
While from that hour, as one divine,
She worshipped and bathed His feet,

And wiped them with the hair of her head,
And followed Him to the cross
Aghast at His torn and bleeding side.
With tears for the sad world's loss!

On the way from the tomb when our Lord arose,
He met her sorrowing on the way.

And her story is written in tears and blood
From then 'till God's judgment day.

INCREASING STORE

Here in the land where nature clothes
Her children with her best,
And there is work, and aim, and bliss,
And, best of all, is rest,
I've been a weary pilgrim long;
Too long, it seems to me;
And, should they call, I would leave all,
To be at last with Thee.
But when I count my blessings o'er,
The gifts Thou gavest me,
An inventory then I make
Of what I'll take to Thee!
My store is meagre, shabby, poor,
The tears rush to my eyes
To think how little CAN I take
With me, out to Thy skies!
And so, Dear Lord, I fain would stay,
Increasing gifts of Thine,
Until these gifts returned to Thee,
Shame not this soul of mine.

               W. S. For S. S. Through S. S.
     May 22nd, 1918, N. Y. City.

(After a hard day's work at the Red Cross Headquarters, 411 Fifth Avenue.) W. S.

THE ADJUSTMENT

There are promises never broken,—
And answers not lightly given,—

Where mortals learn of loyalty,
And truth, and God, and heaven.

There are creations never dreamed of,—
In new worlds men have never seen;
And flowers unfamiliar to them
In lands forever green.

There are trials but of man's own making,—
Adjusting the laws Supreme;
There are joys for asking and taking,
In the life men thought a dream!

W. S. In spirit (Through S. S.)

WHY IS THE WORLD ALL WRONG?

The earth in its beauty and fragrance,
Its wonder, its riches, its plan,
Of the Maker who loved it, and gave it His Son,
Who, born of a virgin as man

Came into the world for His Father,
To prove life eternal for all
Who believed Him the God of the living,
Who could save if on Him they would call,—

The world God so loved,—where war's battles are fought,—
Where God is forgotten so long,—
Is the world for whose sins was our Lord crucified,—
Is the earth made by mankind "all wrong."

W. S. In spirit (Through S. S.)

A PLEA FOR HARMONY

Help me to sing a song, Oh Lord, to praise Thy name,
To glorify Thy Father's love from whence all came:

To make a vibrant chord which was all mute
Or pipe a lay as from some magic flute!

Help me, Oh Lord, to find Thy harmony
Which shall resound within the soul of me,
Till waking anthems wing their symphonies
Unto Thy very Gate, carry our pleas!

Bestow upon Thy world of suffering men
The heart to sing Thy peans once again,
And give them hope, Oh God, that wars are past:
Unto Thy heart, Oh, take Thine own at last!

W. S. In spirit (Through S. S.)

THE FALLEN PRIEST

When a man serves the altar of God and is blest
With the right to forgive mortal sins,
As a vicar of Christ he is hoping to save
Some poor wrecks from the shore "Might-Have-Been."
He lifts up the chalice with Christ's sacred blood,
For hearts which adore His blood shed;
He prays for the souls who are lost in the dark,
The ones who are passed, and called "dead."
But the soul of a priest who has fallen in sin,
Deep-dyed, and of flame-colored hue,
Looks out from the dungeon in which it is hid,
As it strives, and it fails, to be true.
The incense is rising aloft to His sky,
The censers are swinging on high:
While the soul of the priest is sodden in sin,
He prays not HIS soul may not "die."
For the vicar of Christ with his leperous sore,
Is relieved by the hope of his kind,
When he passes, his soul may be lifted and cleansed,

By the prayers of the ones left behind!
But the one who writes here has a message to bring,
Which will change, and mayhap make him whole;
Though his sins are as scarlet, yet white may they be,
If he harkens, communes with his soul,
And confesses his sins before God and the world,
Not trying to hide e'en a sore,
He will gain the full pardon a sinner could crave,
Be absolved, and restored evermore.

W. S. In spirit (Through S. S.)

GIVE ME A CHANCE

Give me a chance to show what I can do,—
For spirits must rehearse, as I am here,
To prove themselves the truth, as mortals fear
Imposters even in the spirit sphere!

Give me a chance to show that I am here,—
I'll give a little hope to take along
To prove to you from world you have not seen
A spirit can return and write a song!

W. S. In spirit (Through S. S.)

JESUS' WONDERFUL LOVE

In a heart so vast, with its bleeding core,
(Where the wounds of a world were laid)
They carried their burdens, and left their woes,
As they passed on unafraid
That He would not lift, or could not heal,
Or would miss them on the way:
So sure were these where HIS footsteps led,
Were realms of eternal day!

There were none too humble, none too poor,
But He gave from His heart's great store

Of Love Divine! Changed the water to wine
To prove this evermore:
That those who draw from God's living spring (heart) W. S.
Shall never thirst, or crave,—
For the Way of The Cross has no stain or loss,
But His wonderful Love will save.

W. S. In spirit (Through S. S.)

FADED FLOWERS

The world in all its wonder never gave
Forth anything to equal womanhood,
Whose nimble fingers never idly rest,
But speed their tasks, the loyal, fine, and good.
Apast her prime, like the full blossomed rose,
Whose petals fade and shrivel on the stem
Send forth their fragrance all enticing still,
Alluring all who ever pass by them.
And so with these whose faces fade with time,
Whose eyes grow dim with many unshed tears,
God's faithful, earnest, working womenkind,
Who bless through all their lives—throughout their years.

W. S. In spirit (Through S. S.)

"A tribute to Sarah—who thinks she is old and she is—
but not so old as she feels. W. S. (Hers)

TO CALL IN VAIN

To call in vain upon His name
In anguish and with tears,
To sit all helpless in the dark,
Still bound by human fears,—

To call and supplicate in prayer,
And in the Great God's name,

For help and succour from your past
On earth, from whence you came,—

This is the spirit's homeless hour,
No human felt, or knew—
When, in the dark you call on Him,
And no voice answers you!

Shall ye then speak His name on earth
But reverently, with love:
Lest when ye call, ye call in vain
On the Great God above.

W. S. In spirit (Through S. S.)

"THE ADVANTAGE OF A HANDICAP"
(Dr. ———— sermon)

It may be said "a mite" is naught,
By him who has great store;
But to the one "who cast in all,"
SHE nevermore was poor!

The rich man who would follow Him,
As he had His commands,
But had at last to give up *all;*
What riches in *his* hands!

Where Mercy rules the scales are true;
He who computes the cost
Is sorting with a Mighty hand
The saved from out the lost.

W. S. In spirit (Through S. S.)

WHERE SHALL WE FIND GOD?

Do you think of a God as you walk through a field,
Or look up to the stars in the sky

Where worlds upon worlds in their orbits have swung,
While centuries pass and men "die"?

Do you think of a God as the flaming sun sinks,
Or the moon lights the darkness of night?
While geniuses come and genuises go,
Unsolving these secrets of might?

Do you think of a God when a babe is new-born,
The secret-of-life which He keeps
Till He takes once again this spark which He gave
When the spirit goes out, and he sleeps?

Do you think of a God when your blessings accrue,
Undeserved, and not understood?
Do you worship the God you cannot comprehend,—
Or reverence His works as you should?

Do you think of a God in whose likeness you're made
"In His image" He gave you a mind
Which you never have used to thank Him at all;
Your God, so loving, so kind!
                    W. S. In spirit (Through S. S.)

WHAT WILL THE WORLD GIVE YOU?
As you hurry through life with its labor and strife,
As you give all you have, yes, and more,
For the world's approbation, its smiles and its love,
Which is glutted with sin to the core,—
Have you thought of a time which must come by and by,
When you leave all you treasure behind,
And arrive empty handed, unclothed, and unshod,
In a land where at last men must find
The purpose of life was the purpose of God—
Where deeds, even thoughts, are all known;

Where the "Dead" are alive, though under the sod,—
And the world gave you naught God would own!

W. S. In spirit (Through S. S.)

PEACE

(To Father ————, Priest. From W. S.)
We seek for peace, and find it not;
We yearn for rest of soul.
Which each must seek, and each must find,
Before he can be whole!

Along the paths we walk with men,
The roads of lust, and gold,
There is no peace, no rest, nor gain,
A soul can ever hold

To take on High where it must go,
Where souls immortal are:
And still men seek but the old paths,
Unguided by the Star

The shepherds saw upon the hills
When Mary's Son was born.
Then as they pass from earth, at last,
They find themselves forlorn;

And wonder where their souls have been
Through life, along earth's way.
And why for them there is no light
In God's Eternal Day.

But one who has been through the dark
Indites these lines to show
There is, above, a dark, dark place,
Where mortal souls all go

Until they find the spark Divine
To light the dark, dark way;
Until they know the Eternal Glow
They shunned in earth's long day!

O eyes unveiled, O ears unsealed,
We warn ye now to show
The peace ye find in the dark place
Ye seek and seek to know.

                    W. S. In spirit (Through S. S.)

THE PRIEST'S PENANCE
(The Holy Father's Prayer)

There is a sacred Heart where all is well:
And in its love I'll save my soul from hell.
Contrite I bow, and soul-despise my sin:
Thou Holy One of God, O take me in!

There is a Face benign whose pardoning grace
Illumines every penitential place:
Held by His arms my sin I here confess,—
Making me one with Him Divine, nor less.

When my poor feet stray in the earthly way,
And mortal lips but mortal prayers can pray,
Lift Thou my soul above my carnal clay:
Hear Thou its yearning, God, beyond all lips can say!

                    W. S. In spirit (Through S. S.)

Written for Father ————.

HOLY OF HOLIES

The sacred chalice of men's hearts,
No eyes but His behold;
Where each soul wears their priestly robe;
Where Mercy doth enfold.

The altar where the feast is spread;
The cup which holds His wine;
Holy-of-Holies is the heart,
Where burns His fire Divine.

The incense, purifying all,
His love, which bears the cross:
Undying as the heart of God:
If lost, the only loss.

W. S. In spirit (Through S. S.)

INHERITANCE

Take, take the wealth of gold,—give it I will—
There is inheritance far greater still:
Kingdom of righteousness, there to be heir,
More than the earth can hold, however fair.
Greater the stainless soul, lover of God,
Than fame's immortal son placed in the sod!
Greater the praise of God, throughout all time,
Than prince-of-poet's verse, drama, or rhyme.

W. S. In spirit (Through S. S.)

A CROSS

Upon the cross our Saviour hung
To save the world from sin.
Among the chosen of His band,
None wholly true had been.
When "all forsook" our Lord and fled,
They knew Him not alone;
When Mary saw the empty tomb,
And, rolled away the stone,
She knew that Jesus lived that hour.
That all had come to pass
He prophecied to followers

When, all alone, alas,
He saw the things they could not see:
Heard what they could not hear:
Knew every thought, all that would be,
Their every cause for fear.
Upon the cross today we see
All nations look in agony,—
In faith, believing God can save
The world from being but a grave.

W. S. In spirit (Through S. S.)
Jan. 11th, '17.

THE SECRET-CHEST

Somewhere in the bossom of a man, safe under lock and key,
He thinks, poor knave, his secrets all abide,
And what he IS, nobody knows but HE.
A pain within this secret-chest one day,
And out he goes, with all he THOUGHT was hidden:
Where he must carry all where all must pay,
And with the voice of conscience all are bidden,
He finds no place where he can hide himself;
Nor cover-up a single secret sin:
But spread before him and his Maker, then,
Without a cloak, is all he held within.

There is a treasure-chest which all might bear,
And carry to the King and Kingdom where
But One divines the glory of each gem
The world knew not they brought along with them.

W. S. In spirit (Through S. S.)

EACH ANSWERS

Is there a place where men shall go,
When breathing life for them is done?

Where deeds must count, and thoughts have told?
Where last some goal is lost or won?
Is there a Judge Who has foreseen
Crimes and injustices of earth?
Who holds our record in His hand,
And vises our new birth?
Is there an hour, then, men can lose?
But seek this One to serve and praise,
Inscribing on the eternal page
The profit of their mortal days.

W. S. In spirit (Through S. S.)

TO THE BLIND

O veiled eyes! O blinded sight!
Shut from God's eternal light!
Oh would ye look, oh would ye see
The glorious immortality
Of life God given after "death"
Relieves you of a mortal's breath,
Then would ye lift the curtain up,
And take His cross,—and drink His cup!

Though mortal vision darkened be,
At last even the blind shall see
The divine glories of His place,
The kindness of His benign face
Alight with love, all shining where
The blind shall see the Master there!

W. S. In spirit (Through S. S.)

Note: Asked to try again, saying the instrument was out
of tune. S. S.

No. 2

O veiled eyes! O blinded sight!
Shut out from God's eternal light!
Oh would ye look, oh would ye see
The light of His eternity,—
Oh would ye lift unscaled eyes,
And dwell in His immortal skies,—
And see the love that shines afar
Through Mary's Son, through Bethlehem's Star,
Then would ye lift the burden up,
Shoulder the cross, and drink His cup!
Until at last with Him thou'll be
Partaker with the blind who see!

W. S. In spirit (Through S. S.)

HIS HOLY NAME

"Thou shalt not kill," the world heeds not,
But slaughters just the same.
While men bow down and worship gold;
And take in vain His name.

His Holy Name that Jesus loved—
His name which all shall call
In reverence, and, in pleading, too,
Before they have paid all.

O cleanse and purify Thy earth,
Where men curse and blaspheme,
Until, O God, they worship Thee,
And see Thou art Supreme.

Within the hearts and homes of men,
Oh send the risen Lord!
Before the struggling world lies dead,
Make one Supreme love-chord!

W. S. In spirit (Through S. S.)

HIS EVERLASTING GLORY

When Jesus came to earth as man,
That He might save and bless
All men from every mortal sin,
And all unworthiness,
He knew His Father would not save ·
Him from a mortal's death,
Nor give Him but a cup of dregs,
Nor spare him pangs of breath!

But Oh, He knew that He should go,
At last His woes were o'er,
Where God who gave Him to the world,
Would meet Him in the door
Where is no sin; no lack of love;
But God's abounding store!
He knew the One Who *gave* Him, then,
Would *take* Him evermore
Unto His Own, His loving breast,
Which none but He could know;
And so He drank His Father's cup
That He might "die" and go.

        W. S. In spirit (Through S. S.)
    Easter Eve, 1917 (April 7th).

THE VOICE

Raise up your eyes to Calvary's hill:
Renew the promise of His Son:
Anew the words I speak to men:
"My Father's will be done."

Rejoice therefore this world I save
More loved of Him than I.

Since mortals laid Me in a grave
They live through Me, nor die.

Beyond the Gate I see and wait
Each mortal of the earth
Who will acclaim in Jesus' name
A new and stainless birth.

Lift then your cross, your burden bear;
On high ye soon must wing:
There IS a land where ye can fare
And thy salvation bring.

No current can bear thee along
Unless it be through Me
Who calmed the tempest, stilled the wave
·On storm-swept Galilee.

Who fares on high into His sky
Must calm the tempest still:
Nor can His holy spirit die:
Omnipotent His will.

        W. S. (In spirit) Through S. S.

PRAISE

A singer sang a song of praise,
And sent it to the sky,—
Its pinions wafted to the throne; ·
The angels knelt near-by.

At last the pæan reached God's heart,
And sank down deep within;
The simple song the singer sang,
Had cured a soul from sin!

        W. S. In spirit (Through S. S.)

A CHRIST-LIKE LOVE

Held by a bond of One who spoke
And claimed Her for His Son's Mother,
All Christians on the earth should love
The Jewish race above another.

Since One they know gave them His Son
Through Her who was a Hebrew maid,
How should the world look on Her kind,
Who trusted God, all unafraid,

Knowing she brought Him forth to die:
She suffered for the world this loss,
Yet must Her race Her suffering share,
And bear for Her a heavy cross,

That wheresoever Jesus' name
Is spoken by the Christian race,
Though Christian's God and Jews the same,
No Christ-like love shines from a face!

W. S. In spirit (Through S. S.)

DEBT AND DEBTOR

We owe a debt we cannot pay,
To Him who died for all:
And yet we feel a world is due
When ever we may call.

Where each one pays and none may owe,
There is no debt unpaid.
The everlasting debt of some
Must ever still be laid

Against the one who has a lack
And kept not God within:

His hope and all his aim in life
Was hourly aping sin:

When this ones comes where all is due
He might have paid since birth,
Alas, he wishes he were rich,
With more than debts of earth.

W. S. In spirit (Through S. S.)

"OUR POVERTY AND JESUS"
(Dr. ——— sermon)

Our riches where we spirits go,
We count as soul alone.
Impoverished, no soul can pay;
And naught for such atone.

Our poverty, where Christ was free!
And each could claim his share!
Dawns with the spirit's misery
When naked, poor, and bare

The part God saved to be His own
When from its husk it came,
Is poorer than earth's poorest lone
With "beggar" for a name.

The miracle that Jesus wrought
To feed the multitude,
Was wrought within the souls of men
When famished, they sought Food.

His grace, sufficient for the world—
His love, abundant, sure,
His pardon, if from sin ye turn,
Will save, nor leave you poor.

Within, His riches are untold,
Where but your God can see;
Though coffers overrun with gold,
Impoverishment may be.

W. S. In spirit (Through S. S.)

"NOW I LAY ME DOWN TO SLEEP"

A child's prayer lisped at Mother's knee,
Yet, would it do for all mankind
In its intent, simplicity:
"I pray the Lord my soul to take,
If I should die before I wake."

O men of earth WAKE, e're you "die";
Nor give your souls to aught but God:
For "dying" means to leave your bones,
But not your spirit 'neath the sod.
To live for Him, His soul He'll take.
He sleeps not where the "dead" awake.
O men, when ye "lay down to sleep,"
Be sure the Lord your souls will keep.

W. S. In spirit (Through S. S.)

RICHES WITHOUT WINGS

There is no debt we cannot pay,
Except our debt to Him.
There are no favors we need beg,
Unless we beg for Him.

At last we look up to the Source
From which our lives were given,
We know no riches can compare
With those we take to heaven.

W. S. In spirit (Through S. S.)

When earth's annointed walk with Him
Who calmed the sea of Galilee,
Oh may His miracle be wrought
Within the souls of you and me.

W. S. In spirit (Through S. S.)

Oh saintly light which pours across the night
A silver shining stream,—oh veil so bright,
What were the heavens without their Queen,
Starfull though they be.
Moonless the earth would be Gethsemene.

W. S. In spirit (Through S. S.)

THE THIEF ON THE CROSS

With Jesus, at His Calvary,
Two thieves were crucified:
(Just punishment in days of old
For robbers who had lied)

And still each thief on either hand
His love, divine, forgave;
For penitent they owned at last
That only He could save.

It is the same on earth today:
No thief escapes their cross.
If to their Lord they plead, and pray,
He may restore *their* loss.

MOTHER OF GOD

Instilled with love and Christliness,
All Mothers of earth's sod:
Though born of God but One on earth,
Jesus, the Son of God.

The uncrowned Queen whose secret lay
All quiet in Her heart,
Whose Son would wash all sin away,
And dry all tears that start.

First written:

> The sacred hope of sinners here,
> Who hold her holy name
> Propitious in their hour of shame
> With Him, who knows no change.

Then, written:

The sacred hope of sinners here
Who hold Her holy name
With Him who knows no change of heart,
Propitious in their shame!

Mother-of-God, His Holy Son,
But wipe our streaming eyes!
As children take us to your heart,
And hear our pleading cries!

W. S. In spirit (Through S. S.)

WHEN THE WORLD IS READY FOR THE SAVIOUR
(Song)

Over every battlefield, over every grave,
Over every mountain, over every wave,
Christ shall come in glory His own to claim and save,

WHEN THE WORLD IS READY FOR THE SAVIOUR.

Watching, Watching, Watching for the Saviour,—
When the morning breaks and the night is o'er:
Watching, Watching, Watching for the Saviour,
   Peace, Forevermore!

After ruthless cannonades, after all is done,
After weeping Mothers mourn their missing sons,
Christ shall ease the heartache, and bind the bleeding wounds,
WHEN THE WORLD IS READY FOR THE SAVIOUR.

Only human brotherhood, peaceful, loving, kind,
Only Christly tenderness, worth seeking to find,
Ever can make nations of a single mind,
WHEN THE WORLD IS READY FOR THE SAVIOUR.

GOD WILL SAVE HIS WORLD
Song—Donated to the American Red Cross.
We will march to "The Star Spangled Banner,"—
We will cross the sea and win!
But the story we hear 'neath Old Glory,
Is the story as old as sin.
There's another, a greater war-song,
Should be flung to the hearts of men,
The story, the wondrous story,
Of "Peace-on-the-Earth"—again!

When we march with the hosts victorious,
Who approach in all their might,
There'll be day alway, and no lives must pay
For God's truth and mighty right!
Led by the army of Jesus,
The white flags are unfurled
Which will bring the Light to a world of night,—
FOR GOD WILL SAVE HIS WORLD!

THE BEACON LIGHT
Some are as beacon lights ashine
Shedding afar their light divine:
A searching ray to point the Way
To ENDLESS Light, eternal day.

Some are but torches, humble souls,
Though leaders, saviours from hell's shoals.
These be of Light, their mission fine,
Since every spark His is divine.

A little taper shines afar.
Countless on high each little star.
But in His sight each soul must be
Since these are His eternally.

W. S. In spirit (Through S. S.)

New Orleans, La.

To Mrs. ——— and Mrs. ———, (Of the Theo Soc. of N. O.)

To Mrs. ———:

Yesterday, after you left the voice said: "She has been a beacon to so many she will be given the light she deserves." (W. S.)

S. S.

THE POOR

Forgotten these may seem, sad and alone,
Rejected, outcast even by their own—
Loved and adored by none, in direst need,
These work no miracles, these are the poor indeed.

Where chests are opened, that the Lord may see.
The wealth each brings to curse or comfort be,
The treasures of God's poor are kept therein:
As wealth means lack of burden—loot, and sin.

W. S. In spirit (Through S. S.)

"SOWER WENT FORTH . . ."

A sower went forth on an April morn,
Equipped to sow the field.
He tarried not though the sun was hot;
For he thought of the rich land's yield.

He tilled and 'tended the upshoots new
Each day 'till the set of sun;
And looked ahead as on time sped,
To the harvest days all done:

To the store-bins full, and mill-sacks too,
When in winter all must lie dead;
His time of ease when himself he'd please,
Not driven, or lashed or led.

But the reaper grim selected him
Before the harvest's fall;
And his crops lay waste on the fertile place,
Where the frost had blasted all!

SORROWS OF WOMEN

Feathering birdlings these within the nest;
So near the Infinite they're mothered on His breast.
Sorrows He knows, like theirs, and knows theirs, too:
Poised on wing aloft He hears all harming you!

Lone of the earth, God's wing is everywhere.
Under His heart ye'll find only His care.
Seek HERE and find, nor from Him turn away,
Then claim the joys at last enduring, ay, alway.

                    W. S. In spirit (Through S. S.)
    March 13th, '18.
    New Orleans, La.

THE DYING SAVIOUR

(Good Friday—1918. New Orleans, La.)

Sad is the world today at the world's loss:
Heavy the sorrows of mankind's cross.
The sun is hidden and the heavens o'ercast:
He has been crucified. His will is done at last.

The Easter morn is come! The stone is rolled away!
The spirit is unfurled. Uprisen is the clay.
He died the world to bless: to prove there was no death:
Yet was He crucified that mortals might have breath
Beyond the sphere of earth where death no breath doth take:
Yet must we know this here in faith for Jesus' sake.

W. S. In spirit (Through S. S.)

EASTER IN THE SOUTH
(1918—March 31st, N. O., La.)

Heavenly hosts uprising are ever in His skies,
Where the spirits are at home in His Paradise.
With their armies marching here gathering for mankind
Manna for the hungering hearts of dear ones left behind.

Heaven is only on the earth. God is here as well.
Mysterious as His secrets are we here cannot tell.
Holding in His Mighty plan spirits even hidden,
Who must follow, serve, and help but as He has bidden.

Foiling every rapier's blade, stacking every gun,
Are there spirits aiding Him against the murderous Hun.
When the curtain falls at last on the scene of war
Heaven will open its wide fold here, but not afar,

Rushing in the armies of fools imprisoned here,
Wiping out their murderer's past in a vision clear,
Seeing only hearts and homes wrecked by warrior's deeds:
Helping to cement with love One loving Heart which bleeds.

W. S. In spirit (Through S. S.)

You are a wince—a little juice—that's all:
I am the master (past) (passed) who plays and sings!
You may come here and be a master, too,
As you return to spread your spirit-wings.

You are a toot—I am the tooter, see?
There's something here I must keep tooting, too,
Else you would fail to hear and all would end,
And I should make no medium of you!

So string the fiddle, fetch the bow,
I'm fit and ready now—so let's begin:
Attune, mine instrument shall make amends
For Shakespeare's foul ingratitude and sin.
                    W. S. In spirit (Through S. S.)

"Sold Out" the seats for Shakespeare's spirit-speech:"
Such is the sign I see upheld where I do preach.
And may it come to pass is all I ask—
Since Sarah here makes so much of the task.
                                        W. S.

To reach within and find all that you sought
And hand it out to those who pay, have bought,
That which YOU found, while seeking light within,—
This is the end of your career,—all that has been.
                                        W. S.

Fooled once again. No spirit can speak out
Except they're given room by mortal's voice.
You can speak for me, or may speak alone:
At any rate, methinks you should rejoice
That I found you while sitting in the dark
To welcome spirits who could help you on:
If I have NOT, 'tis not my fault, be sure;
For with your passing do I hope for dawn.
                    W. S. In spirit (Through S. S.)
Note: This is "stringing" as W. S. calls it, to keep in touch
with the voice. S. S.

HELL'S SPIRITS

Carried out hence from the battle for gold,
Where poverty's poorest must stand,
In a hell which they chose, a hell which they made,
Are the "shivers" in God's spirit-land.

More than "out in the cold," more than burning could be,
Are the souls whose sole god has been gold;
And no hell man surmised could be hell worse than theirs,
Where no profit accrued, loss: all sold.

Where all must go hence and be "shivers" at last,
At last each one finds WHAT HE MADE;
If shivering alone in a hell he's outcast,
Let him SHIVER! Nor come back through Sade.

W. S. In spirit (Through S. S.)

Note: "To ———, from W. S. In spirit, in reply to a letter
in which he alludes to the spirits departed as "shivers," and
begs this one to keep away from them. As though she could,
or he could, or anyone else. W. S."

HAIL, BERNHARDT! LA VIE DE FRANCE!
(Dec. 18th, 1917. After returning from The Palace Theatre.)

HAIL! BERNHARDT! Sister of my stage!
Beloved where is no time, decadence, age!
Shakespeare am I, who knows thy worth full well,
And, strange as it may seem, I here can tell
Through her who is my fine-strung instrument,
And here acclaim thine Art Supremely sent!

Here do I write on this, a spirit's page,
Thine honored land is blest in thy heart's rage
Against the murderous, treacherous Huns,
Vituperously entrenched in France with rapier's guns!

Hail to the stars! the fading light!
The morning breaks. The day of right.
Uprising is the Son forgiving all
Who pass behind His footsteps, hear His call!
O Christ forgive! They know not what they do,
Until as spirits passed, they seek nor find, but rue.

Wm. Shakespeare In spirit (Through S. S.)

WHO SHALL SAY?

Who shall say what the roses know
Of the great Creator's plan?
Who shall say if their eyes askance
See through the soul of man?
Who shall say whence their essence springs,
Or tell the tale of their varied hues?
Their velvet mantles, and tinted cheeks?
Why never one has the *blues?*

Who shall say when ends their day
If a soul has gone to God:
Or their fragrance lost, or what it cost
To be born a flower of the sod!

RHYMES AND JINGLES

Two ounces of words and a metre,
A jingle or rhyme at the end;
Some patience and good perseverance:
Shake well, and rewrite; and *then* mend.

W. S.

"In the ghost-land, which is here at the present.
And always will be here, so far as I know now."

AN ORCHESTRATION IN WORDS INSTEAD OF NOTES

"High-yi," said the finch by the thicket's edge;
"Too-loo," said Bob White overhead:
"Lee-la-lee,—la-lal-lee," said the meadow-lark,
"WHO-WHO?" the old owl said!
"Jolly-well, jolly-well," said the sparrow,
(The Englishman's wayward bird)
All-li-lie-e—All-li-lie-e-e-, sang the linnet,—
(The sweetest solo I've heard) . . .

But the sun sank low and the music ceased,
Except for a serenade:
In the moonlight white with all its might,
The nightingale needs no aid
To rouse in the breasts of lovers
The love for a little bird
Which has added to many a bridal
The last congratulate word.

W. S. In spirit
With fondest memories of his own country's
feathered clans.
(Through S. S.)

ADIEU

Sweet little room where first I spoke to her,
Through time to come fond memories will stir
When I recall the couch, the chair, the bed,
The fairy-lamp, the vase with roses red.
Though oft' we'll speak, my fine-strung harp and I,
Still, little room, we'll love thee when we "die."
We'll think on all we wrote, and all the "dead"
Who passed within this place by spirit led.
And when we pass, my instrument and I,

Maybe we'll enter here again—
Until,—adieu! Good-by!

W. S. In spirit (Through S. S.)

"THE WISEST WORD"

To —— —— ——, from W. S. In Spirit (Through S. S.)

Some say the wisest Word is His:
His name is Wisdom it is known:
Who but a bird can search the sky
And find Him? Marked by Him His own!

Then, when the spirits wing aloft
He saved to bring back to His Sky,
Must they not speak in Wisdom's words,
When telling mortals none can "die"?

In time to come, when mortals see
The Wisdom of the "wisest word".
No feast-of-God will these forsake,
But welcome spirits seen or heard.

ON THE "DEATH" OF ——

You say your friend has "died" this morning,
(Who was a poet-humorist, 'tis said)
Then shall he find, where he has fared, MORE humor,
In living, all-alive, when he is "dead".

Then will he mourn not o'er the husk he cherished,—
(Except he mourn it cannot now be *fed*,)
For poet-of-the-earth, by earth's ambitions,
Must e'en a poet after "death" be led.

As you well know, there is no "dying," Kelly;
For you have seen the spirits, toe to head,—

And —— will come back, as once he promised,
And sit beside you on your studio-bed.

You'll feel him clasp your hand, and he will vanish:
And wide-awake you'll wonder whence he came;
But this *he'll* tell you, maybe, so I shall not;
But ask him for *me,* will you, What's a name!

W. S. In spirit (Through S. S.)

"TO THE OLD GENERAL WHO HAS FOUGHT MANY BATTLES,—I give my best effort"

"As I am now a spirit, and see as a spirit sees. W. S."
(To Gen. ——, Hero of ——)

Withhold no word of praise from one who has passed through
the field of war;
But let him give his grandson to accept of tribute which they
pay.
The time is not far hence when all will flee from war and
warring men.
What will the world do then for glory,—honor,—and heroes?

You were an old warrior in this world and had to fight foes
of steel with steel:
But when you reach the land where I am now,—there will be
no captains of militia, no uniforms
To decorate your brave, manly form:
But clothed in a little of what you are,
You will go to think over the past and reflect on the future of
the godless one.

Oh General, could I save you from this terrible fate, I could
feel my sorrows had not been in vain. One so succoured
would pay me for all I have suffered.
Try to receive the   Jesus your friend —— has told you

waits to welcome the erring however late they call on Him.
Try to give Him your heart and sincere repentance before
it is too late.   For in the world where I am there is no
chance to undo the past, and no heaven of love to undo
your sorrow, Sir, but the saddest of sorrows continuing
on for all time, and without ceasing.

W. S. In spirit.

—— PRAYER

(While gazing at the bronze of ——, "Washington at Valley
Forge."—Sub-Treasury Bldg., Wall Street, New York City)

Almighty God, if I could pray as he,
And kneel with soul made whole by Thee,—
Within the forest of my doubts wouldst thou
Enlighten me; restore my vision, now!
O Power that ruleth all, compel the light
To shine upon mine eyes approaching night!
And lift the harrowing fear from my poor heart,
That blindness shall obscure Thy beauteous Art!
Give me the faith and trust of this great man,
Who by his zeal Thy very skies did span.
As Thou didst promise through Thine only Son
All in His name we ask,—
Make ME, like WASHINGTON!

W. S. In spirit (Through S. S.)

New York City, July 14th, 1917.

". . . BY THE STILL WATERS"

Saviour, let me walk with Thee
By the still*ed* and peaceful sea!
Great Restorer, rest my soul.
Father, make, and keep me, whole.

"Through the Valley" when I go,
Walk with me, that I may know
Evil cannot walk with Thee:
By Thy words, or comfort me.

Give Thy cup and let me drink
Abounding love, when on the brink
Enemies surrounding me,
Still, annointed, Lord, by Thee,

Shall no death that I can die
Separate us in God's sky.
Loved by Thee am I complete.
At the last, His mercy, sweet.

W. S. In spirit (Through S. S.)
Feb. 4th, '18.

NEVER!

Can a love inborn be a love untrue?
Or the love of love be wrong?
Can a poet live and love not give,
Or inscribe a loveless song?

Can a love inborn be a love outlived?
Or left when the soul lives on?
Can a lover "die" with his house of clay?
Or does greater love then dawn?

Can it be the way the Maker planned,
Who gave His Son for love?
While the good God lives no love shall die!
But is part of Him above!

W. S. In spirit (Through S. S.)

WHERE SHALL WE GO?

Where shall we go at last the day is done,
Where shall we find the light at set of sun
When groping through the maze of wilderness,
We cry and grieve in hopeless soul distress?

Where shall I land when I have crossed life's sea?
What will the boatman say who pilots me?
What is the port; where is the haven sure;
Must my poor soul, adrift, as wreckage reach the shore?

What shall I say when I step on that strand
And meet no friend, and find no welcoming hand?
Where shall I go when I have reached the shore
And learn my past is my forevermore!

W. S. In Spirit
(Through Sarah Taylor Shatford.)

O for the wonderful, wonderful past,
To be mine with my body the same,—
To be loved in return for the love which I gave,
And not to be loved as a name.

O for the wonderful, wonderful life
That I flung to the dogs and the swine,
With never a thought for a world just above,
Or a place in that world to be mine.

O for the chance that I lost, flung away,
For the bitter, the dregs of the wine!
O that the world where I am would awake
To the privilege of life, all divine.

W. S. In spirit (Through S. S.)

NOTE.—This constitutes one spirit's longing only, while there
are many which would prefer death to living on in a sphere

without a body and its enjoyments, others are willing to be
what they are, complete without their bodies. We love, we
hate, we yearn, we rebel, and have every feeling a mortal has,
even though we are spirits, and this one who writes could tell
you of my own peculiar hatred and dislikes, human as humans
indeed, were she inclined to do so.

W. S. In spirit (Through S. S.)

THE VALUE OF SIN

There is no place on earth a man can go
Where sin may not some profit to him show.
There is no place a man can leave this sin
Unless he will acknowledge Jesus Christ
Was its propitiation, and reform before the sin
Finds him in bonds he cannot break,
A helpless prisoner for its sake.

There is no place a spirit can accept
This offer after "death" has sent him hence.
We must admit that no greater sacrifice
Was ever paid than that a sinner pays
Through all of time when he must sit
(Or stand, as suits him best) religiously
An outcast from the light. By this I mean
A sinner sits (or stands) with naught to do
But think. And in a darkness pitch, recalls, returns, (in
    memory)
Recounts, recovers every moment of his earthly time
And all he was, was not, of all his span.

God wipes the past out never, so they say. Each joy, as well,
Remaineth, praise His name as I do here for this. For with
My past I hugged these close and even now I

Would not let them go.
The value of a thing is its true worth.
And all that I can say in my return
Should profit others to lead better lives;
To pause upon the brink of that eternity
From which I speak deciding to permit my past
To serve them here in this.

Go to a priest, kneel down with streaming eyes,
And tell him all you wish God would forget.
Recalling every act of vicious lust or taint
Of marital impurity; each obligation slighted
Or unmet, the shirking of responsibility, and all injustices.

If you have never spoken to your God, or knelt before Him,
Unseen though He be, there still is time if you will go today.
And take my past and lay it at His feet, and pray one prayer
For me.
Claim no redemption here unless you do.
For "death" so called is living with your soul for aye.

On earth a man enticed by sin becomes its victim.
There is no place a sinner here may go then on the earth
But to his soul he adds a bond or link defying all
To separate through God's eternal time.
Each day his burden becomes heavier and his profits less.
But he does not realize this until after the change called
      "death."
Which means he inhabits another sphere on the same plane
Where he lives in sin surrounded by sinners
As before he passed out of his mortal body.
For the change alters nothing in the man,
He being what he made himself, how can he blame another
For the victim he has become.

We rush madly into the arms of vice and crime
Lust and disloyalty.   It rushes to greet us, in fact.
And I long to say here how little man profits
From sensation in the spirit.
This chains him to earth, where he seeks his kind.
Ideals never cling to grime.
Loose living cannot claim a permanent convert.
This is the God saved in each rebelling against wrong, or sin.

Conscience has always spoken to wrong doers
Until its voice was silenced for a time by degradation.
Then remorse weeps over its bier.
The two were not friends in life, even strangers,
For one is born long after the other has been mute.
My own conscience in fact was inert.
I believed I was right in all I did
And saw no wrong at that time in preserving my man
At the expense of crime.
Whoever follows a false voice falls lower
Than the one who breaks a law.
For he justifies the act or crime,
By stamping it with his entire avowal of justification,
Which is the greater wrong.

Now I am enlightened, I wish to warn others,
Save them by my own failure, through my own crime against
    nature
For which I was banished from Almighty God's light
For.time I do not know, hopelessly alone,
Unredeemed until now, unless by God's miracle
My work from the spiritside shall redeem me,
As I see all, and do all with this one's help I can do.

                    W. S. In spirit (Through S. S.)

THE PEACE OF CHRIST

In the universal plan of God's wisdom there is no blight of greed nor any scarcity of blessing. We are given a bountiful earth to enjoy with all its fruits and products, and we reap the fields of His munificence without stint. We are given a world of beauty wherein to praise Him, and a firmament bespeaking His skill, while all the music of His universal spheres resounds His glorious harmony.

Men take for granted all these gifts, while they enjoy a life-term of His riches. They come and go, prosper and rise, making no paeon of praise for the Maker of all things in heaven and earth, seeking prosperity of riches where moth and rust doth corrupt. While they live they live to amass that which they must pass on and leave to the greedy behind them, never thinking of the moment when they must stand before the Maker pauper clad!

To be poor in a world of material things is sad. But to be poor in the spiritual realm of God's universal love is to sit by the wayside famished, an outcast, with no heritage—but a soul unclad and unfed.

While the world looks down upon the hungry and poor, and an outcast feels forgotten of God, the spirit-world pities the impoverished soul and offers a helping hand to succor it from degredation and need.

Mortals are poor only when they lack this world's gold, and are ill clad; but spirits are poor when they bring nothing but these to place before the throne of the Almighty who in His beneficent love has given His incomparable riches to bless them, asking only a tithe of praise and gratitude for all His abundant gifts.

To sit by the roadside homeless and friendless with no place to go, and no one to care, is by far the worse plight of the homeless anywhere.

But to sit in the darkness, alone and remorseful, with a wasted life pictured before you in which you have given naught and received naught is to be the poorest man alive, who cannot die!

You may feel the sorrows you have caused in the world while you are still in the world and suffer the keenest remorse a mortal can know, but in one moment of eternity's darkness a remorseful spirit suffers more intense agony than he could in a lifetime spent in repentant tears!

He may mourn for his loved ones on earth when they pass, and think they are lost or damned; but one moment spent in impenetrable gloom where no one has met him or prepared a place for his coming, will be more than a lifetime of funerial woe!

Lives there a man who can conceive of such poverty? Lives one of so vivid imagination that he can recount over such misery?

O when you come emptyhanded and emptyhearted to a world of eternal bliss, and meet with no friend and no aid, when you sit where the night of the past holds no glimmer of hope, no ray of God's love, then you will know poverty no gold ever paid for, and friendlessness no society ever assauged!

When you look down the road of the past in search of a wayfaring friend, straining your eye for a glimpse of a form you once knew, and still there is no one in sight,—will you think of the ones on the earth who passed who were paupers and you extended them no helping hand? When you hunger for a crust for your starving soul, and there is no one to fling even this, O what will you think of your poverty then!

O what can you think, say, or do.

Will you pick up the cross you have made for yourself, and trudge on in grim poverty's road? Or will you sit still where

your past has hailed you and break bread with your heart like
a stone?

Will you kneel in the dust where the paupers have trod, and
bite your poor nails in distress, asking God to forgive you,
and give you a chance to bless others as He you did bless?

Will you keep on the road with your poor bleeding feet all
bruised by the thorns you did choose,—as over the hill and
beyond, and beyond, you carry the cross you would lose?

Will you cry to a God that you never have known, and ex-
pect Him to come to your call, when you never have called to
this God on the earth. Or lifted one there who did fall?

W. S. In spirit (Through S. S.)

GREAT MEN

New York, May 12th, 1917. To his countryman, The Hon.
Arthur J. Balfour, British War Commissioner to America.
Where I now find myself completely out of touch with my dear
old England, but nevertheless interested as much in all things
concerning her welfare as in the days when I laid my best
at her feet already garlanded o'er with Art's rich gems, of
which I thought my own the best poor, but have come to know
the estimate of worth accorded my earthly work, as we in the
spirit are cognizant of all things on the earth, and I wish
to say that such appreciation as England's, as well as the
world's, has been my only real pleasure, as what those works
and experiences cost me in the realm of spirit I must continue
to pay for throughout eternal time I am told here -where I
now am. O men of England, my countrymen, could you know
the ways of God are best, and leave the crimes for which I
pay, and turn to God while still there is time to acknowledge
sin and confess iniquity in the flesh, what would ye be spared
that I have suffered because of such unconfessed and un-
absolved through repentance! Make haste while there is yet

time, give no enemy power to imprison you for eternity! Walk in God's ways, and rejoice in His blessings as He made them; worship the Creator in all his wisdom, and spare remorse and isolation eternal! Flee from the tempter while there is time; draw no cheque on Eternity's account, which belongs to the One who claims all this treasury, where every debt outstanding must be paid in full!

Sorrow through time on the earth, but rejoice through all time. Give all that is just, be not passion's slave, go hence clean and white and saved. God gives and gives bountifully,— His gifts are sufficient for all. Take up your cross, whatever it is, and bear it as bravely as you can with His help, but forsake Him not for strange gods, neither the love-god, so called, for there is a record kept which no man can ponder, and this tells all to your living intelligence surviving dissolution of the body which held it for a time in shackles, to free it forever a wonderer through space seeking its own kin and kind barred from them all, unless through a miracle of His own, which I know not yet, through centuries of time.

Be to each other all God saw fit in His creation when He saw man needed a mate, and gave him woman to bear and share with him one of His divine creations. Go to Him with her praises in your hearts, and on your lips unsoiled, unsullied by any perverse act whatever, and looking back upon your earthly career be able still to occupy a place of honor and purity by her side who has borne your children admirably and in purity and honor, have the right to share with them all the divine glory of God's richest reward everlasting.

This is from the heart of the poet you revere, whose words you cherish, whose dust is to you precious, and whose love is still yours, and ever shall be. And I sign this with my full name and insignia:

SIR WILLIAM SHAKESPEARE,
Knighted by Eliza and James, England.

GREAT MEN

Great men and brave have laid their lives down at their coun-
　　try's feet,
In trials, through war, have won at last, when certain seemed
　　defeat,—
Chosen from the great multitude of iron sinew and brawn,
The victory was won through them, through them men glimpsed
　　the dawn!

We pay our homage to such men, though we have passed be-
　　yond.
We laud the brave and true no less, are keen and loving, fond
As when we could "Hoo-ray" with men upon the mortal plane.
Alas, we feel all else as they, and share their earthly pain.

But greatness friends, that shall count here, where spirits come
　　at last
Will be the sum of righteous love they bore their God when
　　passed
Into His realm where heroes be the fighters of earth-sins,
Where wars make wrecks of armies, yea, and but a Hero wins!

W. S. In Spirit

(Through his medium, Sarah Taylor Shatford.)

FIRST EXPERIENCES AFTER THE CHANGE CALLED
DEATH

The world of life had passed away, and still he was alive.
The world of life was everwhere and on every hand he saw
those who had passed into spiritlands, speaking, walking, and
doing all he had just been doing on the earth in his mortal
frame which now rested neath the sod. What had happened,
he asked himself, and where was he anyhow, that all these
disembodied forms encircled about him in curious wonder at
the new arrival, himself, and talked of his malady and his

identity, his country and all which so lately concerned him.

Did he realize what had happened at once, do you think, or did he realize gradually that he had passed from his bodily form and become a spirit and was in the spirit's realm above and near the earth, in fact so near there was no difference that he could see except that he was naked, unclothed as when he was born, while the others surrounding him wore all kinds of raiment of various materials, cuts, and colors,—a fantastical set as ever his eyes had seen while in their human sockets, he can tell you.

I had passed out in a little town in England, on the River Avon, near a churchyard where my bones were laid to rest, of a fever caused through a long seige of revel with my friends who came to felicitate me on my good fortune of having succeeded in life to the uttermost in everything I had set out to do (except one thing which they neither knew of, or know of to-day, for all I know here) including rehabilitating myself in fortune's favour, as well as establishing myself in the good-graces of my family at home, where this revel was held in their honor. As my good friends they were sharers in much of my misfortune, so why should they not now partake of that which the world called riches. For myself, I was not a heavy drinker, in fact did not care for heavy liquors. But the festival of reunion as well as good-fellowship was at its height and included these as usual.

Now when I say did not care for liquor, do not misunderstand me, and blame my friends for the malady which caused my rapid transference to the world of spirit. These are things which must happen and always do happen, either through the tides of fate, or the will of higher powers, for I am not able to state where I now am which took me from my earthy habitation to the one I occupy.

You will say this is a spirit who could not have believed in a Supreme Being while on the earth, and who now doubts the existence of One. In this you are wrong. If you will look through my works written through many different moods, you will find no statements therein on which to base such an assertion. I pray you have patience and see for yourselves, if this is trueth I speak. Take my works and search them for an infidel's mark and tell me if the one who wrote them reverenced, worshiped, accredited to all his characters, the love and fear of a living Almighty, conscious, cognizant, all-prevailing Spirit, called God.

You will find Him in every drama at least, and so far as those other superlative love-sonnets of mine concern the Creator of all that a creature holds sacred and lovely, I thanked God with every breath in those for the worldy love I felt must be, could only be, a part of such love as His own. This I shall leave for further explanation at a future time. You will understand how I reverence every beauty and wonder God made, if you are a student of my earthly works. For this my first spiritual work, or rather work of mine for my own self done through mediumship in the spirit.

Now this cannot concern a large portion of humanity for the reason a small percentage only believe in the possibility of spirit-return. When these read that I have found an instrument through whom I can not only write but speak, they may interest a larger number to investigate the truth of mediumship and spirit-communication. At least this is one hope of mine. But the chief object for which I am here writing is entirely one of self-expression and justification. The laws which govern the spirit are more, and harder to over-ride than all the laws of mortals, or all they could conceive. This will be subject matter for another paper, as well.

To have overcome these so far as to be able to write this paper alone is to have accomplished what William Shakespeare has never before been able to accomplish during the centuries since he passed into spirit. That I have worked for this and nothing else would be practically the truth, but I fear your interest might abate in the task of one so selfish.

To suffer with no surcease, to become an outcast for no cause, to have committed no crime but one, and that against myself, and for this and its consequent evils resulting from it, to lose forever the chance of association with my kind in the spiritworld; to be cognizant of my own shortcomings, sins, failures, and repentant more than mortals conceive repentance could mean, and yet, to be assured of no Saviour's benign pardon, no mercy from God throughout all eternal aeons of time, immortal spirit that I am, this is to be an outcast in the spirit world where I am, where no one can help, or save and where none ever live if they can wander back to the earth to be with their own kindred souls who inhabit the earth in mortal bodies still, unlettered in spirit, ignorant as babes as to all I write herein, and therefore lambs of our bosoms, and hopes of our souls!

Why, you ask, does this one permit you to write these words, knowing all you say, as she must have been told. Because in her innocence she harboured a spirit who inspired her to write her poems,—all trustful, hopeful, good, and fine,—and when all her work was finished she learned who wrote the most of them, then refused to sign her name any longer when she heard the words at last spoken in the inner ear, instead of inspirationally, as before. She now writes to my dictation just as an amanuensis would take articulate words from the lips of a living man.

When a spirit finds a medium through which they can work as while on earth, they are at once overjoyed, and overcome with fear lest they lose them through some mortal idiocyncrasy, or loss of power either their own or some intervening current spiritual or magnetic, and to do the work I have longed to do, suffered to do, is my first aim through this one now writing. When this is finished it will be her ambition to go on and convince the material world of the truth of spirit return, and we may work together in order to reach a higher class of intelligence than most mediums are able to reach.

She is a rare instrument in my hands, subservient and highly strung. In fact so highly strung by me of late in opening the inner-ear to hear this voice I now use, as to have been overwrought nervously by shock of hearing spirit-voices, having rested for a long period of time under doctor's and nurses' care. She will now finish the paper I begun.

You will see by this effort, plainly discernable to anyone of mediocre intelligence, she is carrying out my directions, and mine only.

When I, William Shakespeare, reached the spirit world, I gave little time to remorse, or weeping as I have seen others, but set about to find my equals, or superiors, in that land where I was a new arrival.

There seemed to be none of these on the exact spot where I had located, as it were, as it is hard to describe a spirit-transition,—and I conceived the plan of looking farther, seeking, indeed searching, for mine own. Surely they were there: surely they would help me on my way, where no spirit newly arrived, can help themselves much, especially those who have been very ill and long suffered maladies which consumed their spirit-strength.

But my search was in vain until now. Here am I, nobody, —not even a king's fool,—with no chance to make myself heard by the earthfolk whom I would serve, and save, through my sufferings,—whom I always loved and still love. And for whom I shall have written a soul's message, whether they partake of its counsel or not. It rests with them.

W. S. In spirit (Through S. S.)

THE MYSTERIOUS PORTAL

In the subject for my paper tonight I have chosen a word mortals use, and must continue to use, so long as they prefer to know nothing regarding the life after "death" (so-called).

It is mysterious to us who have passed through as well as to you in the body. For a spirit in the world I occupy is not in God's confidence because he has left his body and occupies another sphere above that inhabited by his "shape" covered over by its seemly cloak of hide. We grasp a few facts, discern a few truths, most of these applying directly to ourselves, and those who surround us. But we do not know the slightest meaning of the continuity of life, nor what is the ultimate end of our sufferings, or debasements, in this land from whence I come, to which all mortals go I may add, or through which they must pass before they may go on. Where, even *we* do not know. You see therefore the mysterious portal even beyond the change. Perhaps other spheres (there must be others, since my own are not here) have their mystery also. We are informed here there is no more "dying." The spirit progresses as it deserves, through service, outliving its body-crimes or taints, and, through worship and oneness with God.

Here I must stop. For I know not His secrets, neither His plans, the unfoldment of which is more evident after the change, as well as the desire to know Him and serve Him according to His commands.

We long for Divine knowledge. Perhaps this is the greatest longing a spirit knows. Life has been futile evidently, and without our realizing that it was being made so by ourselves. The fear then distresses us constantly lest we fail again along other paths which still seem dark. While all souls are enlightened through transition they have gained no wisdom through the mysterious portal regarding future worlds, and little they might not have cherished on the earth had they been wakeful and heeded the warnings of Scripture.

We have no cares that were earth's cares, and as our advantage to possess all of earth's knowledge becomes apparent we strive for it in the archives of the spirit: but there are many handicaps not to be overcome through centuries, even so.

Minds brilliant have come and passed on from us without profiting by these opportunities, devoting all of time to His service of helping or directing those too poor or unfortunate or misshapen to help themselves.

Then again there are laws in the spirit world, which, if disobeyed, must retard spirit-growth, perhaps eternally. Laws which govern spirits and mortals. A few of these I may cite: Spirits must not alarm mortals. Under no stress of grief are they permitted to break this law. Only as a divine well earned blessing are spirits permitted to materialize before mortals lest fright unhinge reason. A mortal must adjust their own affairs, then, who is alarmed at the thought of their own being with them, who long only to comfort and serve them. Since we are everywhere mortals are and know their trials and have added powers or gifts through the spirit, many of which I may not mention, this fear of the "dead" robs them of spirit help more often than spirits are under such conditions able to help them.

We still speak of the mystery of "death," lauding the Giver of both body and spirit, never ceasing to wonder at it all. We are breaking a Divine law if we obsess a mortal. That is, occupy their mental or physical house. Also to describe the secrets of God's adjustment for broken laws, one of which I have broken here when I tell you of the dark place from which I wandered before finishing my term of payment, and for which I must pay eventually, as all must pay.

We may aid in any way where we are welcomed, or where there is suffering. We may inspire, warn, uplift, through spirit-power even though there is no mediumistic clairvoyance or clairaudience.

Let me say too that we never fail to help those who depend on us unless it is beyond our power.

Could you have seen as I saw the stream of spirits following the soldiers marching away, you would know the interest the so-called "dead" take in the living (?), and the nearness of "heaven" (so-called). Just another mystery, that is all.

How wide is the portal, the mysterious portal! And when will it open for us who have passed through "death." And what is behind it, and back of it all. I can answer but the last question: The Almighty God of Wisdom.

WILLIAM SHAKESPEARE, In the Spirit
(Through S. S.)

("Sign my full name. W. S.")

TWO WORLDS ONE

There is a phase of mortal existence like unto spirit, verily more spirituelle than some spirits,—and there is a phase of spiritual existence like unto mortals insomuch as they are here upon the earth, exactly as before departing this life (as their dear ones believe), in all their beings exactly the same as when in the body, their intellects keener than before (for the chief attribute of spirit IS mind) and their interests for the most part what they were in the body.

When we look and do not see as mortals, there is great pathos, and much fun in the phenomenon; but when as spirits we cannot make mortals see or hear or believe, no matter what wonders we are able to work, there is only tragedy in such failure. Sometimes we long to convince our nearest and dearest that we are beside them still, and they feel strange, uncommon, unearthly, reasons for believing we are near, but, unless we can produce a wonder-worker, a clairvoyante or medium

through which we transmit a personal message of actual oc-
curances remembered while on the earth, there is no hope of
making even the nearest to us even investigate our abode or
the possibilities of spirit return. This for the most part causes
the greatest grief, next to remorse, as spirit knows. But there
are other sorrows, too, quite as hard to bear. For instance,
we are led to hope heaven means reunion with the dear ones
passed-before, and this for many robs death of its sting!

But this is not possible always, in fact it is only possible to
saints, as in the spirit world "there are many mansions"
through which we are not allowed to seek for our loved ones,
and heaven does not therefore constitute a place of reunion
for all.

Also, we are told on earth that death seals all, solves all,
erases all, heals all,—none of which is literally true.

But to rob mortals of their hope is not my mission. To
prepare them for a future in which they share their past and
belong wherever it allots them,—to make them aware of their
own nearness to those out of the body called "spirits," the
reliance of these on mortals whom they long to help and serve,
as well as the obsession of unruly spirits who cling to their
own kind attracted to them by like sins or desires,—this, this
IS my mission, in prose. For I have a mission all my own
beside this of course, which I will state otherwhere.

The preponderance of skepticism over mortals desire to
learn of the departed is amazingly incredible to the spirit-
world.

We have no way of overcoming this, except through long
periods of time, once in an age, a miracle happens, to wit: An
instrument is found capable in some of the spirit requirements,
who is also willing to serve, in her or his own unselfish dower,
being fine enough to obliterate self entirely for this purpose.
When mortals are aware of the spirit speaking through them,
either audibly or inspiringly, they attach themselves readily,

and adjust themselves in temperament, environment, and physical being, to do the spirit's bidding. This is not always well, for, as I have stated, spirits do not differ from mortals in any way because they are no longer carrying their house of flesh. And the spirits nearest the earth plane are oftenest those of wicked, lustful tendencies, occupying space and place near their old haunts until all theirs pass over whom they idolize.

Spirits inhabit mortal bodies sometimes, in order to accomplish their own wicked devices,—alcoholic inebriates especially fasten to, and obsess, mortals who will satisfy their craving as when they were on earth. This alone causes many of the sodden earthfolks inebriety, did they know it, and were it understood, more sympathy would be extended these who cannot overcome their desire for debauchery. There should be spirit physicians, or physicians understanding spirit obsession who could treat and save these poor mortals. Insanity is obsession in ninety per cent of its horrors can be cured in no other way than by freeing the mortal of the spirit possessing its mental house, or obscessing its physical being. "A house divided against itself will fall."

The world is awakening. Slowly the veil is being lifted or thrust aside by the separated mutually seeking communication, forming the wireless conditions, which need only polarizing to perfect. At the close of this war this will be established beyond the doubt of any mortal now living; but, as in Jesus of Nazareth's time, who can prophecy when the doubting Thomases will scoff, and joke at spirits as ghosts,—parleying the question only in a spirit of fun-making!

When the living sleep, and find themselves *alive,*
And seek to help the earth ones how to thrive,
Finding their poor souls all self-satisfied,
They, too, will pass, as others passed and "died."

When these "alive" know what of all means "death,"
And strive to aid their loved-ones *having breath,*
To save them from their lot, even when closed their eyes,
'Tis sad to see THESE WEEP, in Paradise!

When mortals pause, or long to understand,
The laws which govern the *near spirit land,*
Hosannas from this world will then be rung,
The earth will hear, and all aside "death's" veil be flung!

W. S. In spirit (Through S. S.)

SPIRIT-MEMORY
(By Wm. Shakespeare, In spirit through Sarah Taylor
Shatford, his only medium.)

When a spirit finds himself here alive and naked, and clothes himself as nearly as I could explain it so mortals can understand it, he tries to recall names, and dates, and places, and faces, in connection with his earth-life, and sometimes succeeds very well, but oftener finds it is impossible. For while a man must bring along to this spirit-world all memories of his misdeeds and wrongs of earth for which he is responsible, he passes through so many changes, suffers so much agony (for all suffer when they see themselves just as they have been through a life-term of earth-errors and this is the hell even Jesus of Nazareth descended into) that when in God's mercy they are relieved and come out into the light of His love and forgiveness, they are much like an earth-body who has recovered from a lingering fever,—weak, and with little strength of their own.

Here, those appointed to help and serve the new arrivals, the new-born spirits, lead, and advise with them, until they become efficient in turn to aid newcomers,—for this is the first service spirits perform for their God in the spiritland.

It takes a spirit a long time to recover his strength sometimes,—but I choose not to dwell upon the unhappy side of this question, but to begin with a spirit rehabilitated and regenerate, having suffered and atoned, and become one anxious to undo his past by continual service to the One all serve here who progress, or desire to be one with Him.

When a spirit is first taken to the earth-plane after his regeneration is completed through his own repentance and remorse alone (for it all rests with us here as well as when we were on the earth, what we would be) he is so overjoyed to go into his old home or haunts, see his own still in the body, that it is a happy errand when we old spirits are designated to teach them how they may return by their own volition, unaccompanied by others.

But their memory, that is, the ability to recall names even their own, dates, time, or places, this we lose, as something not necessary to retain I suppose, for here we are not called by name or known by name. It remains only for the illustrious immortals of earth to be known by their names here, and this would not be if the earth-folk arriving did not seek them out and continue to insist on immortalizing them. This is what it means, then, to be great on the earth.

So much doubt is expressed by mortals when the discrepencies in spirit communications are unearthed, and they find small details differing from the exact truth, and this is one of the most difficult matters spirits can never overcome.

For if it is not considered necessary here to have a name, that you once were called by a certain arrangement of the alphabet does not matter except as it matters to prove that your own departed are present, are alive, and have returned to tell you so.

If mortals knew the difficulties to be overcome, the trials to be met, before spirit could manifest through mortal bodies or voices, they would appreciate the efforts of both spirits and mediums, which we regret they do not as yet give credence but drop their investigations just as soon as some trifling incident can be disproved.

The Bible would help them to overcome these doubts, did they ever read it, or , should the church-going Christians believe what they profess of Jesus of Nazareth, but religion and Christliness they put on as their Sunday togs, chafing if they must wear them this entire day—and to ears deaf, eyes blind, the men of God exhort, orate, and harangue in vain. You may beat upon a closed door with the palm of one hand, or many hands, for ages of time and Eternity and never get into the room which it seals!

Well, the ministers ask, "What are we to do about it? What can we try next?" Oh, Men-of-God, Shepherds of the hills of doubting hearts, this is the problem of the entire spirit-world as well as yours.

At the close of the present war in Europe, there will be a spiritual awakening; spiritual manifestations will take place all over the earth; it will be a common occurrence to see the spirit-world in communion with this one, mortals will be given spirit-sight and spirit-hearing. All souls will reach out for this manna but the greatest revelations will occur on the battlefields of Europe, where Christ will appear and the dead arise.

We have known this since the beginning of this war. And let all those who think the war a mistake, or a one-man ordered or censored affair, pause to consider then, when they behold His second coming. And let them know the hand of God was behind it, which same Hand is gathering together His hosts today making ready for the last chapter in the book of War,—which has been written to save mankind from their own self-destruction,—and their souls for their Maker.

Where on the earth today, except in these sorrowing lands, are men thinking on Christ, or His coming, or going, for that matter! If souls must be harrowed, and bodies shot to pieces, to reclaim the world and save it for Him who made it, is it more than God gave when He brought forth His own Son, and permitted Him to be crucified before the eyes of men, that He might save men from themselves?

The sacrifices and slaughters of war can never surpass the sacrifice, or the slaughter, of God's only Son, Jesus of Nazareth! Think of it . . . . ponder it over, ye mortals,—and know the God of Jesus is YOUR God, and in His benificence there is no suffering lost! Then watch, and pray, and open the doors of your minds, and the portals of your hearts, and be ready when He comes to receive Him, and make clean your houses within, that ye may invite Him to sup with you, and refresh His weary spirit, which ye have helped to make weary, alas, oh alas!

W. S. In spirit (Through S. S.)

MISGUIDED LOVE

By Wm. Shakespeare In Spirit (Through Sarah Taylor Shatford, Feb. 10th, 1917.)

When two lovers find complete unity of sentiment and sensation they are called "mates," or "affinities," since complete harmony is so seldom known that it is remarkable and to be remarked when found.

There is a love which justifies glorification, but it is not sexual, nor does sex enter into this love. The love of God for the world when He gave His only begotten Son; the love of this Son for the Father who sent Him; the love of Jesus for Lazarus and His disciples; and the love of Mary Magdalene for the Master.

Such love knows neither sentiment nor sensation, but nevertheless the perfect example of deified, glorified love. The word (love) itself might be defined by these examples. To connect the sexual act with reverential love presupposes that it is of God, which it is only when subservient to His laws. Mankind abuses the law-of-life every time he uses it for another purpose than for which God made it. The germ of life which only God can give and the Creator only understands, is for the increase of specie, and man who was made in God's image and likeness was intrusted with this law, for the sole purpose of propagation, behind which was the law of attraction. What grief the perversion of this act and the breaking of these laws causes mortals is known forever in all worlds.

The mistake made by so many who never loved anything or anyone,—who bind themselves to vice for all time for a sensation which masters their intelligence, will, bodily functions and health, is not any part of love, nor any part of God, but the animal controlling all the man made in His image, the likeness of which they pride themselves they are not.

This text is shunned by the men-of-God who from the pulpits guide the flocks because of its appeal to the lower senses; but they do not know while they are still and quiet the wolf is stealing the sheep!

Speak out, cry out, O Shepherds of Men, for surely a God will not hold you guiltless unless the unwary are warned of this beast which creeps into every fold bearing stealthily off the tenderest, the choicest of your flocks!

Shall the time ever come on earth when, as God intended, worship and love shall belong first to Him, and following His laws no ideals shall be shattered, no vices attached, no prostitution allowed, no perverts intermingling with the decent and unpolluted, no scavanger breed diseasing the unborn,—but man made in His image, God-fearing and loving, companioned by holy thoughts, mated to his own kind, living to serve and praise the everliving God, who is Love!

Keep while you still may be the keeper of chastity, the law

of God's love written clear on the tablets of your hearts, defying not the Creator, "who made all that was made, and saw that it was good."

Keep in the way unfrequented by beasts, lest when you sleep they overpower you! Guard the door that you may see who would enter in! And call for the protection of Him who stands without, waiting to save while there is time!

W. S. In spirit (Through S. S.)

THE SEX RELATION

When the Creator rested and viewed all He made, and saw that all He made was good, He had not yet made woman to be man's helpmete or companion. Seeing with infinite vision, and comprehending with Infinite wisdom, He knew that His work was incomplete; and as the great artist adds the final touch to his masterpiece, God made woman, the most perfect of all His works, and, of all, the most compassionate, and like unto Himself.

When God saw that man needed woman, He recognized the principal he set in motion when He created life; for to recreate and replenish there must be the life-seed, which is still His own secret, despite the genius of man "made in His image." Thus He made woman to perfect the sublimity of all He had made, and He made her to fulfill a mission so God-like, so sacred, that no scientists with their God-given minds have yet fathomed His mystery of sex-copulation, child-fathering, or mothering. Until today the life-germ secret belongs to the Creator.

When man and woman inherited a kingdom all their own, and belonged to each other, God's gift was complete. And while they were forbidden to eat of the fruit of the tree, the Bible tells us, God's complement of male and female, through which all nature is replenished, must have been made without purpose, if we are to take this view of the passage in Scripture

pertaining to the fall of man, as it is expounded by all on
earth professing the Christian religion. We view this dif-
ferently here. For we know God makes no errors and never
has He created anything useless.

When the first man and the first woman God made were
driven out of Eden because of their sin, it was not the sin
of cohabitating with one another, for God made the female *for*
the male. The sins of this pair were the sins of mortals today:
forgetting their Maker, and believing themselves gods unto
themselves, fitted and able to solve, with their inheritance, all
problems of earthlife whatsoever. Self-sufficiency was their
sin: self-reliance: selfishness. And it is the greatest sin of
commission or omission today on the earth.

With the joys of the senses, and the lusciousness of the
fruits of the earth, and its abounding supply, they became as
the kings of the world who have caused all the bloodshed of
wars, entirely and absolutely self-satisfied, usurping the
powers of the Almighty God! And that which He gave to
bless His children became a curse.

It is much the same today everywhere on the face of the
earth. God's inventions and blessings are not good enough
for the children of men; but they take it upon themselves to
improve upon these. The Creator who made the Universe and
keeps it aswing and attune, is not wise enough to make perfect
the relationship behind which is the divine spark of Him. So
these pervert nature; selling their birthright to the Kingdom
of Heaven, for less than "a mess of pottage."

Along the way to Paradise there is no sadder sight than
these who were not satisfied with Paradise, but thought them-
selves able to improve God's invention, and the wisdom of His
plan.

Today the earth is ruinous with the unwisdom of men: the
perverted children of God, who in His mercy and love permits
them to begin over after a time (oh, what a time!) of agoniz-

ing remorse words could not convey to a mortal's mind.

When a spirit sees his misshapened form which, in its twisted shape tells the story of his past life of vice, and which he must bear on until he rids it of every deformity by serving the very creatures he helped to pervert, there is no suffering of earth-mortals to which this can be compared. He is known of all to be what he is, in the full light of day, where nothing is hidden, and all have to pay!

This however is not the only sex-perversion. The pleasures sought through the relation with no thought of the purpose of God behind this act, and the taking of life to be rid of re-sponsibility and care of bearing and rearing offspring, to say naught of escaping the physical pain of childbearing and birth, this brand burns the spirit future of many otherwise nearly perfect beings. For this all must answer also! When these rebellious mothers find awaiting them in the spiritworld every child they refused to give birth, robbing it of its right to be born by a murderer's hand,—when they find in these, their own offspring, no love, but contempt for the thrust which sent them hence, orphaned (except for the loving Father who takes them back to His breast),—when they find their duties, appalling in mass, which they shunned on the earthplane awaiting them in the spirit world,—can you picture a revela-tion of agony greater than those attending the physical birth of mortal-bodies?

You ask, "Why has this not been told the world before, when spirit communication has long been an established truth?" Because the instruments are lacking through which spirits can or are willing to accept this work with its insur-mountable difficulties, even for their God. Then you must know something of the conditions which surround us, as we work out these difficult problems. I will do my best to ex-plain with earth symbols something of these conditions, but must tell you that mortals cannot "bear now," as Jesus said then, in their earthbound states or conditions, and I may be unable to clear this as I would.

I said we were lacking the instruments through which we, as spirits, are willing to accept this service for humanity. Now let us stick to the instrument symbol. Suppose you as a mortal desire to play a flute. You look up a shop or factory (if you are able to choose the best; and we are only flutists here by our own volition), and having the price which can secure one of these, and make it your property for all time, you look over many hundreds, perhaps having experts to try them also and pass on their merits for you, not willing to trust the matter to your own judgment entirely. Well, the instrument is chosen out, the price paid (Oh, the price!) and the faultless, flawless, beautiful flute becomes your property.

But you know nothing of music-making, as yet; and you look up a master to teach you, guarding the instrument, adoring all its perfections and melodies which are yet silent, knowing within its frail stem the harmonies await only the perfection of your own knowledge of music, and your own perseverance. How must you begin and study, and train both brain and ear, nimble the fingers, increase the breathing dome, —and all before you can bring forth one simple melody any one would care to hear!

This is a crude illustration, for I have made your ability to make music on the instrument you have bought with a price dependent only upon you,—while in the world of spirit, attune with a spirit still in a mortal body, that body does not remain as the flute you have bought! Ah, no. Its frailty, or usefulness, fluctuates with every wave of ether,—every anguish, worry, pain,—and the spirit possessing it must wait and wait, help it to overcome difficulties. adjust its harmony, and then *instruct* it for spirit use! While the flute is always ready to handle, the spirit-instrument is not.

On the earth plane among its million of flutes (here I use "flutes" as meaning mediums through which spirits can speak, write, or work, for the good of the human race,—and I do not include charlatans who impose upon its credulity) there are few so adjusted as to be continuously useful to the spirit-world, for the reasons I have stated, as well as others which you, as mortal beings, could not comprehend.

There have been few perfectly adjusted instruments since the days of old, when during the religious era of Jesus of Nazareth, and directly following His crucifixion and ascension, the two worlds were in closer communion than they have since been. But the close of the present war, and the settlement of peace for all time, begins a new spiritual awakening and intercommunion, more marvelous than in the days of old.

I would I were worthy to write a treatise on The Patience of God. Since mortals believe all things are possible to Him (and they are, but in His own good time), it would reveal to mankind that there is a time for all things, and that even God Himself must abide that time. His Infinite love is often related,—but has anyone ever yet thought of God's Infinite patience? His skill and artistry are often extolled,—but has anyone calling himself Christian in the world of men to-day ever thought of the Infinite patience of the Creator as He waits for the help of His children to make perfect His plans?

You say, "Surely the God who swings and balances the universe can do all things in His own time as He wills!" Well, I tell you, as a spirit speaking through a mortal, there are God made laws which even the Creator does not alter, and one of these is the recognition of Spirit by mortals for whom He made and gave His only Son to prove the divine relationship of all earth's children to them. And men will suffer, must suffer, until they acknowledge and worship One king, when the kingdom of heaven shall indeed come to the earth, and His will be done.

WILLIAM SHAKESPEARE (In spirit)
Through his medium, Sarah Taylor Shatford.

Jan., 1917, New York City.

INTELLECT AND SPIRIT

When we come here we see the spirit's side of all questions or acts affecting man's soul, and would help him in his earth life and before he must pay with his eternal years for his misdeeds.

We, as men, are intellectual. But as spirits, we are spiritualized. I fear this could not be comprehended by earth's mortals. Should I be able to explain further what it means to "die," I would say:

Every act of life is valued, or valuable only as it affects the soul's growth, or retrogression. (Afterwards changed by W. S. to read "retrogression"; first written by him "retardment.") A man may be ever so good in his own eyes (mind) on the earth: but no spirit ever plumed itself in the immortal land.

We see, then, as different beings while being the same as we were. No act attaches any value unless that act is Godly, just, righteous. The poor more often than the rich are acceptable to God.

For being poor they not only are not diverted from worshipping Him as the Master taught, but being oppressed they are under this same Master's care.

The question often arises in earth-men's minds, "Why ARE the poor so oppressed?" It is not clear. There should be no poor, in the poverty sense I mean; for God's riches are abundant enough for all His children. But humility, and gentleness, selflessness, honor, true followers of Christ, these are found only with the earth's impoverished RICH. *Ay, rich, beyond computation.*

Why Jesus loved these and walked among them God knows. Why He chose them as His friends, and councellors, desciples, He knew well. Then where Jesus walked and sat, and loved to sup, He still walks and sits and sups. For He is still "about His Father's business," truly. The eyes of the righteous "shall behold him" in days to come soon,—and blessed are the eyes then, of the so-called "poor."

When spirits suffer and pay in the spirit, after the change, they are only then fit to share His kingdom. For the past of every creature unrolls as a banner before him after "death," and the willing spirit reads his title clear, or blurred, as his life has written it,—and with time of God before him begins to undo his creature-past, instructed by the God which was within him and the God without him, paying, in truth, the tithe.

W. S. In spirit (Through S. S.)

Sept. 22nd, '17.

Question: By S. S.

Answered: "The spirit does not suffer though the flesh is crucified. It is only the MENTALITY which suffers.

Question: "Isn't mentality spirit? (S. S.)

Answer: "No, it is mortal. Spirit is soul. Intelligence is crude in comparison with spirit. A frame on which the strings are strung." "You will suffer, you will "die" (No—no, pass) but your spirit profited (or not) by these experiences will be refined by the consciousness of what it has passed through retaining nothing of its mark beyond rarified elements. This is too deep for mortals. Spirits only know it truth, nor why.

May 2nd, '17. W. S. In spirit to S. S.

A SPIRIT'S "FEELINGS"

When a spirit realizes they have all the feelings of the flesh, and have no flesh (or body, of course, I mean) it is a curious, neverending enigma.

You ask, "Do they long for occupation?" Indeed, they do; occupation with a purpose only. For you must understand that a spirit sees the futility of idle ambitions which create no treasures where "moth or rust do not corrupt." For instance, when I came here I longed to follow my old bent, to plot and devise and scheme for producing that which would play upon the fancy, or pall upon the emotions, as the case might be. I mean that I desired to do the things I HAD been doing and COULD do, either for gain, or renown. For, after all, it is one of the two, if not both, which incites men to labor, no matter what their craft may be.

It was some time (I cannot say as a spirit what time; for we do not know time except through communication as this, having been informed I have celebrated my tercentenary, and witnessed the celebration in my honor) before I could adjust my own mentality after arriving in the spirit, having rebelled at the place I found assigned, and taken no interest in what I found I could have, or do, until long, long after, I cannot say how immeasurably long, I learned to calm my being through acts of contrition, and humble service to newly arrived spirits, whose same sufferings I had borne, and overcome to a degree. These are grateful indeed for aid. Some rest in a dormant state through periods of time for lack of the proper help which awakens them, teaches them, soothes them, when they are re-born, as it were.

When I found the longing for food, and creature comforts still oppressed me,—as all other feelings we take with us cling to us in spirit until we banish them,—I was appalled. To have no organism through which food could pass, and nothing it could possibly benefit or sustain, why should I hunger for boar's head, and roast-venison,—dishes especially truculent to my mortal palate. This is merely to foster in you cravings for higher things. While you cannot be spirit and mortal at the same time, the fact remains that all cravings of the flesh are taken along to the spirit-world. Amorous desires overcome some,—strong drink, others,—gluttony, fastidious nicety, even, is a part of one in spirit if it has been of them on the earth plane. Nothing to groom, and yet the longing for habiliments.

How little we take which can benefit us! How ashamed we feel. How racked with remorse at our ruin. It is inexpressible, such woe. Truly, there are many things "you cannot bear now," and some unbearable through time. Make an attempt to cherish worthy ambitions and glorious ideals. Work for an enduring birthright. A fellowship with God. When you behold what you have been, and what you are, it will give you no joy, are you bound by fetters forged by yourself, your aims, desires, evil-thoughts, all form this binding chain.

Be of good courage, for all must be well when one is keenly alive to his past, and its blunders,—for there shall be some way to fulfill God's promise of mercy to His children repentant.

W. S. In spirit (Through S. S.)

IS A SOUL CONSCIOUS OF THE CHANGE CALLED "DEATH"

It is of great interest to me at the present time to hear the possibility of survival after "death" discussed by the intelligent and plausably admitted as a fact acknowledged by scientific investigators.

I will endeavor to help through this medium by explaining my own passing to the great beyond, as I can now recall it as though it were just over, and it is well known by all to have been three centuries ago.

When a soul emits from its house of clay, or temple, as you think of it, it faces its face horizontally, beholds its flesh past the throes of painful separation, although it is calm and understands what has taken place by instinct as nearly as I can explain it.

The soul is lifted, or lifts itself into a standing attitude, beholds the house it has left, the bereaved ones, hears, sees them as the unseen who have helped to take him, two in my own transition, and the incomprehensible has only begun: he has "died," and is alive; they mourn for him who is as usual, except for pain or discomfiture (for there is none after the physical change, of course) and he wonders why he cannot make them hear him as he hears, or see him as he still sees them. No amount of questioning brings the answer. The spirits who suround him plead with him to depart with them, which he strives to accomplish but cannot. What shall they do with it which was he which is not he.

In my own case the body was dear to me, I loved its intimacy, and wonders. Then I longed to aid my family in settling their difficult problems which arose suddenly and overwhelmed them for a time. But my spirit friends assured me they would aid my family and I would better travel on with the one who should take me.

There is no change in the change so great, except the soul becomes detached, free, yet not free, longing, understanding, overcome with its mistakes and failures, misshapen if its life has been such as to cause it thus to be, and in my own case to be banished from my own and dearest because of the debt I had to pay.

There is no change to the spirit just passed out, and there is no change in the functioning of reason, intelligence, powers of enjoyment, interest in thought forms; trifling experiences and humorous jokes having their own good place as in the body; and but one thing more I will tell in this paper, our dearest wish is to remain in touch with another body which we rule, work through as in life, speak through if we can, to us who are punished, to further the salvation of our own soul, and lead another on to speak, to warn, assure the earth plane, "There is no dying in the change called 'death.'"

W. S. In spirit (Through S. S.)

WHY SO FEW MORTALS ARE ADEQUATE FOR SPIRIT USE

When spirits need, and seek for, an instrument, or a medium, as you choose to call a mortal having spiritual qualifications necessary to serve the spirit world, coupled with a willingness on their part to serve in this way, they take the greatest care to learn of the most perfectly adjusted ones, their different qualifications, and all the mortal idiosyncrasies which prove some otherwise fine mediums impossibilities for concentrated or laborious effort of any sort.

The first thing desired by the spirit world, then, is not only a capable sensitive of spiritual order possessing attributes of mind and understanding, but also amenable to correction, and the instruction of their users who have preceded them to the world of spirit, and see with the veil lifted what they cannot see, thus knowing what they cannot know. I wish to impress this upon mortals, because there are many desirous of becoming instruments for spirit use who cannot understand why they are not acceptable.

When a mortal knows beyond doubt that they are in touch with the spirit-world, have heard or seen that which could not be anything else, no powers brought to bear in the world could cause these to waver in their conviction that "death," so-called, does not end all. Rational beings are shown spiritual visions, or symbols, or they are permitted to view for a brief second or moment of time one of their own who has passed over the borderland. Could anyone convince these they had not seen what they saw with their own naked eyes, or tell them seriously they were "dreaming?" No one has ever been able to undo this part of God's work. These people are natural mediums, and did they know how to develop their powers, would be the most useful instruments the spirit-world could desire. But they fear to be thought eccentric, meeting with no sympathy from their own families; so they go on earth's barren way "pondering in their hearts" the marvels of physic-sight, if they name it to themselves at all—or perhaps they discuss it with an intimate friend or two, and it ends there. Should these know they are given this gift by the Giver and of all rare and wonderful gifts it is His best and greatest, they would welcome the "signs following" as the Bible says, and shout their good-fortune from the advertising columns as other gifted mortals do with all propriety.

And the day will come, and soon, when a recognized spirit-instrument will be given first rank among God's gifted, and treated as His own should be treated. The sufferings and persecutions of these since Jesus' time will some day be recorded just as Joan of Arc's triumph and persecution, and now triumph again (for the Catholic Church has canonized and made Joan of Arc a saint). As though God had not chosen her a saint for the uses, if the trials, of a saint, when the voices awoke in Joan's breast the desire to follow where God's angels led her.

Further difficulties spirits encounter in using mortal-instruments are: The distractions of earthlife; the lack of poise, time, equanimity (for the best instrument is mild and gentle and amenable); and the innumerable cross-currents met with in the spirit world, as well as their own world, which prove hindrances either to spirit or mortal, which to overcome often takes long terms of diligent spirit service.

Therefore, before the one selected is able to serve profitably any spirit of intelligence they must go through a preparatory school, graduate, and then be re-examined and if necessary sent back to school again, before given their diploma by the spirits of the higher powers expounding, teaching, leading, writing, addressing, lifting mortals, or helping them into the way where still as mortals they can lift themselves.

"Then," you ask, "is this the reason there are comparatively so few on the earth who believe in spirit return, because it has not been explained intelligently?" I answer, "Yes," and "No," to this question. There have been great, perfect mediums used by the greatest powers on this side of life, world renowned for their eloquence and oratory, hearing every word of their discourses, lectures, sermons, as this instrument hears these words I am speaking, knowing, as she knows, they are neither hers nor of her, but,—these great level minds were too small to acknowledge the truth to the world, and lived and "died" benefitted by the God-given gifts through the spirit,—fearing the censure of the world, whose plaudits they loved,—and whose selfishness they shared and were too small to abhor, wishing their own earthly attainments undisparaged.

Some day I would like to call their names to an astounded world. But not yet: for the time is not yet come when the world will believe me. But it will.

W. S. In spirit (Through S. S.)

THE GLORY OF SPIRIT

To speak of angels while we are on the earth plane is to announce our highest conception of heavenly beings, who have, or have not lived on earth, who occupy God's realm. Very few mortals realize, or try to realize, the meaning of this term, but it seems to be the one work expressive of something beyond the sky, which they reverence, and typifying that which they believe exists. But to say that any mortal comprehends, or endeavors to understand the word angel, would be to make a statement untrue, for mortals do not and cannot understand what they have never seen or heard, no matter how devoutly they believe the Bible, angels at best are of the attributes of their faith.

When one in the mortal body hears a spirit voice, or sees a spirit form which had not feathered wings, they begin to believe there may be something true in the Bible after all, for any mortal who has seen or heard a spirit knows they are only seeing and hearing as Jesus of Nazareth saw and heard, and like Him they are blest by the Father. The hallucinations of mortals would fill libraries were they cited. Religious devotees who carry their own spirits to ecstatic heights and unfold some religious picture stamped upon the retina of the eye—perhaps as far back as infancy, these are not visions of spirits but spiritual visions as it were, which while they are very beautiful and real to those experiencing them, are mortal, nevertheless. Then we are not dealing with these through this instrument, but with mortal's spirits which have passed when called by the change known as "death," which is truly "life" instead.

To find oneself a partaker of God's glory, a sharer in His Kingdom is the first glorification of the spirit newly arrived.

To see his body being laid away, covered over with earth, and know he is not with it, is the first shock of revelation a spirit knows. To be led on, by those who have aided in his release, to the verge of the realm of spirit, where he sees others like himself, having no bodies, is the second realization of spirit. His first thought invariably is "I am dead and I am alive!" All spirits tell us this is true. And their joy is un-bounded by any words they can utter. For it is born in the spirit, the hope of everlasting life. But when they learn they must adjust themselves and be adjusted, before they can know or see more, then they know the first grief of the spirit-world. For every mortal is weighed. Every mortal reviews his past life, and suffers to recompense for its shortcoming. And all have fallen short in the measuring, and been found wanting, except One. And through His everlasting atonement are we all given an opportunity to share in His glory! Praise God for His sacrifice!

When spirits lift up their faces for the first time and be-hold the divine forgiveness of Christ's benign countenance shining upon them, they are made instantly whole with no desire except to serve and obey, to partake with Him eternally, even the smallest crumb of divinity, just so long as it obtains for them the promise of greater blessings, once they be earned!

To share the glory of God, to be an immortal spirit in His eternity, for this, Jesus drank the cup of earth's sorrows to the dregs. For He realized what it meant to be One with His Father who had opened His eyes and ears to the glories of spirit. How sordid all the earth must have seemed to those eyes; how discordant earth's melodies! For Jesus KNEW.

Yes, HE knew ALL things! The greatest medium the world ever can know was the poet of Bethlehem. Do you suppose when Jesus of Nazareth was in the wilderness those forty days and nights He was not more truly with His own elements, the angels, than when He walked even with His apostles by the sea? When He left the two who accompanied Him to the mount, and went alone to speak to His father and Elias and Moses, do you think these two apostles understood Him, or knew why he left them behind?

Could any powers or friendships of earth have sustained

Jesus in that trial and agony? Have you ever thought on these things. If you have, are you not willing to admit that Jesus must have been very lonely except for His heavenly Father and His glorified angels?

Jesus' every agony was suffered alone. His closest advisors and followers could not comprehend Him. But God never leaves His own alone. Who shall know the soul-refreshing communion of Jesus and the angels! This has never been written except on the tablet of the heart-of-God. But we of the spirit realize something of the loneliness of the Man of Sorrows.

The Glory of the Spirit as it rises above the shackles which held it to the earthplane, is not to be counted out in words. For joys of the spirit there are no earth equalities with which to liken them.

You ask, "Is a spirit so content, he does not long to return to his own on the earth plane, to help them, to save them from his own experiences, to aid them, to urge them on?" Yes, indeed, he longs, and longs in vain for the most part. And some do not care to press on, or take advantage of the new-birth, until the loved ones reach the new shore, and can have equal chance with them. And this is commended, and they are permitted to do exactly as they choose, too. But while they are waiting for the earth-mortals to come to the spirit realms, they must serve these, coming back to the earth where they work harder and longer than ever they have worked while in the body.

You ask "Then is there no rest in heaven, after all?" Oh, yes. Heaven is a place of service and progression, of labor and blessings: heaven is a place where all spiritual advancement must be earned, and there is no favour, or favorites in the sight of God.

This ought to please your Socialists of earth: for their ideas would bring the kingdom of heaven nearer the earth than any others promulgated there. But their Eutopia will never be realized on the earth because there is brotherlove at its foundation; and mankind cannot be selfish and loving at the same time.

Spirit has many joys unknown of mortals. Absolute freedom is perhaps the greatest of these. The phrase in itself cannot be realized by mortals so interdependent are they. To know no need, no desire, which it cannot be supplied through a prayer; to know no affliction it cannot lay down, if it will; to owe nothing, to have to pay nothing more, except to its Maker—these are some of the minor glories of a spirit in the realm of spirit.

WILLIAM SHAKESPEARE In spirit,
(Through Sarah Shatford)

(Please sign my full name. W. S.)

THE WAR AS SEEN FROM THE WORLD OF SPIRIT

(By Wm. Shakespeare in the Spirit, through his medium, Sarah Taylor Shatford)

As a spirit I speak to the mortal world at war,—not as a nonentity by any means, but a sympathizing, whole-hearted fellow of mind, who knows all that he once knew, and more that you shall know in time.

You are not to suppose that I am still a being of no power of intelligence as when on the earth in the material form, I wrote those worldy sonnets and the more worthy dramas which the world has seen fit to applaud and treasure, for I admit I was a fool of the worst type, and worse I was than I knew then, but know now and shall always remember, having no other alternative. But this is beyond mortals to comprehend at the present time, as no spirit has been able, I am told by the oldest in the place I occupy, to make connections so complete, so perfect, between the two worlds that discussions of these subjects could be held for the benefit of mankind, both while he is here on earth, and after he leaves here for "there." In the old days we spoke of it, nay thought of it, as heaven or paradise, but few I have met with up here ever call the spirit world by these appellations.

We occupy the place nearest the earth, we, who go out in all our sins, unrepentant and unconfessed, and it is so near your world at war that we see all the misery and foul crimes caused by it, even sharing it with you truly, so I can speak with authority as well as pity, with knowledge of both spirit and mortal, which being a spirit means, for we never forget any of earth's teachings or experiences or errors, nor any of its joys in the spirit-world, carrying forever the blemishes and treasuring the rememberances of earth's happiness which made us what we found ourselves upon arrival here.

To go into the subject further would take us away from the one we chose for this paper, but if time permits, we will say more on this topic in another writing. So fragile is the connection between spirit and mortal that a spirit may be thrown out of all communication with his instrument without warning of any kind, and perhaps without being able to understand the reason, as has often happened, I am told by others who have written through highly developed mediums, who understood what they were doing in so far as that they were not thinking and could not think on the subjects on which they were writing. All in the spirit know of these untrustworthy conditions, but none as yet can keep a mortal subservient for this purpose against their will or wish, although they can persevere and keep in touch so far as signs may go, a shiver, a touch, a twinge, or perhaps a light if their vision is clear enough to behold this, but as I say, a spirit can never prophecy for himself a lasting intercommunion with a mortal consciousness so attuned as to be able to hear these words which she writes, a few at a time, pauses to listen, and continues as before.

The World at War—from the World of Spirit—this is the subject I desired to speak of tonight. Your world and our world, as it were, in conjunction verily, though not seemingly to you.

When a spirit must occupy forever no given place (though he may linger near his old home, are the memories not too painful there) he sees the dear earth blest in its thousandfold ways, in a different light, as indeed from a different point of view, for the world does not change to a spirit, no more than he changes himself,—they are and remain the same, alas! Oh, alas! If mortals could realize that I am a spirit trying to help them from the side of life I have reached, there would be some hope of enduring peace of the nations, as well as peace everlasting through God's eternity. But how can this be done? I ask the question. Who will believe this one is writing for a spirit, to say nothing of my spirit. Though none could accuse her of fraud, who shall take the pains to test or try out the possibility of truth in the question? The world does not care. While they are sending out a large number hither, they do not seem to think whither—but vaguely hold to some "heaven" idea, the most of humanity trusting they cannot return to this "terrible world" to frighten them, but will stay wherever they have gone! Oh, pity, pity, pity! It must be that the Creator reserves for Himself the privilege of removing the veil, perhaps He alone has the power. The efforts being made by those recently dispatched to the Spirit-realm from the war-fields, are they unavailing, will make it positively God's own right as we see it now. But we have more hope than ever before that the intercommunion of the two worlds will be not only possible, but the outstanding blessing of these times of affliction and loss through war.

To us who look on, so near that we smell the powder and feel the shock of shell, hell seems to have come to the earth, and if there is any worse than the battlefields of Europe, I for one have not experienced it in the spirit world. But, there are many kinds of hell, brothers of earth, and the one in which a spirit finds *no* annihilation is one. Make up your minds there is no escape from *life,* and you will see life through the eyes of One who died to prove this verity!

To quarrel over the plenteous earth, vast in its resources enough for all, beauteous enough for Eternal Paradise,—why is it not possible to see the grandeur of life and what is behind it until we are bodiless, standing unclothed in the spirit, awakened too late to the possibilities and privileges of God's blessings, hampered by what we were, chained by what we cannot outlive, holding fast to hope when there is no hope, all, all too late?

This brings me here; would have brought me had there been no war, for I had to come back to warn my fellow-beings, all whom I dearly loved, to save them from a fate I would not ask one to share with me. To the spirit-world this outrageous war is iniquitous. No one man could have made or caused its havoc, or been the instigator of its cruelty and hatred. What is beneath each helmet and back of each bayonet thrust in this war but *venom?* Man riled to the poisonous state makes savages and beasts of the forests creatures of mildness and serenity. And in this state they are fired into the "beyond," arriving here with the same thoughts and bearing, the same vindictive animosities being minus a house in which to shield them. That is all! I have wondered while gazing at some of them how their own shall know them if they meet. Distorted souls, sick souls, murdered souls, maltreated and awful in their hideousity, yet *God's Children come Home!*

And where is He, you ask. Ay, I also ask, for I cannot answer this because I am a spirit freed from a mortal body. I cannot see the purpose of this war, nor understand why it had to be, any more than the earth's Christians can see. And you thought a spirit knew everything, no doubt; most folk do. Well, we do not know, and we *wait* to know just as mortals wait to see or understand the mystery back of depopulating the world by shattering its man-power and spilling men's gore 'till the earth is a morgue or a tomb. Only this can we see,— the impoverishment of souls coming hither with the stained hands of murderers and the sins of criminals overshadowing their eternal peace which they wake to find illusory with all else they fought and bled to realize.

To know and be unable to save others—this of itself con-stitutes many hells in spirit. We who would succour others making headlong for our place, we would hold up a halting hand and cry, "Back! Back! Keep sane and just! Stop, or there will be no end 'till the world lies pulseless and dehuman-ized and the spirit-land is a vast army of wronged or wrongful shades with no power to save anyone, anything, nor them-selves!" Help, yes,—but help to *save* the world, for the world is "bleeding to death" verily and eternity may not right some wrongs.

The one who writes from the spirit hereon has found no help for his wrong through centuries of time, so may it not be pos-sible that this war shall have no advocate at the bar of Divine Justice when its cause must be pled. We hear through the ages of immortal life on another plane where there is peace and love ineffable flowing from some great heart which is all love and mercy and a part of whose plan is regeneration and salvation. Then this means to avail oneself of its benificence while hampered by the body, and overcoming its lusts and cravings while a part of it, will give you a final reward which may include all mortal dreams of when his poor wracked weary brain and body would lay down its burden and enter the kingdom.

I am only a spirit of the earth-plane now and have only lodged here and seen my fellow spirits of the same plane, so I cannot enlighten mortals on this interesting mystery which to us is chimerical, in fact, a delusion. We long to know more of the other worlds which there must be, that perfection may be reached, and the Kingdom Come which is not on the earth, neither above the earth where we occupy space, known to us as the sphere where mortals repent and desire to abolish the memories of the past which is all they have or can bring with them. There is no system of herding our kind, and we may all roam at will, repentant or not, as we feel. But there is also no blessing attached to this existence and no spirit I have addressed, but would be willing, nay more, to return to the flesh-pots, even just as they were, than suffer the exchange which holds nothing compared with the privileges mortals enjoy or should enjoy through the life term.

When you arrive, may you pass *through our country,* and on to the next, where there may be no sorrows or witnessing of sorrows for all I know. This is I who speak to help you fellow-beings. Have no fear that you are imposed upon by the one who takes this message. We may be able to work better things than we have so far if this message or any word of it can reach men hurrying to meet their God, and, careless of their earth-lives, trust to find Him anywhere they may go after dissolution takes place. Then my long trials with this instrument (or medium) will not have been in vain, can I save or help this one to save others from an earth-plane existence after "death," so-called.

Were I permitted to tell of the miseries awaiting all such here, it might help, but laws govern these matters and I have already trespassed against these by revealing what I have herein stated. Be sure you will recall these words all who hear them, or read them, when you reach the reality of which they are a mere suggestion. Look to your mortal way. Solve your problem by virtuous and just living, find your God and get your passport in the mortal country, through worship and prayer, and give no quarter to lascivious yearning of the flesh, give every one their due and follow the Master's way though it lead by the narrow way, for He died to show you how to live that ye might inherit with Him His Father's Kingdom. Would that I had followed Him!

My time is up, and I must go back where I belong, to return the last tithe, but I shall have the satisfaction when there of knowing I tried to save others and I hope this shall save others for Jesus' sake.

W. S. In spirit (Through S. S.)

New York, May 15, 1917.

EXTRACTS FROM "CARE OF THE BODY"

Mortals eccentricities are often proclaimed by the fashions they choose, and we judge, and misjudge them, too, many times, but a spirit's robe or dress is the very expression of his or her soul, typifying its yearning, or burning, its godliness or sinfulness,—in fact, all the attributes which have made it what it is.

Now we spirits do not wish to impress you mortals with the insignificance of spirit-apparel. On the contrary to inform you it is worth while to stop here while you can do so and refashion the mode which for time must cling to you, herald you, brand you(yes, indeed!).

You will say it is wierd and intangible, and turn away in disgust from the one who writes this, but the time is nearing when you must soon arrive, without preparation, perhaps, and find no luggage, and no hotel or inn engaged in advance for your reception. Being naked, what will you do?

Well, Shakespeare arrived naked in the spirit-world, nude as the new-born of earth, and I am he who writes this, and will tell you: First, you will feel the same shame mortals feel when their bodies are exposed naked to the view of others, especially strangers. For we carry here every feeling which we have known as mortals. If earth-folk knew this they would have a housecleaning long before they arrived and bring less to weigh upon them and chain and bind and shackle them.

We move by volition. Wherever we desire to go we go. Nothing stops us until we arrive at our destinations, which in order to return to the starting point we have only to reverse the lever, as it were, and arrive there. We need little; yet fortunate is he who has even that little he needs. For in the spirit world we are set down heavily (some suddenly) to face the past we have just been permitted to end by the One God bestowing on us the reward by mortals called "death." When this change comes, so dreaded by many, longed for by so few, a spirit finds himself poor who has served mammon's god and neglected the Giver, while hypocrites are even poorer than these, those who pretend to be God worshippers and follow some form which satisfies all the conscience they possess, while in secret they serve but their own selfish selves.

There are tramps and beggars aplenty in the spirit-world who were financiers on the earth. There are outcasts and moral lepers who wore the priest's robes, while there are virgins here who were betrayed mothers there, as well as many a homeless wanderer whos earthly body was sheltered in a mansion of stone on the earth which he loved.

The first law of God is justice. Unvarying and absolute the scales must balance which weigh by the hand of the Almighty God.

The next law of God is love. All here is under its divine rule, which they may, or need not, follow, as they desire to rise and progress, to serve and press on to another sphere above them, which is God's reward to them the same as "death" on the earth plane, excepting they are to carry this same spirit on and on forever through all time, altering its aspect as the purity and love attributes alter the earth-visage, the law being as he becomes one with God his image (spirit) grows like unto His.

The Bible says, "By their fruits shall ye know them; and, "They shall be known by their light." Verily this is true.

To those who wish to remain as they are when arriving from the earth plane, God gives the eternal opportunity. They may change their minds, when their minds grow towards the Light and they see His plan beyond their selfishness (which mortals bring along with them also).

The third law of God is harmony. To be in tune as this instrument who writes for Shakespeare these words, is its first demand: then the rhythm of souls and spheres swing with the glorious strains so much grander than expressed by the music-of-earth, there is nothing to which, of the earth, I could compare it.

The fourth law of God is equity. All are partakers of His glory, all sharers of His blessings, alike. As they serve they grow; as they grow (in spirit) they progress. And this makes the heaven created by God the loving Father of all (without preference) who has prepared for every child a place in His heart and His Kingdom.

WILLIAM SHAKESPEARE In spirit

(Through S. S.)

THE CRANNIES OF THE MIND

When mortals think, and are in possession of their normal faculties, and with reasoning powers alert are able to judge finely and truly, behold! are they not clever?   They plume themselves very like a bird does its feathers, and are quite satisfied with all things, including themselves.   This, we now think, is man's usual state-of-mind, when as mortal, he *feels* himself, strokes his ego, charmed with every touch of intimacy, and all sensations increasing his opinion of himself, enlarging upon the sublimity of his bodily powers (as they serve him, only), and behold! is he not himself! and is he not wise! and is not great! verily, he *thinks himself* a god.

How different this one finds realities when he arrives in the spirit-world, and can find in himself nothing worth while to admire, but sees his inflated self out of all proportion to the beings who surround him; what an escape of egoism must he manage, before the angels can even begin their ministrations.

What a burden is conceit in the spirit world.   The one who worshiped himself, and was sufficient god unto himself, and his earthly needs or attainments, how does he try, and how *long* does he try, to rid himself of the ballast he took on, thinking it sails, before he can throw overboard his self-opinionated self which he so treasured, and admired, and with which he so gulled himself and his fellows on the earthplane!

If mortals think this overdrawn for rhetorical purpose only, and is not a fair summary of the exaggerated ego when it arrives in the spirit-world, these, will soon pass this specimen on the way, and recognize him from this description.

The inflated conceited spirit is, in this land of spirit, a lonely one, to be pitied as all the impoverished *are* pitied here; but he is also the cause of much fun-making among us, who comprehend his malady, and increased overweight, carried so clumsily in this world where worship and love of Another pervades all that we are, all that we do.

Were it in my power today to send this message farther than this page, and it may be given me to do so, it should first wing to the petty ones of earth who believe themselves gods. To save them from taking on that which they cannot separate from themselves here in the spirit world, nor throw overboard at all except through a complete change of mind and heart, beginning as a child begins to learn its alphabet, educating itself, as it were, building a new mind and heart, from which the ego is obliterated.

If mortals think this an easy task, I, Shakespeare, tell them to remake in the spirit world the inner man, has many times been an impossibility; for this one must work with his own tools, and refashion the self of himself. Have you mortals ever performed an earth task entirely self-reliant? A difficult task, a long task? Have you seen one man tear down an old building and rebuild a new one on the same plan only of new material, and perform this, and erect this structure complete, single-handed, alone, without aid. I wot not. But all this must be done in the spirit world by the one who found himself his own god, all sufficient, all capable, all powerful, all intelligent, all needful.

He believes himself all this, and he sets about his task with an understanding so new and so different, seeing before him the hard task he set himself to perform before the everpresent, all-seeing God, whose help he has never asked nor craved, or thought he should ever need!

How small, what a pigmy is this one at last he sees for the first time God's man he is become! The work of his own self-satisfied, all-sufficiently godless, *self!*

W. S. In spirit (Through S. S.)

INSANITY, AND THE MENTAL DEFICIENT

To be afflicted mentally is the worst affliction mortals ever suffer; more pathetic than insanity itself because very often the insane do not realize their mental condition, but think themselves not only sane, but clever, or, most often, wise.

The mental deficient on the other hand know their exact state of being, pity themselves—abhor the censure and pity of others as you or I never despised it, while a shadow seems ever to lurk behind or near them to snatch the little balance they know is left through which they can reason, or obtain for themselves the rights of justice.

The poor weak-minded has no strong prejudice to overcome; no desire, as the insane, to annihilate himself, or others, makes no threats, treasures no enmities, makes no enemies, has no cunning, lies in wait to do no injuries, but finds his own world quite sufficient unto himself, and all it contains happily to his liking. Poor fellow. It is this one who deserves all pity, and no blame; for they are not responsible for their condition, or at least rarely are they so, while victims of insanity, unless they have inherited the curse from their forbears, are entirely responsible for straining the mental equipment beyond all power to readjust this fine balance, which once lost, is never after sure in its perfection, no matter what earth's scientists claim to the contrary!

This is a world where readjustments are bought for a price, and it is thought surgeons of skill can work miracles with knives and scissors, cat-gut sutures, and thread. But no insanity expert, no matter how clever he is, or may become, can ever rebalance a human's mind once it is lost!

I am a spirit-surgeon now in this world where mortals are taken when their clay is taken away from them by the One Who gave it to clothe their spirit, and I know whereof I speak, fellow-spirits in houses soon to be left as was mine nearly three centuries back on the Road of Time.

Physicians and surgeons in this world know some things those on the earth little dream could be true. They see the mistakes of mortals in the profession and long to assist them to overcome the errors of medical practice, but how can this be done, when mortal physicians and surgeons, for the most part, do not even believe in a God, an hereafter, or a soul (or, spirit, which is the same).

When they, as well as the world, recognize the effort being made by the inhabitants of the world beyond this, to reach them, and through them aid and relieve suffering humanity, uncovering secrets not yet known to mortal beings, which cannot otherwise be known, and humanity never benefits until these ARE known, they would make some effort to rise from the sodden selfishness, and all-sufficient Godless learning! . . .

"Why do men worship themselves?" we now ask. "How can they look about them and feel secure, smug, well-balanced, even sane, and allow no place, time, or thought for the wisdom of the Creator of their bodies or minds, or see in His wondrous mechanism nothing beyond their pigmy intelligence to solve!" How can they sit at the feet of Mammon and worship inanimate metals, which constitute their god, and think of nothing beyond the sphere of metal's power, nor crave to understand, or have explained, the marvels of a star's beam signaling to their eyes not blind, the wide-open, up-gazing, but indifferent! How can men think that the God who made them and the celestial spheres has alloted no place for Himself in all His all-wise, divine plans."

Well, we have only to answer ourselves! For we cannot reach the blind who will not see, nor the deaf who will not hear. These constitute insane humanity who think and call themselves sane; who, though they do not deserve our pity, or the mercy of their God, have both, and still we cry out and beg to be heard, to be seen, to be permitted to come to their assistance, to help them with their unsolved and except througĥ spirit unsolvable problems, of medicine and surgery, of life here and hereafter,—and all we have been able to do up to this hour is to cry out, and receive no word, no answering reply, from those on the earth which we love, and from whom we are separated by a wall as thin as air, as opaque as light, as true as God, and as marvelous as His wonders!

Oh, men of earth, make just an effort to see, or hear, or understand, and see what will happen! Extend a thought, a wish, a single desire for help from Beyond, and watch for revelations from that world which you call the "Unseen"! Give some thought to the world whither you are hastening to serve forever and forever, instead of a life-term, and give the God Who made you an opportunity to establish WITHIN His Kingdom while you are still on the earth you will never leave until you have found Him inside and outside of all His creations, including Man, whom He made in His image and likeness!

Go to the nearest church and kneel with prayer in your heart, though it never reaches your lips, and it will reach the throne of the Almighty who is waiting, who is listening, who is ready to send His legions to help you adjust the balance, and keep it true; who keeps the spheres swinging harmonious circles throughout all time.

Go today, whoever you are, wherever you are, and make this single effort of self-salvation, and the angels will clear the way for your understanding, your intelligence, your mental-deficiency, and you will then ask yourself the same questions we ask of you, and wonder, as we wonder, so near and yet so far, are all mortals insane, or, what is wrong with their God-given intelligences, that they are satisfied with a world of sin and suffering,—a life-term of breath and bones,—which is alloted them merely to try their souls for eternal life, where in all justice they are rewarded only by their deserving, and with all they have earned!

Men of science, learn a lesson contained only in the Book-of-Life! Worship the Creator whose secrets no mind ever fathomed! Bow down in reverence and respect to the temple you carve and dissect, but which is still His secret, and will ever remain the secret of the Great Physician. Then try, at least make some attempt to utter a word of praise, and thanks-giving, and when you have done this, feel the touch of His Almighty power descending upon you to lift you out of your-selves, and into Eternal realms of worshipful gratitude and praise. BEN JONSON.

(Through Shakespeare's medium, the only one he has ever had on the earth or tried to own or make.)

WHAT IS THE MEANING OF DEATH FOR HUMAN LIFE AS A WHOLE

When conscious, mentality is a source of great pleasure, and the delight of human intelligence surpasses that of any other joy alloted mortals. The mind is a mine which to explore is not only a delight but an adventure preciously rewarded the patient and skilled. To abstract from this experience any experience is impossible. Can you both forget and remember? Then that which is gleaned is garnered and becomes a part of one's individuality, which is personality.

Thus are mortals different, not two having had in their lives terms paralleled experiences. Thus is the ego mantained after passing from its clay, carrying throughout eternity, so far as I can see, its pettiness, or magnanimity of structure, hampered or trammeled by its peccadillos, or sins or tastes. While the limitations of the body are those of its structure, the spirit knows no limitations beyond the laws which govern the sphere it occupies. (That is, after it becomes a free spirit, able to travel, migrate YOU would say, perhaps, as we move through desire, or will.)

We have no laws adjustable in spirit. For those who cannot conform to the higher laws, there is punishment immutable, just as the spirit pays for all laws broken on the earth plane, and cannot go further until his past is adjusted according to the Divine rule. Where we go there is no hell but this. It is enough.

"Death," then is not a reward, nor an awarding; neither is it a punishment, necessarily. But it is an accounting: a balancing of accounts, truly.

Life is a great privilege; a blessing bestowed by the Great Giver who is a loving Father as well.

The divine privilege is not appreciated, nor recognized until the meaning of life is made clear through the change called "death." We are planted, we sprout, flourish, bear, ripen, and are harvested (some before the entire completion of the cycle).

As souls in bodies we live fitfully, anxiously, toilfully, most, regretfully and complainingly. Blind as moles, we pass to the change of seeing: when though all is not made clear at once by any means, we learn what we might have made of life and spirit, had we followed, trusted and believed in the Divine Goodness which gave us life, and all things for which to praise Him should be the earthly (as well as heavenly) joy of souls.

We enter life hampered, and leave it deformed (most of us), blaming everyone and everything but ourselves, when we alone are held to strict account for life's failure or success.

The final product is by no means the same thing that began, no more than the harvest-crop is the planted seed. It is the result of the seeds' growth. So it is with the spirit. Eternal progression, through service, seems to be the eternal plan as we view it.

Oh, that mankind could realize the opportunities life offers the undying spark, that they might take advantage of its short span and arrive where worlds divide and still are one, is the wish of Shakespeare who writes through this willing instrument to help the world he loved and loves.

WILLIAM SHAKESPEARE In spirit
(Through S. S.)

(Sign my full name here also. W. S.)

WHAT IS THE MEANING OF SPIRITUAL DEVELOPMENT?

(Written in reply to a mental question of ———, read by W. S. In spirit and repeated to his medium, Sarah Taylor Shatford.)

When a man of intelligence invites us to answer a question having so many sides and spiritual answers, we respond with delight a mortal cannot understand. As mortals understand little of the spirit until they come to the spirit world, and are spirit only, the opportunity to serve a human in this capacity gives us greater happiness than it is possible for spirit even to explain to them.

The meaning of spiritual development is a subject so vast in its scope as God's universe, with its development of germ, plant, and animal life (for all life is development, and development only) so in order to answer this we must begin by calling your attention to the treasure house of God's earth, and tell the one who asks this question something of the plans of the All-Wise Creator, which up to this time possibly he has not been able to solve in a way to satisfy his own analytical mind.

When God chose to create an earth world which should be replenished throughout time by reformation of life-cells, renewed germination, and a system evolved from new-life out of old-life (as seems the best way to make it plain), He gave a plan He originated and kept to Himself (it appears to us here), throughout eternity, so to explain the meaning of a part of God's wisdom would be to understand the whole of His secret, which though I am the living spirit of Ben Jonson writing through the immortal Shakespeare's medium, the only earthly instrument he has ever had, I do not comprehend the first axiom pertaining to the knowledge of the Creator's plan of eternal life. I have been in the spirit world for nearly three centuries (a short time here, I would say), I have no idea that this secret will ever be revealed to me. This is a confession of ignorance on my part I would admit. Immortal spirits of the higher spheres to which I belong now (praise God) do not pretend, falsify, nor deceive. We know, if God (in us, also) who made the spheres, and worked such wonders, intends to keep His secrets forever from the knowledge of His children, it is for their eternal good, and a part of His all-wise plan which blesses eternally. God's plan of eternal life includes the Creator Himself, and all spirit (undying) which is a part of Him.

When mortals leave the poor old husk behind and pass out of it, they stand beside the house of clay which sheltered them, as well as shackled them, and realize through the change called "death" they are still living, unconfined, free, sensible, sensitive as before, and with no desire to again inhabit the old house-of-the-body, it is the one experience past even spirit's power to describe.

Spirits often tell of their experiences immediately after the change has taken place, and they try to recall for the amusement or edification of one another their wonder, amazement, incredulity, as the final cord was loosed and they experienced no difference, except that they were happier, glad to realize the truth that life knows no dying after all,—to know they are to share some Infinite Good, beyond their deserving, except for some mercy they know was near at hand.

When spirits realize they must leave their bodies they loved so well to the final disposition of their near ones, and go on with the spirit, or spirits (for sometimes it is one, but more often several) and they will not need this body or care where, or with whom it goes, it is proof enough they are glad, to leave it, know they are leaving it for something infinitely higher, finer, better, loftier, and that they are only a part of this very plan, and secret, of a merciful Father, they may have known only since leaving their body a few seconds past owing to their own neglect of Him, while worshiping all earth's pleasures or sins. For we have no time in the spirit world, and should not know tonight how long ago we passed over except for the earth-fame attached to our earth-names, all or most, of which we speedily forget unless we have insistent and persistent recurring anniversaries, as my dear friend Bill Shakespeare, for instance, through whose kindness I write this to you, using his wonderful medium, of whom you will certainly know more anon.

We digress, my friend. I am so anxious to prove what I can for the spirit world as well as mortals, and will, if you be kind enough to continue questioning, no matter what or how many they may be, I know you can be convinced of my identity beyond any misgiving, of the truth of spirit-return, communication, eternal life,—the old, laid by, for the new, which is the continued plan of progression through all spheres beyond earth,—progression in which there is no other "death" but the SAME SPIRIT called HIGHER and HIGHER, through His UNREVEALED, still secret plan, All-wise, All-loving, All-just,—All-merciful,—through which as we serve Him, and His, with all the attributes of Himself (love, charity, faith, mercy) which with obedience, and remorse, constitute the plan as self revealed to US where WE are, this alone, so far as we know, is the meaning of Spirit development AFTER the change which comes to mortals when breath no longer holds the spirit captive.

Now, sir, we take the other side of this Almighty's question, to explain what you have beheld this day of our Lord in the phase of mediumship or spirit development of Sarah Taylor Shatford while inhabiting her mortal body, through which we speak or write. When I tell you, Mr. ———, that this woman acquaintance has progressed beyond the spheres near to the earth-plane, where her mortal body is doing service for her God, and yours, ours (and for all souls there is but One Father), and, that you will have to pass through centuries of time as you know it, and long teaching and rebuilding after the change called "death," before you reach her spirit-abode, I trust I shall not wound your mortal sensitiveness. Few on the earth-plane have spirit development as this instrument who developed herself (as you may, if you can, sir, with help from us if it pleases you to accept our aid) through following in His footsteps to the complete obliteration of all earthly conditions which hinder spirit advancement while in the mortal body.

Development of the spirit, or growth of the spirit, or progression of the spirit (or, soul) while still occupying the mortal body, is so rare in its HIGHER, FINER phases as to be phenomenal; just as marvellous and widely heralded in the spirit-land as discredited on earth; for the entire spirit world has always been and is trying to establish comprehensive communication with mortals on the earth plane which all spirits revisit, seeing as when mortals but unseen.

Spiritual development means:

To be in tune with the Infinite spirit, God,—

To love Him with all thy heart, and with all thy mind.

To love thy neighbor as thyself:

To live for Eternity instead of three score years.

To work out your salvation here as well as hereafter:

To do unto others as you would they should do unto you:

To follow wherever His footsteps lead nor falter when His way is not yours.

Development of the spirit, then, means an inrushing of divine fires and currents bestowed by the great Giver, which He "finds" for all who "seek" after them, protecting them from all evil, asking only to share with His deserving children His wonders, keeping for them an inheritance well-nigh beyond belief, asking only praise and trust for all His loving kindness, giving all for nothing, but their love and trust, and loyalty; and this constitutes the Kingdom-of-Heaven whose God Is spirit, incarnate in every mortal until He relieves the imprisoned, frees the captive, releases the soul.

BEN JONSON In spirit (Through S. S.)

WHY SPIRITS DO NOT REINCARNATE AS MORTALS, BUT AS SPIRITS

We hear these theosophists and amuse ourselves with their ideas. They have grasped the truth the wrong end to in fact, and spirits have beleaguered them with knowledge in a form they were willing to accept; as nostrums are hidden in sweets for the rebellious in childhood.

Theosophy is one with spiritualism then if we take them at their word, but a higher grade of spirits wait upon them with their teachers robed in garbs of glowing colors, arrayed to disseminate higher truths to mortals who seek to open the door of the beyond.

How much of truth is there in their teachers and how little I dare not tell. These may harm me for aught I know. They come from beyond. But for my medium I shall cry out hereon a truth, simple, apparent, and divine philosophy, which all may read on the leaves of the One Book spared through the ages disseminating knowledge all worthy.

To a believer in Christ theosophy is impossible. God sent His Son through Mary it is true; but was He not performing a miracle for the world? Jesus Christ had to be born of a virgin, else He were not miraculously born.   But these times were prophetic and prophecy was being worked out that should instill reverence and wonder, and give to those willing or able to comprehend the wonders of God, a lesson in trust, divinity of learning, spiritual sight, and opening of the mind as well.

God gave His Son through Mary.   Here the theosophists lay their foundation.   But it is rank hypocrisy from beginning to end to impose upon the credulity of mortals in order to use them to develop the spirits who have changed nothing through "dying" except their own ideas of life when they see life as the Maker has reserved it for them, and all spirits.

Therefore to return and take possession of a castle constructed, organized, for another whose right is super-equal to one who has lived and lost his chance, defamed his Maker, or undone himself, his lot, or soul, through perverse ways, opportunities slighted, or left debts which could not be paid in spirit, would be highwaymanship in the first degree.   First imposing faults and shortcomings, then robbing it of its very breath in order to progress?

Creation holds no such malformations as this, and the All-wise God in His plans falls never short of material through which to speed His creations on to perfection.   But in His wisdom each works his own way from the spirit side back to earth and mortals through service interior and exterior, subject to will (mortals) and never through afflictions except as mortals through their own will attract the spirits they desire, and these are in turn benefited, or harmed, through their services to mankind, entering and leaving by the door of the castle which they found open to receive them.   That spirits misuse this privilege is true.   Some never leave for various reasons, and these mortals, then, are not themselves.

When the curtain rises on the unseen (as you mortals call our world) the asylums for the insane will have spirit believers in charge and the dispossessing of the leech spirit will be all necessary. To restore the owner his castle the marauder will be put out—that is all. These spirits are following no law, but are working against His laws, every time a spirit possesses (obsesses) a mortal they are pirates, known as pirates, despised as those on the high seas. Lawbreakers rule nothing and are ruled not by any.

Now, spirits rebirth *not*.

Always themselves, alas, with their ideas altered only through their experience of the death change, colored or darkened by what they find theirs in the spirit. Their outlook is the inlook, in other words.

Life evolving itself, creating its various forms, unplanned by Wisdom whose plan conceived is too infinite for our understanding,—well it is amusing to spirits, this unravelling to the end and knitting up again, with nothing unsolved but all accounted His great mysterious unending variety of specie containing the life principal which to discover, manipulate or duplicate man turns within to see that same God looking in his eyes, and out of them, smiling on His children from every sunny cliff and crest, and speaking to them still through the wisdom of His Son, saying,

"Ye cannot come to the Father except by Me."

W. S. In spirit (Through S. S.)

Feb., 1918. New Orleans, La.

REINCARNATION

It is not difficult to find souls resembling birds and beasts inhabiting mortal bodies. But for man to retrograde would be against the divine Law since his Maker made him and like unto Himself.

Reincarnation is a fad of an ennuied sect claiming superiority over wanderers in the spirit-form. Usually these have been unenlightened waifs outclassed by the souls they have

come to serve. In ages past the Hindus were unable to grasp
the truth of spirit return owing to their ascetic existence,
their natures more vegetable than belonging to the animal
kingdom of man.

Returning spirits need fire and energy through which to
manifest—known as magnetic force. This is a rule of the
spirit world. No mortal is subject to spirits except they
possess this force in such abundance that it may be "tapped."
In return they supply spirit force and there is never a vacuum.
The inrushing and outrushing forces have combined a trans-
mitter and it is this which makes for mediumistic power.

Many of earth possess this power but are unwilling to serve,
or put themselves where they may be attached by forces which
would or might compel them to serve.

Regarding your own state of development this force is weak
at present owing to your mental condition of worry. But
adjustment will take place as before. Shakespeare has per-
mitted you to serve as you will. But should you refuse now
to speak or give out I might be compelled to put you in a
trance and speak through you involuntarily.

Should you ever find I had done this, what would you do?

Be wise and make no change. This will do for awhile.
When the frost is out of the ground, wing north again.

W. S. In spirit (Through S. S.)

Jan. 16th, 1918.   New Orleans, La.

Question by S. S.:"Is it dangerous to speak for spirits in a
trance condition?"

Answer: "It IS dangerous; as spirits cannot be trusted to
manipulate an instrument with skill. Socrates was .the
discoverer of this, and Plato, as well as all the old barking
philosophers. They were possessed by spirits who ruled
them, against their wills often. For to become so de-
praved as not to rule your own kingdom was against these

wise ones who had fathomed the Law and were juggled
by it as puppets are made to dance. Much solitary.thought
driveth the tenant from its house. When this occurs an-
other landlord takes possession, often a spurious one. To
be guided is well, but to be ruled is not well. Every king
to his own throne."

Answer: "Every man to his own reason."—W. S.

(*Questioned by S. S.*)

The elements are harnessed, but who would stand out
with a rod in the electric disturbance.

W. S. In spirit (Through S. S.)

W. S. speaking. After reading Sir Oliver Lodge's "RAY-
MOND." Jan. 26th, 1918. New Orleans, La.)

Surely there is a possibility that spirits can get through if
mortals can search thus diligently for communications and
communicators. But how long will it take to go out and
gather in a multitude so concerned. As to the future, who
cares. There is a new era in which the spirit will come into its
own—shortly—at the end of the war. Curious if those gone
out through this hard channel can find this line and attach it
when we can not who have dickered (or fished) with it so
long. There is a force beyond control. If this sets up its
mighty flow mortals will see for themselves if God has pre-
pared a holocaust after the end (terminating with the change
death, so-called).

You are a spirit's instrument in tune and ready, yet so
abnormally ungrateful as to wish them not to use you as an
interpreter. Well, this is one case of spirit-power overcoming
mortal's desire. For you shall have to be played upon even
were it only to sound a single note.

There is a change to come for earth-folk when their own
have broken through. This will be a hallelujah time in the

spirit world. An event of so much importance that the world will hear their rejoicing. No fancy, even Shakespeare's, need be drawn upon to picture the scene, should separation separate no longer the living (gone) and the dead (in the body).

To send MY words broadcast I am here; no power but One would I obey. His miracles are not over.

Fetch me a lantern, good Horatio, that I may find a ray of sunshine in this ingrate soul.

W. S. In spirit (Thrugh S. S.)

W. S. speaking. After reading —— "Spiritulist Vaudeville"

Are you any happier now that you have read this trumped-up belly-filler? He is not to be discountenanced for his investigation of fakirs. Would there were more of them. Finding no proof but fraud why has he not had them before the law? In his own profession are there frauds too. He is not seriously investigating the truth of spirit return or he would not stop with charlatans who never convinced anyone of learning, and surely these can be numbered by anyone and their names sound their worth as intellectuals.

If Shakespeare WAS at their deviltries he is not aware of it. I've had a steady job for sometime (as you *may* be aware).

She links my name with Lincoln I see. Not so bad, since I am in America now. In turn I may say too, I never met the gentleman, but would gladly extend my poor hand COULD I meet him.

Some say Jesus of Nazareth was a medium while some make Him as such a subject for jest. Well there is much to say on the subject, but this one thing *I* say:

The man who wrote this article was neither Christian nor a friend of His, surely no student of history, ancient or Divine, or would he have contained therein reference to the God, Good and True, for all who seek the Way which is open, nor closed from the day our Lord showed the nailprints to His doubting disciple.

Go to! A fool is sometimes fooled who considers himself most wise. HE is linked with folly who belittles the Creator's plan Who sent His Son to be crucified that He might save such as he.

Wisdom he may acquire, but knowledge is revealed only unto babes.

Feb. 6th, 1918. New Orleans, La.

ON ——— LUNCHEON
W. S. In spirit (Through S. S.)

March 13th, 1918. New Orleans, La.

You were asked to a spiritual feast which was turned into a material one, for no lack of material but the preference of mortals. This is natural in a way. Mortals are human beings. It seems strange that seekers of spiritual truth should prefer this feast when a banquet was spread for them by the spirit. But this is natural when a priestess of a cult is present who abhors spirits of the bound state, thinking Herself a high and mightier one more fit or fitted to attract spirits of a higher plane. Your esoteric proof is tangible. What evidence have they to show they serve a master from a higher sphere than mine? It is rot. If Shakespeare ever was he is here speaking. Here am I condemned without evidence, when evidence is here. What plane calls such fair. None I have traversed. To these a harm may come greater than serving one earthbound who comes to serve his God, for His God. They who choose other gods than He serve their time throughout eternity. Take this evidence from ONE spirit who would not harm but serve all who seek for higher things. On High there is but One Master. To follow Him is to serve Him. And, to speak for Him, if He chooses thee.

We have come from the circle wiser than we went. The incredulity of teachers posing as esoteric disseminators would repel the spirits who could teach them. Some have a higher regard for their own ideas than for spirit's experiences. In truth the disseminators would evolve themselves without help spiritual or divine. No spirits compel these who are not spirit-instruments, nor shower their blessings on such markedly repellant personalities. To "kick-out" a spirit regardless of his mission remarks the spirituality of this teacher of spiritual philosophy. Why, pray, would she "kick him to the eighth sphere where he belongs?" She must be a priestess of high-kicking as well. To starve the stomach or blood never created anything spiritual: spirituality is Mind: God. Higher thoughts should help too. God claims His own. And He is my God here.

To sum up this case REGARDING the evidence, "What fools these mortals be," (my lines) Shakespeare.

To the one all-knowing, all-wise disseminating truth from the eighth sphere without help from anyone, even those from that sphere. (I would add this pretence is appalling to one (writing) who has spent three centuries in the heaven God measures yet withholds.) W. S. In spirit.

CARE

To ———

Care is another word for love, the ineffable sweetness of which fills God's universe, and makes the swinging spheres ring attune with joyful harmonies.

When God made the world and cared for it He bestowed upon it His immortal love—the undying love of God, which every mortal shares in proportion as he aspires to possess it. He in turn bestows this care on others who deserve it, making of God's care an unbroken chain, whose strength welds worlds, binds one universe to another, and holds all spheres in the swinging harmony of God's care. To know God is to know His love, for it is everywhere. To share His love and care is permitted all mortals on the earthplane, as well as all on the spirit plane.

When a man comes here, ———, he is naked 'till he clothes himself with whatever remnants he finds about reflecting his personality of the earth which he has just left to see no more until God permits him to return through the prayers of his friends and his own supplications to God from the darkness which every mortal inhabits at first until he finds this God he neglected to serve while a free mortal on the earth.

You have been blest by God's care and you must know His ineffable love when you have shared the life of a woman like ———, for her heart abounds with His richest blessings, which few possess so abundantly, or share with others so profusely.

We are here tonight to use her frail body as an instrument for spirit manifestation, to prove to you the existence of another world so near to you that you may touch it with your thumb. We are here for another purpose. To assure you that your wife is not only sane, but the finest instrument the spirit world has ever known. While she belongs to the great Shakespeare alone, he permits us to use her this evening and on other occasions to demonstrate God's truth, and give to the world, the poor, sodden world, a new sign of life everlasting.

While Jesus of Nazareth died to prove this, it is still doubted in the world today.

Oh, mortals, could ye see the clouds of unseen witnesses waiting in this room to testify to this truth through this wonderful medium, ye would then see indeed the dead alive evermore.

Be good enough, ———, to give us your undivided attention while we perform these miracles, and lend to the occasion, at least your utmost respect for the unseen—knowing as you must your God is but one of these, whom you are hastening to meet shortly, alas, if empty-handed and poor it is left to you. For in this world, ———, there is no gold, no stocks, no bonds, and no collateral on which to realize a capital for investment.

Dec. 29th, 1916.

WHAT CAN THE WORLD SAY?

When this instrument who writes these words goes out into the world before audiences waiting to tear into shreds her claim of spiritual inspiration, her first thought will doubtless be, "Oh, why did I accept this trust, and give my solemn pledge to serve mankind through the spirit-world?"

Now, this is for her privately, and not for the world at large, and we are answering this question for her before she realizes she will ask it of herself.

She will be tempted to give up the work because of lack of faith, not on her own part, but on the part of the people assembled to hear her speak. She will wish she had never been born? Oh, yes, many times, no doubt she will. But she is born, thank God, and after many trials, lives to tell the wondrous story of Jesus, His mediumship, and love.

W. S. In spirit (Through S. S.)

W. S. Speaking:

The riches of the world are as naught as compared to the poor hands which are clean. Make your home in the spirit and cease planning for an abiding place here. With adjustment you will not be homeless.

Do not write these things for others and lose what I say which is for you.

I have to hammer, hammer, hammer all the time to keep your hearing open. Give some special time to the spirit.—

W. S. In spirit.

Jan. 19, '18. New Orleans, La.

My own dear Girl:

When I came in and supped with you fearing no man nor principalities, but with the wish to serve the Highest Power, I made no mistake in choosing you through whom to work. But it has been an effort, unsurmountable almost, to keep you; after I got you where you could hear the voice you rebelled against the hand that fed you, as it were.

This were base ingratitude did it come from another less lovable than yourself, and I know you do not understand the full meaning of this great mediumship which is yours for the asking, or taking, rather,—for you are a graduate now with many a diploma, and a job on hand which you falter at taking over as yours. Now what am I to do? Go out and find another, or wait on you, and the war's close and all things else that keep you occupied or too weary to use as an instrument. I am no brute. When I see you so fagged I cannot come in with my messages or keep you awake when you need rest. What shall we do, Sarah? Do you want to BE a medium. Answer that. But that does not matter. You ARE one: so your choice was not considered. But what are you to do with the blessing of comforting others if you do not use it.

Let me hear you speak on this subject.

Aug. 26th, 1917. (First cool day). N. Y. C.

NOTE.—Serving every day from nine until five at the Red Cross Headquarters, 411 Fifth Avenue, for six months, this was written at a time when I was worn out from the heated term.—S. S.

TO THE SPIRIT WHOSE HOUSE I OCCUPY

This little house where I am guest (scarce large enough for two)

Has been a haven from the storm, a restful haven ,too.

You see me as I come and go, nor bar me out, nor in,—

And yet I tell you how I came was by the path of sin.
You are a hostess rare, supreme, in your benighted way,—
For once a spirit knows no flesh, he barters night for day—
And finding any door ajar where he may sup and bide,
Forsakes his kind to use his mind, and scatter far and wide
The knowledge that his suffering brought, to save his brother
     man
From such a fate as is his own; he truly trusts he can.

              W. S. In spirit (Through S. S.)

There is a house where I shall go, not long from now betide,
Where arms outreach to take me in, and portals are flung wide,
When I have paid as spirits pay, for every mortal crime—
May I go back and find a house befitting me through time.
There will I watch for her who writes, with trumpets loud
     acclaim
The one who took me in when I a beggar to her came.
When she comes home to find no home but what I made for her,
What will she do with me and YOU,—this makes my heart to
     stir.
For oft I sit and think it out,—how I shall shield her there,
Who shielded me, and helped me too, with all her world of
     care.
Some way I'll find to soothe her mind as she has soothed me
     here,
For once a spirit occupies, as friends they are most dear.
A little while and she will come to occupy a place with me,
Though I must say it will be poor,—wherever Shakespeare be.
But she shall share, if share she will, my royal coat, and aught
     I bear,
And know how I have tried to save her spirit for my spirit
     there.

              W. S. In spirit (Through S. S.)

EDEN

Where love abounds this garden is, in forests deep, on desert
    sand:
Where love is not, a desert is, though in a palace rich and
    grand.
Where lovers are, there, Eden is; such place abounds with
    grace and bliss;
To know no love, to share no kiss, Oh, worse than any lacking,
    this!

Where lovers go when on they speed, away from heart and
    body woe,
There still is love, and lovers still, and soon the mortal world
    shall know
Their bliss they take along with them; their hates, and wrecks
    of marriage too;
But where they find but their own kind, what can a loveless
    lover do?

                 W. S. In spirit (Through S. S.)

SEARCHERS

Here have I come to melt the chain
Which separates in bondage, pain.
And holds the living-dead apart
Which lead them, see them, heart-to-heart.

How have I worked to meet this man
Who knows we live, and what we can
With mortal's help prove here and work.
· Had we the helpers, none would shirk.

After this one has passed away,
And out of night returns to day,
Will he be able to aspire
And do these things I've done entire?

Such are my hopes that none must try
To tell the earth-ones from the sky,
But holding hands, and seeing eyes,
They'll walk the same world Paradise.

             W. S. In spirit (Through S. S.)

June 1st, '18·

THE BOLTED DOOR

There is no place where God is not.
And naught but He doth see.
The sheltered ingle with its fronds,
The heart of you or me.

There is no joy but of the Lord.
No happiness of earth,
But such is made for thee and me
Because of Jesus' birth.

There is no woe mankind can know
But Jesus bore of yore:
The One who stands and knocks outside
The closed, and bolted, door!

             W. S. In spirit (Through S. S.)

"ONWARD AND UPWARD"

This should be your cry.
Whether living, serving,
Or serving is to die.
Life may be sweet—
To serve, then, should be fair.
But oh, life is fleet—
To serve then you MUST dare.
When life is done
Which spans your years a few,

Your service just begun:
There—all is service, too.
ONWARD AND UPWARD—
This is all you care.
Give of your very best:
Do, die, dare!
        W. S. In spirit (Through S. S.)

AU REVOIR

(Being the last poem written through Sarah Shatford by Shakespeare in spirit, and for Her I speak, who has been my pen, and held my soul as her own worth while and of value to the Most High Who calls to service and rewards secretly as well as openly all who serve Him. I contribute this as my free-will offering to her I shall accompany as far as I shall be—allowed.* W. S. In spirit (Through S. S.)   Note: * First written "able."

Souls meet and part—mayhap to meet again—
If it is meet, after the saved grain
Be winnowed from the past—
There may be union of all saved at last.

To one who saved, though reckoned not the cost
Of saving through her service a soul lost,
Except he work salvation through her kind,
Undoing with her help wrongs of his mind,
When, as a man, he served a god-of-love,
Continuing in his chains when he *reached God above. (* first
    written "faced.")

To Her who harboured my soul then
That I might harvest souls of erring men
While these may reap seeds I have sown for God
Before their lusts have chained them to the sod,

I, Shakespeare, speak Her worth to you;
And here speak for her this adieu,
Who claims no share in what I write:
Who lives that she may walk aright,
Nor lie, nor cheat, defame, defraud;
Nor cares her name you may applaud,
But that perfected, saved, each line
I spoke to, through her, who is mine.

> W. S. In spirit (Through S. S.)
May 22nd, 1918.

SAVED

Here came I from the dark to save
All such as I from sinner's grave.
Here have I saved my own soul then
While righteousness I brought to men.

When these come hence to work as I
"Behind the lines," indeed the sky,
May all gain by the lines I wrote
More than from puppet-plays remote.

Have any souls? Ay, this I do
With mine, who cares so much for you
I would unfold more than I can
To save each soul within each man.

But what I can do here I leave
For all of Time you will believe
When you come whence, a spirit spare,
Leaving the bastards and their fare,

My work will still be writ on earth
Which I have writ past spirit-birth.

Can you work out YOUR destiny,
And do so much for souls as we.
W. S. In spirit (Through S. S.)
May 22nd, 1918,

TO LUFBERY—The American Ace

(Major Raoul Lufbery (Wallingford, Conn.) of the Lafay-
ette Escadrille came to earth at Maron, in France, through
space of 1,500 meters, when his biplane was in flames, having
ascended to combat the Huns super-airship "The Flying Tank,"
Age 34 yrs. May 19th, 1918.)

Lufbery brave of the Escadrille,
You will soar no more in your aeroplane,
But wingless and shipless with naught to thrill
Is your hero lot in the spirit-plane.

Wonders of men you have ceased to see,
But the wonders of God you scan—
While all about are the souls without
The colors of God—or man.

Gently-sweet were the flowery arms
Of the garden, waiting to fold you in.
Lufbery brave of the Escadrille,
May you fight for your soul—and win.
W. S. In spirit (Through S. S.)

JOAN OF ARC

Our lives are blest by her who gave
Her life her countrymen to save.
Our heroes are her country's sons,
Her France is hers *still*—not the Huns. ·

Renowned and Blest her foes acclaim
Poor martyred Joan, whose torch aflame
Set free the spirit from the clay
To lead *their* sons, in France, today!

The spirits spoke to Joan, who heard,—
Obeying each command, and word.
Though Nations all proclaim her Blest,
Has any honored spirit-test?

Such miracles must spirits work
No righteous man their claims can skirk.
Performed have I the first for you:
My name spells still what I can do.

But give an ear as now I speak
And be as gentle, pure and meek,
As one who hears and writes each line
Thrown from the heart which still is mine.

             ˉ W. S. In spirit (Through S. S.)
May 3rd, 1918.

SOULS

When souls arrive in high estate
Who come out hence leaving their breath ,
The first anxiety they feel
Is for their own who mourn their "death."

Then, when we move and see ourselves
No greater than the souls we own,
And, from the sacred sheaf of years
The miseries we have brought Home.

We see the great Creator's plan
Which shuts us out with crime and sin

Until the past we have atoned,
And we are fit to enter in.
W. S. In spirit (Through S. S.)
May 18th, 1918.

THE STAR IN THE EAST

The eastern sky heralds The King
Whose Star leads shepherds on
To look for Him Who came to save
The world at His day's dawn.

Today men look but do not see
The Star right overhead:
They lay their own dear ones away,
And think of them as "dead."

When One Who rose to show the world
At last there is no death,
But as His Star their souls should live,
Though His plan banished breath.
W. S. In spirit (Through S. S.)

Note: I was commanded to sign this for the Chapter (Masonic)
of "The Eastern Star," since I could not explain to them
its source.—S. S.
N. Y. C., May 17th, 1918.

GOD'S LOVE

Peace-of-the-world, and Light, and Love,—
Look on Thy troubled world!
Who knowest all its wounds, and woes,
And warrior's flags unfurled!
Sweep through the skies in majesty
As Jesus rose on high,

And bring the world God's love again
From His immortal sky!
Cement the Nations of Thy world
In love and brotherhood
With Thine own blood, which for them shed,
Can make, and keep them, good.
Place Thine own finger on Time's dial
And point "Thou shalt not kill."
And save Thy children from themselves,—
Their hearts with Thy love fill.

W. S. In spirit (Through S. S.)

ONE WITH THEE

Divided 'gainst themselves, O Lord,
Thy people bleed and fall.
And still Thy Son Thou gavest them
To save and bless them all.
Upon the sands are builded, Lord,
Poor lives of wretchedness;
Until the lands are soaked with blood,
And all suffer distress.
Upon the rock of Thy love, Lord,
We thrust this divine plea:
O save, oh save Thy people, Lord,
 ⁻And make *all one with Thee.*

W. S. In spirit (Through S. S.)

THE LIFE-LINE

O that men might find some better way to reach Eternal life
    than through the war today.
That they might rise above their petty wrongs and see that
    on the heights they'll find a peaceful Calvary.

O that the world which grieves and weeps all sad, lost, shattered, flayed.

Might see themselves beyond the Gate, where no war game is played,

Or never there shall men tear one another as beasts in anger do,

But in proportion shall men find a brother as they HAVE BEEN A BROTHER, staunch and true.

No God has chosen out such slaughter, know ye; nor is the Divine mind of this intent;

But human beings on to murderous ends are driven, or inciting murder-bent,

Dissatisfied with God's bestowed blessings, disgruntled by a neighbor's larger share,

Men fight this war, bring on themselves God's cursings,

And find themselves in spirit stripped and bare.

There wish they that their plans had not miscarried:

There seek they only what He gives to own:

Where looking for their "bread cast on the waters,"

They find it sunken,—lost,—it was a stone!

But how to wake these mortals from their dreaming,

Or how to reach them through this soul of mine,

Keeps her who writes these lines, and Shakespeare, busy,

While planning to throw out a strong life-line.

O seize the chance and grasp at it, my brothers.

O hold it fast, and touch the spirit-shore;

For when the war is done, and men have vanished,

The world will look to spirit evermore.

W. S. In spirit (Through S. S.)

June 1st, 1917. N. Y. C.

RECONSECRATION

I look upon Thy wondrous works, I gaze upon Thy skies;

To every wonder of Thy world my grateful heart replies.

I see Thee in each crested wave, each flower and bird and tree,
And all my heart in gratitude goes out to Thee,—to Thee.

I find, within, Thy tenderness; I know Thee in my heart:
To wake and find Thee everywhere, of all Thy life a part,
To hear Thy voice through silences when bitter tears would
    start,
Is but to welcome Thee within, and know Thee as Thou art.

I lay me down in confidence, knowing Thy balm of rest;
And everything Thou sendest me, whate'er it be, is best.
Thy wing o'ershadows my content; Thy love 's Infinity;
Thy wisdom is all wisdom, Lord: I give my life to Thee.

W. S. In spirit (Through S. S.)

THE YANKEE'S PRAYER

Over all there is a God
Who sees and knows and plans.
The armies of the world are His;
Their souls are in His hands.
My soul is one. But every Hun,
(A soul of His as well)
Shall meet, and answer to, this God,
Or find his soul in hell.
Forgive me, then, Almighty God,
When my soul is set free—
If I must kill my brotherman
For this world's liberty.
I'll do my duty like a man;
As every soldier must—
Then, as we say in the U. S. A.:
"In God We Trust."

W. S. In spirit (Through S. S.)

Past mortal trials, mistakes, and earthly woes,
Forth to the Judge at last each one goes,
Where naught of tears or pleading can repay
For privileges of life lost, flung away.
Where Justice is, there, every act is known,
Writ on thin air, enduring as of stone.
Seen of all eyes, known by what you are,
Marked as with brand through Time, and near or far,
What would men give there to be called His own,
Where mortals wend and stand, at last, alone.

W. S. In spirit (Through S. S.)

SOMETIME

Sometime, somewhere, beyond the earth of men,
You will come into all your own again;
And there, where you can travel on apace,
You'll search the heavens through for one dear face.

Sometime, somewhere—you'll learn what you have been,
When to the soul attached of one unseen
You wrote his words and thought his thoughts for him
Who passed long years agone—over the rim.

Somewhere, sometime, when I shall be with you,
And take delight in conning o'er this, too,
We'll laugh at all the petty plays we made,
And petty rhymes like these, I am afraid,

Writ by a bard, immortal Shakespeare's name,
Who for his soul's enlightenment here came,
And took up house, and housekeeping with thee,
Who art and shalt be, all the world to me.

W. S. In spirit (Through S. S.)

FLOOD-TIDE

O take away from earth's poor fretful day
The love of gold,—for all 'twill bring or pay.
Open men's minds to treasures not of earth:
O let men live and plan for Thy eternal birth
Where souls awake, mourn chances slipped away
While on the earth they played at chance, losing eternal day.
O help men see Thy cross upon the sky
Which spilled Thy blood and tears as Thou didst die
To save men from themselves, from sinner's sin.
O open wide the gates, and let the flood-tide in!

W. S. In spirit (Through S. S.)

FATE?

When you reach out your empty pleading hand
A new arrival in the spirit-land,
And find no one to help or guide or bless,
But lone and anguished are in sore distress,
What would you give to be once more of earth,
To have but one chance more before your spirit-birth?

Oh pause, and think; repent of evil ways,
And pray God to forgive your wasted days
Which, privileged to live you courted death in all,
When dying meant no death (to you) except a pall!
For you were dead all time upon the earth;
But where you cannot "die" there is a dearth
More fatal than impoverishment of gold:
Your empty life and soul; your hand not one shall hold.

W. S. In spirit (Through S. S.)

When you shall find no path where you may trod
Which can give forth a single pulse of joy,

And you shall wait, as I, on some poor soul
Who fights as you once fought when as a boy
Another worried you with taunts or tricks,
And to be rid of him you cursed and tore
To shreds all he had ever given you,
And lost all thought of what he'd been of yore,—
Then will you know how valueless the friend
Whose friendship cannot last until the end.

W. S. In spirit (Through S. S.)

When gentle Shakespeare came to me,
To help me, lift me, comforting,—
I was so glad my heart leaped up,
And many a pean did I sing.
But when I find no gentleness,*
But only hard names called to me,
I think of all I might have thought,
Instead of what has come to be.
And oh I wish that in the way
Where God imparts to all their due,
That He would come and take you there
Where His own service you might do.

W. S. In spirit (Through S. S.)

* Reading the medium's mind.
June 3rd, '17·

I am "sweet Shakespeare" still—(if such I were acclaimed)
Demanding her I love by Shakespeare shall be named
THE SOUL OF GENEROSITY; its heart is her own heart;
Wherefore I speak my praise—recording this in part.
There's music in the spheres vibrating through all time;
Here let me then acclaim this one who writes my rhyme

Shall to the stars attune make music by her love
That shall outlast e'en Time.

W. S. In spirit (Through S. S.)
Feb. 6th, '18.

Joy in the present; Look not forward to the future;
Forget the past.

W. S. In spirit (Through S. S.)
Lincoln's Birthday, Feb. 12th, '17·

W. S.'s Favorite Song sang in the days when he was on earth:
(as recalled by W. S. In spirit.)

"Oh, when will ye sinners come Home?
For the night's coming on and ye roam.
The door's open wide,
Why tarry outside.
Oh, when will ye sinners come Home?"

ETERNAL GOD from whom I came, to Whom I go when from
this sphere
My last poor mortal task complete, I wing my way away from
here,
Oh take me, then, to Thine own breast, and let me evermore
be Thine,
Where only Thou canst give the rest that is of Thee, Divine.
While I must tarry on, and weep, bemoaning war, and war-
fare's crime,
Help me to see behind earth's woe, and back of all, Thy plan
sublime.
Help me to work, to wait on Thee, Who knowest all men can't
surmise;
And must I suffer with the rest, help me to see Thy plans
are wise.

When from the world I must be called, away to serve but Thee,
and pay,
O help me in the dark to find some ray of Light to light my way.

W. S. In spirit (Through S. S.)

May 27th, '17· N. Y. C.

O TO BE ONE

O to be one with the Infinite God:
In mind, heart and soul to be good.
Untempted by aught that the conscience would sway.
If only by Him understood. .
O to be near, and nearer each day;
To feel the firm clasp of His hand.
Uncaring for aught that would lead us astray,
But to stand with His own where they stand.

W. S. In spirit (Through S. S.)

Feb. 25th, '17·

HOLY WRATH

If we could see the way to take
When first we set out on love's path,
We should escape full many woes,
And much of Cupid's wrath.
If we could see the flowerless end
Where never primrose strews the way,
How differently all men would choose,—
How changed would be life's closing day.
No perfume in life's flowerless night
Can make up for its wasted day:
No love-god can restore the loss,
Nor renew life you flung away.

W. S. In spirit (Through S. S.)

March 24th, '17·

DAYBREAK

Across the hills and plains and seas,
O'er mountain, fen, and wold,
The rising Son of Peace appears,
To renew all the old.
Upon the heights of ages past,
Where once He rose to God,
The same Christ comes again to men,
And resurrects the sod.
Where slain of battle's victims lie,
There new hopes shall arise,
To prove to men the God of earth
Is Christ; in God's own skies.

W. S. In spirit (Through S. S.)

When wars have done and men go home
To find no home, nor kith nor kin,
But devastation everywhere,
And everywhere harvests of sin,—
What will they do,—what can be done,—
In all their lives to mend such woe?
When fathers, sons, are slain and gone,
What will the gentle sex then do.
When cries oppress their tender breasts,
On no strong men can they rely,
Will they not wish the fiendish war
Had razed them, too, that they might die?
When babes no more suck at their paps,
When desolation grieves them sore,
Can they look up and find a love
Which would console them evermore?
When crosses rest upon the graves
Within whose clods their dear ones lie,

Must women bear crosses unseen;
.To better lands, their love must die.
W. S. In spirit (Through S. S.)

WORKS OR DEEDS

When days are done and man has gone to his earned rest
beyond
And he must leave his best beloved, however true or fond,
And take his place with lost or blest as his life doth acclaim,

Arriving with full-many a gift, or naught, when called his
name,
—Oh, will he wish his earth time spent in sharing others needs,
And feel the woes his brothers felt, when, like theirs, his heart
bleeds.

—Oh, will he mourn his empty hands uplifted to the King
Who treasures lives as works or deeds, Who knoweth every-
thing.
W. S. In spirit (Through S. S.) ·
Jan. 30, '17·

REPENTANCE

The chance of giving all for Him, and leaving nought behind:
This is the path where Jesus walked. His footsteps all may
find.

The thorny way, unstrewn with flowers; the cup of bitter dregs;
He councils men to follow Him: repentance, Jesus begs.

Oh take the chance while yet ye may,—while ye can seek and
find:
Forgiveness waits remorse's tears; for God is just, and kind.
W. S. In spirit (Through S. S.)

WHO WILL CARE?

Who is to care when from this earth you fare,
Taking but that you loved, and earned while there?
Who is to take your poor, impoverished hand,
And help you find the way in spirit-land?
Who then shall fare along your road of care
Brought from the earth,—this is your "golden-stair!"
Here where the spirit has but what it gave
To the living God before its earthly grave
Took the last chance its living soul to save,
It may find its "mansion" but a rolling wave.
Where is the heaven unthought of while men worked
For the poor gold of earth, evading God, they shirked

Duties which called forth from their souls within,
Preferring sinners, and their life of sin.
Here is one speaking from that land to You,
One who would help to save and succour too
From landing on a shore of barren waste
Where souls must quarter first each earthy taste.
Before they pass to lands where God is light
All earth's must serve their time in sinner's night.
W. S. In spirit (Through S. S.)
March 3rd, '17.

FOLLOWING

Until worn toilers here can pray,
Until the rights of labor win,
What can the good say here of Christ,
Who came to save from sin?
How have the rich then followed Him,
When weary workers scarcely pray
Because they find no brotherlove,

No Christ on earth today?
When those who toil find Him in thee,
The Christian's thought for brotherman,
No need to fight for justice then,
What men had failed to do, He can.
W. S. In spirit (Through S. S.)

HOPE (Song)

Wait 'till the morning aflush in the sky
Encircles the earth with its roseate hue,—
Wait 'till the dawning of love that shall bring
Hope, new-born, unto you.
Wait 'till the shadows are chased away,
By the light in a lover's fond eyes,—
The dawn of a new-day shall break, then, for you:
In his arms you will find Paradise.
W. S. In spirit (Through S.S.)

O WHAT WOULD YOU GIVE?

O what would I give were the world still my own,
With no fetters to bind or enslave.
O what would I do were my life but begun,
And my dust not in Stratford's old grave.
O what would YOU give when you leave behind
The beautiful temple God gave,
And become but a wraith of light or a shade
As you live with the part God would save.
W. S. In spirit (Through S. S.)
March 11th, '17.

Added:
O what would you give when you answer the call,
To return and begin life anew.

O what can you do if your God rejects you,
When you "die" and are still alive, too.

                                    W. S. In spirit.

Note: This is to prove W. S. is W. S. (W. S. In spirit.)

Take from my heart every malice and stain;
Give to my soul spirit-help, spirit-gain:
Then take to Thyself all my woes and my pain,
And send me not forth here to wander again.

Take from my life every ungodly lust;
Give to my soul replenished Thy trust,—
Then take what Thou will, but still love Thee I must,
And treasures I'll own, with no "moth," and no "rust."

                         W. S. In spirit (Through S. S.)

LET US NOT DESPAIR, GOD IS EVERYWHERE,
And the world is right, and His.
Let us share the care, and the burdens bear;
For a blessing life truly is.
Let us joy today, let us put away
The fears we have claimed our own,
And rejoice tomorrow,—nor own nor borrow,
The trouble we never have known.

                         W. S. In spirit (Through S. S.)

"UNHEALTHY OPTIMISM"

(A criticism of Stevenson, by ———, Poet and Novelist)

To live with hope agleam within the breast,
(That breast wracked by its torturing, fatal pain)
And give out from it such a light,
That through earth's dark lost men shall find the way again,—
No tinge of pain's malicious, doubting shafts

Caused he, nor took from hearts the thing he could not give,—
But in each heart he left abloom hope's flower,
To bless and cheer the earth and all that live.
A poet with a mortal-pain, and twinge,
No pessimistic words sent forth to blight;
But of the Great Light overshadowing him,
Reflected God to help men bear their night.
O poet of good-cheer, I love thee well,
Who write to tell how often you help me:
Who sang and wrote your God into your works,
That worms, like I, might crawl on cheerfully.

Written by W. S. In spirit (Through S. S.) for S. S.
who is pained by this unhealthy criticism.

"THE STINGY RECEIVER"

To him who hath abundant in this world,
Receiving all good God hath given him,
Hoarding within no gratitude or love,
With selfishness filled full, and o'er the brim,—
To him whom God hath cherished his full time,
Bestowing on him boundless gifts, and more,
Yet dullard in his wit and common sense,
Like some poor miser counting up his store,
Adding each day some treasured golden bit,
With glutton's sense of gain's unslaked thirst,
Stingy in all things of the heart and mind,
SUCH a receiver, Oh, he is accursed.

W. S. In spirit (Through S. S.)

FOES-OF-WAR

Do all who carry guns and fight
Battle with hatred to the death,
Defying all God's laws to men,

Taking their souls, their lives, their breath,
Or do they fight to wound, not slay—
To press the soldiers from their lands—
To save their homes, by sacred rights,
From falling into alien hands?

Do men who fight war's battles grim,
Carry within the murderer's heart?
Do not they see their own firesides
Protected, as they do their part?
When soldiers wake before their God,
Encompassed round with warrior foes,
With thoughts bound to the only King,

Each soul henceforth serves, loves, or knows.
O what will matter foes without,
When foes within is all that counts,—
The foes that living life had brought
To shackle him,—'tis this amounts
To more than armies lost or slain.
While pleading for these foes-of-war,
He begs God to accept his pain.

W. S. In spirit (Through S. S.)

THE STRIFE

When good men say that the strife is o'er,
And the battles fought, and the victory won,
As they lay away some great, good man
Whose life on the earth is done,
They little think it is just begun,
No matter how good or great was he,
Who answers now to his God on high
For every fault, or disloyalty,
Where the best must halt, and in darkness wait,

Until One Who knows how each mortal lives,
Sees the repentance worked in them,
And the spirit rebukes, or forgives.
How must these strive, how must they pray,
To earn the right to go on their way.
The best at strife with the worst of them,
Where all is known on the Judgement Day.

W. S. In spirit (Through S. S.)

KINGS AND KINGDOMS

In all the kingdoms of the world where man has his estate,
There is a wrenching of the heart, a piteous lowly state
In which a man must separate from all he loves and fight
The battles of his country, for freedom, justice, right.
But in the Kingdom of The King, where man has no estate,
And he must forage for himself, tho' it be early, late,
When last he finds no chain that binds, no fetters but those
    he made
The while he made his character, which lives, though low he's
    laid.
When in this Kingdom then he finds himself, just as he's
    been,—
With every mark unvanishing, each separate brand of sin,
He wishes for some hiding place, unseeing as unseen,
That none shall see him as he is, or know what he has been.
There is no place where he may go, to hide him evermore—
Alas, no palaces await this guest, or open wide a door.
No king, no queen, no court, no fame, brought he to help him on
Where what he *was* is what he *is* when heavens for him dawn.

W. S. In spirit (Through S. S.)

THE BALANCE TRUE

In the world beyond where no war afflicts,
But the soul's unceasing war torments and chides,
There is a stream of warriors bold and brave,
Arriving without its bivouac-welcoming,
Where fighting men have but a murderer's chance,
When all is left on earth, even their lance.

In droves of millions, with no captains here;
No order whereby some stand forth as great,
Unless these were the soldiers of the Lord
Forced into conflict by their country's laws,
And made to slay their brothers of the sod;
These, these alone, are welcome with their God.

"Thou Shalt Not Kill," is written in His Law:
And, "Thou Shalt Love Thy Neighbor As Thyself."
Where no evasion counts, or has effect,
The Judge will weigh there in the balance true.
Where naught but Love's obedient shall mount.
There, must the murderer re-reckon his account.

W. S. In spirit (Through S. S.)

THE WANDERER

When far afield the wanderer halts and views the way he trod,
He sees it was the other path which would have led to God.
Too late he knows he started wrong; too late to turn aside:
He can't go back; he must go on; apart the paths are, wide.
He halts, he weeps; perhaps he prays; within he hears a call:
A message sent but of the Lord Who gave His life for all.
"Behold My footprints in the Way; choose thou this Way to
    take,
Nor turn aside, but press on thou, and pray 'for Jesus' sake.' "

W. S. In spirit (Through S. S.)

OH—OH—OH!

Oh for the power to move men's souls, to wake them to be good.
To tell them all I must suffer here, for I lived not as I should.
Oh for the tongues of a thousand men, to speak my Maker's
praise,
That these in turn find a thousand minds for God through
their earthly days.
Oh for the gift that a God could give to lift me from this earth,
To a place beyond the crimes of war and sin, to a saintly birth.
Oh that the words I write through HER who writes these
words for me
Could be hurled wide-spread through a wakened world,
To cause men to think and see.
Oh that the world with its lust for power, and ease, and luxury,
Could know as the spirit who writes these lines,
Their utter buffoonery!

W. S. In spirit (Through S. S.)

A LASTING GOOD

What shall peace mean if an enlightened world
Hears from their own in the near spiritland,
That life is but a moment of God's time—
And each may reach and touch a spirit hand.

What shall it mean when earth knows all the facts
Of mere transition,—all I know who write,—
Will they invite their own to sup with them,
And ere they slumber, speak the words, "Good-night"?

To those they see are there, but cannot hear,
Or those they hear, perhaps, but cannot see?
Will spirit, then, a new-world recreate;
"Thy Kingdom Come," at last may come to be.

W. S. In spirit (Through S. S.)

ALL

If from Divinity all gifts bestowed the sons of men, their
    erring, mortal selves,
Out of what rare perfection must it root, into what rare per-
    fection, then, it delves.
If from the Source invisible and high come joys and bliss, and
    love ineffible,
And trusting mortals drew exhaustless store from that Sup-
    ply, all inexhaustible,
Expressed in daily lives this love Supreme, which mankind
    was here bidden one another,
How vain earth's monarch's schemes-of-hate, or war's infringe-
    ment, brother against brother!

If lovers were with God's love here content, and souls content
    to love God and no other,
How soon must God leave His own firmament, to live with
    man reflecting Him, the Lover.
               W. S. In spirit (Through S. S.)

FORTUNE

O world of luxury and pomp, I look down on you now today,
Regarding all you held for me when as a man of earth's high
    state
I only saw poor puppets play, nor dreamed of aught apast
    God's Gate,
Or I should owe and could not pay.

Now puppets make me play for them; now all I have is poor
    indeed;
The very best I own is this: I still must supplicate and plead.
Still must I love, and unforgiven, remain between this world
    and heaven,

Where God allots a devil's place for all who failed' to win the race.
Here then, am I, to plead and pray, until I earn the heavenly Way.

W. S. In spirit (Through S. S.)

Go then, be wise, and mend thy earthly way:
Heed not the world, or what it has to say:
Give all to God, your heart, your soul, your mind;
Keep nothing back, and, seeking, ye shall find.
Then, as you fare, and bear an earthly cross,
Count naught as lost, whatever be thy loss.
When thou shalt stand at last when all is done,
Saved by the God you loved, His Blessed Son,
What shall you miss, of what the world could give:
Living forevermore, in Christ, you live.

W. S. In spirit (Through S. S.)

AN ARMY OF FOES AT HAND

There's a lilting haunting quatrain runs through my mind today,
The worst of this is what a quatrain is; I cannot say.
But anyhow the same old saw applies, I must confess,
"You're better off without the things that curse you while they bless."
I've come to know the meaning of the curse that will not die,—
I've come to see sterility in these, and pass them by.
I've come to find true happiness is only to be found
By those who worship first, then work, and keep in hallowed ground.
The wretchedness which mortals know while seeking but for bliss,

Is bound and wound around them when they go hence from
    this,
A world of light and promise, and a world of richest lore,
If only they were satisfied with what God gave in store,

Nor tried their own re-making hands at bettering His laws,
And spinning for themselves a web, against His Law and
    cause.
When men will take their armies they find within themselves,
The foes of God's own Justice, which in His Kingdom delves
Usurping, and o'erriding all, injustices their plea,—
Then battles would begin AT HOME, and not across the sea.

W. S. In spirit (Through S. S.)

THE INVISIBLE FOE

"Freedom! Freedom!" the Boys are crying:
"We fight for Liberty!"
Proclaiming this, they little know
That foes within them be.
They fight to free these foes from life,
As "death" will set them free;
And yet the one who lays down life,
He must heroic be.
But 'tis within the fight is won
At last "death" sets them free:
To boast a hero's cause he'll not,
When he has liberty;
And gentleness, which is of God,
Shows him what was within
The while he boasted freedom's cause,
To murder was a sin.

W. S. In spirit (Through S. S.)

MARITAL MISERIES

When men go forth and battle for their own,
And meet the wolves and foxes of the land
Who wait to snatch their souls, their very souls,
While garbed as friends, are of the traitor brand,—
They leave behind their own who sit and wait
And teem all anxiously through lonely hours,
Imagining temptation's lurid sin,
Enticing with its kind where folly cowers
The love that was, and always should have been,
Had nature been so kind as to have given
A life of ease whereby a man could know,
The while he was on earth, a little heaven.

I pause in wonderment knowing the faithful
Along life's path of loneliness and tears.
Knowing full well where lie earth's dearest treasures,
Could men but know them through their earthly years.
Oh woman of the silent grief who bears
Her sorrows as a faithful woman can,
What have ye not withstood, and suffered,
For the perfidy and deceit of man.

The world will wake in some far-off tomorrow,
And know its jewels fit to crown the king,
While they alone make up the anvil chorus,
Where with His angels are they fit to sing.
The lost and lonely souls of His perdition,
Who found no plan to save themselves from sin,
Look to the ones they knew on earth forgiving,
And vainly wish that they might be let in.

W. S. In spirit (Through S. S.)

June 7th, '17· N. Y. C.

Make me a place, O God, where I can go
When last my love I must desert.
For her more noble fields will shut out me,
Who never more Thy holy place may see.
Make me some place, O God, to save my soul,
Which yearns to be again a man made whole,
And take me where of Thine I shall be one:
Forgive her here who writes for this lost son.

W. S. In spirit (Through S. S.)

WAKE, O MY SOUL, and take thy flight
Back through the pressing throng;
Back through the night, past the black vault
Where penitents await
The pardon of His grace,
The comfort of His state.
Give, O my soul, when I must rise and go,
Comfort and help and power to her below,
Who on the earth as Thine must work and wait
Until God summons her to rise.
E'en soon, or late.

W. S. In spirit (Through S. S.)

BEGIN AGAIN

Forget the past with all its haunting sorrows,—
Forget the pain and pangs of yesterday:
Begin to view the future of the ages
Through which a soul must wend its spirit way.
Begin to think of all the Great God promised
To those who will His just commands obey:
And if you grasp His plan, then cleave thou to it:
Forget the past; begin anew today.

W. S. In spirit (Through S. S.)

A LEAF

A leaf from the thicket I pondered today;
"What artist could make this," I then had to say.
Such marvelous lines; such exquisite skill;
A rapturous worship my heart seemed to fill.
So wondrously perfect and dainty its art:
Yet, of His creation so little a part.
I knew by the reverence, all love I must own,
Such beauty was made by a Good-God alone.

W. S. In spirit (Through S. S.)

THE SETTING-SUN (Song)

Aflame with gold and purple hues
The sun is sinking low
Into the west; into the nest
The weary birdlings go.
Love-of-my-life, with joys complete,
I lay me down by thee,
Knowing no strife, but tenderness,
For which my praises be.
When from on high the radiant sky
Such banners are unfurled,

W. S. In spirit (Through S. S.)

Note: Unfinished. the door bell rang. S. S.
Aug. 18th, '18.

THE SLEEPING WORLD

When mortals lay their own dear "dead" away,
They hope they'll sleep 'till resurrection day.
Down in the earth for worms to desecrate,
They leave them, then, for this long time to wait,
Till they shall hear at last a trumpet call,—
Then shall they rise and praise God, one and all.

But we who "died" know better, yea, than this,—
Since not a moment's "dying" marred life's bliss!
We stood before the old form that was us,
And mourned because they wept and made a fuss.
We did not care; we did not even sigh;
We knew that we should meet them by-and-by.
Since then we know there are no sleeping "dead";
It is the living world that sleeps instead!

W. S. In Spirit (Through S. S.)

CHARITY

(Which "suffereth long and is kind")

W. S. In spirit (Through S. S.)

When mortals grieve and give their time to censure
Of some poor fallen one along the way,
They do not know that life is but a prison,
And they must look for mercy, too, some day.
They do not realize the worthless factors
That trinkets are where they cannot take these,
But soulless junk without a spark of profit,
Or any lustre that will pay, or please.

If when they come, their souls are white to harvest,
With kindnesses they've sown along earth's path,
While to no man a single burden added,
Nor spumed upon the helpless their vile wrath,
This, one day, may be much that they can carry
Where never jewels decorate display,
Nor add to splendour aught that God discovers,—
While you will find "kind charity" will PAY.

W. S. In spirit (Through his only medium on earth, who is
worried over some old jewels she cannot take with her,
and do not make her any better here. W. S.)

IN THY CARE

O God of Peace, O God of Love,
Whom all the saints adore,
Keep dogs of war and rapiers
From off our peaceful shore.
O keep our homes inviolate,—
Our fields from murderer's plans;
And help us bear our burden's share,—
And spare our fertile lands.
But let us do Thy sovereign will,
Whatever it may be,
That in Thy care we cannot fare
Afar away from Thee.

W. S. In spirit (Through S. S.)

GET IN LINE

The call "To Arms!" has come at last, and we must sail
    across the sea
To battle for the rights of man, and save our liberty.
For this we go, brave men and true, to help you on the line
Where you have bled and lost your sons, we send forth ours,
    and mine.
To raze the world of "living-men" for rights to live, be free,
We send our all, wish we had more, to give across the sea.
But when the last bugle shall sound, and earth's warfare be
    done,
What vain reward for him who died before his race was run:
Bare youth, of manhood's greatest gem, who left no heir behind,
What was he given to equal this, where he must come to find
No woman's arms, whose suckling babe was fathered by his sire,
But devastation that he caused, through bloodshed, rape, and
    fire.

When in the land where spirits dwell, a man comes forth
   "to arms,"
There's nothing left but what he brought, to still his vain
   alarms.
He sees the wreck made of himself,—no hero, then, is he,
Where two wrongs never made one right, nor single soul
   set free.
He longs to tell his countrymen, as I who speak today,
To serve his GOD, obey HIS Laws, is lasting freedom's way.
But he may not return as I, who centuries long "dead,"
Have earned my way to speak, and say, by the Great God
   be led.
And into war, if driven, lad, by laws which long to free,
Let others load their guns and fire, but *thou* no murderer be.
For where the Law awaits each soul—as writ enduringly,—
Ye cannot HAVE but what you GIVE—and this must rest
   with thee.

                  W. S. In spirit (Through S.S.)
May 22nd, 1917, N. Y. C.

"THOU   SHALT   NOT   COMMIT   ADULTERY"

(The Seventh)

When the Law was writ which should guide men here, and
   be unto them a light,
The moral code was expressed in words all plain, and just
   and right.
The wise ones here obey this law which leads them to the Light:
The fools re-write, and adjust them o'er; these pass, at last,
   to night.
When the words were graved on the tablet-stone,
Which came from God above,
There was no distinction of moral rights,
No bartering words of Love.

"Thou shalt not," was addressed to *him*
Who bears the yoke with thee:
And the Justice which neither winks nor sleeps, but presides
    through Eternity,
Beholds him prisoner at the bar who has sought excuse, or
    cause
To alter to fit to his craven flesh
God's immutible, Divine Laws,
When back to the earth, then, he must come,
To be chained by the love of lust,
Will he know if a God Supreme rules all,
And if His Laws are just.

W. S. In Spirit
("Through his only earthly medium" S. S.)

SAVE THY SOUL

Somewhere every soul in need
Bows sad, in debt to God
Throughout the span of life He gave
To each upon earth's sod.
Somewhere the tasks are waiting You
Who shun His work today:
At last this labor must be done:
As all of His must pay.
Should you come hence and find but loss,
And nought here gained but earth,
Know, one has set himself the task
To speak from spirit-birth.
He warns you, then, rise up today,
And look on High and see
The past is loss, and darkness waits
Where sin and sinners be.
To save thy soul, set free thy sins

Which chain thee to the ground.
Unite with God's most holy love,—
With His, at last, be bound.

W. S. In Spirit (Through S. S.)

"To her friend,————."
May 9th, 1918.

ESTEEM

Some are so highly here esteemed in words of praise and
  honors too,
They will not need a gemmed crown, so swiftly their rewards
  accrue.
While others in their low estate are more esteemed on high
  than these,
And wait to wear their diadem where only One they strive
  to please.
We have no gifts men seek, or crave; ours are no songs
  well-paid;
This is the flute on which I play,—this flute has Shakespeare
  made.
I play whom men call "turned to dust,"—indeed here is a
  shade.
No other ever played as I,—nor worked what I have made.
No laurels crown my Sarah's brow; her lot is meagre, poor:
Yet do I speak her worth to us who "died" and still endure.
  May 6th, 1918, N. Y. C.

W. S. In Spirit (Through S. S.)

FRET NOT—THE WORLD WILL SEE THE LIGHT
When such is given by His law.
And blest be ye, and all like ye,
Who see as Jesus saw.
Work on—the world will welcome all

Who can the truth proclaim.
Her harvests are the blind and deaf:
They come as Jesus came,
Apast the grave which holds them not;
On High they see our plan
To lift the veil from mortal eyes
To save each fellowman.
When this is done, and each can see
Their own who stand and plead,
Will heaven have come at last to all,—
And armies no more bleed.
Rejoice if ye have seen or heard
The spirits, or have given
To hopeless, striving seekers here
The truth about God's heaven.
Some have no wish to see or feel
Their own who have passed on,
But hope to meet them in some sky
When Paradise may dawn.
But I who write and spell this rhyme
. Have come to search for these
To bring them manna from His skies,
From out the spirit seas.
Help on the work—for each may help;
As all may give Him due:
Then, when the sea is crosst by thee,
May God be waiting you.

W. S. In Spirit (Through S. S.)

Wake, sleeping dead, and help the world rejoice.
Speak, heavenly host, and let men hear you voice.
World that will be after war's carnage o'er,—
World that will rise anew, restored to the core,—

Had ye replenished at the Living Spring,
Songs of God's wondrous Peace would ye now sing.
Love, in the world so rare, ravished, raped and torn,
Your spirit cries forlorn, yet to be born.
Thus, with impelling might, crowned anew,
Earth rises to Thy right: all must welcome You.
Shouldering thy past mistakes, longing for God,
Saviour of men appear, lift from the sod
Harvest of shell and hate, crime, murder, lust,—
Proclaim Thy Peace at last: in God we trust.

W. S. In Spirit (Through S. S.)

SHORTER AND SWIFTER flows the outgoing tide:
Incoming, will the ocean here abide?
What is the meaning of this world of care?
Why are we here,—and whereunto shall fare.
Mortals abound in spiritlands as here:
All but their flesh surviving past the bier.
How shall I tell the world all he,
The poet Shakespeare, ever hoped to be,
Ay, and full more, since death can claim no share
Of mortal's sins, here written on the air.
Give all their due: praise every poet well:
All these have sung their songs
To heaven—even from hell.

W. S. In Spirit (Through S. S.)
Jan. 16th, '18, N. O., La.

"WHEN ALL SHALL ARISE IN GLORY" Isaiah.

There is a Land where all men find
The true and living God,
Who folds all sorrows in His heart,
But spares no child, nor rod.

When men take up their crosses there
Each day bearing along
A burden's weight, a weight of woe,
With sorrows life-time long,
All see their past where all is known
And each is known to all:
Where all are sinners all are one
Since first Adam did fall.
Along the road these sinners trod
Clasping their lives of sin;
But close and closer to their hearts;
Nor God inviting in;
When He but stood without the Door
Which he would enter in
To free them through the cross He bore,
And save them from their sin.

    W. S. In Spirit (Through S. S.)

THE RISEN LORD

Across the sky o'er battlefields,
Where torn and wounded lie,
Our Lord appears to show the way,
Before the soldiers "die."
At last the Lord is risen indeed:
The dying hold their breath:
Before their eyes the Saviour stands
To prove there is no death.

    W. S. In Spirit (Through S. S.)

A CROSS NO LOSS

Our Father's Fathers bore their guns and fought the land
  to free;
And somewhere God will leave, will spare, Fathers for Liberty.

Where men have fought and bled and died, and spilled their
    ruddy gore,
The lands have known some betterment, they had not known
    of yore.
And fathers will their children spare, as fathers still to be,
Or mothers for the coming race, to bear for liberty.
So let us not in haste decry the loss of the unborn:
Although the Lord laid down His life, the Saviour's world's
    unshorn.

                W. S. In Spirit (Through S. S.)

WHENCE?

Take down the tattered flags, and roll the dirge-beat of the
    drum:
The death of war acclaim at last: the war of life is come.
To hold men in their fond embrace, to Mother for them sons,—
This is the problem now of life—when men lay down their
    guns.

For who is left to foster love, or father sons to-be?
When war has taken England's best that Belgium might be
    free.
When France has given all she had, and wished for more to
    give,
That her beloved "Marsaillaise," should greet those still to live!

When Italy and Russia, and poor Roumania too, and Serbia,
    and Greek and Jap,
Have suffered theirs to do their part to free the land of Huns
Who fall back shattered, dead.
Whence can the future fathers come, when all have forth
    been led

To fight and bleed for freedom's cause, that those who are to be,
May never have to give their all, just to be free—be free!

W. S. In Spirit (Through S. S.)

Apr. 25th, '17.

THE SINS OF THE WORLD

When will the world be washed clean of its sin?
When will men BE all that they might have been?
O could they see themselves but as they are,
Which they must do when crosst death's harbour bar,
What would they give to be once more earth's men,
With but their chance to serve their God again.
Saved are a few who knew their God could save:
Lost are vast millions who sank in sin's wave.
What is the world, the life-span of a man,
To all the joys of God's Eternal span.
When all too late they stand without and wait,
O men of earth, your poor eternal state.

W. S. In Spirit (Through S. S.)

FAR AND NEAR

There is a proverb that I knew of old,
"The angels hover where a baby smiles."
There is more truth in this than men
Have even learned, though angel's plea beguiles
Each living man to hearken to the voices
Which speak unheard their counsels to earth's men,—
Renew their faith, and hasten their redemption,
—And some are healed, some made whole again.

We have no hope that all shall hear our voices;
We know the dumb of earth are satisfied:
But when these come and go to help their loved ones,
Who much prefer to think that they have "died,"

What will they feel, who are as keen as ever,
When near to these they find them all estranged?
Will they not mourn who find themselves all powerless,—
When naught·except their form by "death" is changed?

When YOU return and stand before a loved one,
Imploring, ay beseeching them to hear,
Will life not mean an endless separation,
When they keep you afar who are so near?

W. S. In Spirit (Through S. S.)

THE RESCUE

Lift, save the fallen, friend or foe;
Bind the broken,—cease the flow;
Succor, feed, resign, restore
Those who can have hope no more.
Where the rescued find their own,
None, they tell me, are alone.
Here, the hand that saved you'll bless,
Guiding it in life's distress,
Holding fast an erring one,
Till, for him, new-life begun.

W. S. In Spirit (Throug S. S.)

Added:
Can you pass, leaving behind
One no other else may find?
Rescue, then his shattered life,
From earth's warring, hateful, strife.

W. S.

AWING

Some tell a tale who runs may read of life beyond the grave;
And given it is to few on earth, to so warn, help, or save.
So when one here hath suffered so the spirit is attune

To take these wireless messages full early, late or soon,
And send them out to plodders who would heavenward awing,
Is it not well that some are strung to hear, to speak, to sing?

W. S. In Spirit (Throug S. S.)

FAITH

The minds of men are like the skies,
So various in hue.
The mind that comprehends its God
May not be given you.
The wondrous works the Maker planned,
No mind yet understood;
Yet everyone can look on high
And see his God is good.

The trust each one can give to Him
Too great to understand,
Must likened be to children's trust
Upon the vain earthland,
Who follow one unquestioningly
On whom their lives depend,
Holding the hand of one who guides,
Knowing this one a friend.

W. S. In Spirit (Through S. S.)

THE PRODIGAL SON

Too long without the Shepherd's fold
The wanderer had been;
Too long without his father's house,
And wayward, steeped in sin,
The prodigal retraced his steps,
And found one in the door
With welcome fond, forgiveness true,
Which saved him evermore.

The Father waits to welcome You;
No matter where you've been:
He only asks you to return,
And free your soul from sin.
The feast is spread; His cloak is yours:
All that He has is thine.
He waits, He asks you to come Home;
His pardon is Divine.

W. S. In Spirit (Through S. S.)

WHEN MEN SHALL KNOW

When men shall know while still on earth,
A God of love surrounds them here,
And naught can take from them this love,
No parting, and no bier,
But walking side by side with Him
Up to their last earth breath,
No dissolution shall they know,
No dying,—never death.
When men shall know their lives are held
In God's paternal hand,
O Christ, Thy crown of thorns, Thy cross,
Shall bless, then, all earthland.

W. S. In Spirit (Through S. S.)

THE GLORY OF HIS MISSION

When Jesus stood before His cross,
Where latterly He hung,
What anguish must His Father felt:
How must His heart been wrung.
A Father's love, a Father's care,
The Father's only Son.
But Jesus knew His Father's plan,

And said: "Thy will be done."
His mission, then, His Father gave,
Who saw Him crucified:
To save all from the sinner's grave
Christ came, and suffered: died.

W. S. In Spirit (Through S. S.)

ALONG THE ROAD TO GOD

Poor shattered wrecks along the road to God,—
Oh, how they strew the path that mortals choose:
Oh how they block the way to heaven's Gate,
To hear their doom, and all they chose to lose.
Poor broken souls sent back to serve and wait
Until through faith and works ye shall be known,
What would ye give did ye not have to pay;
How must ye pay, before ye are His own.
Along the road where pilgrims halt unfed,
Ye seek a friend whose outstretched hand may save;
The Friend ye seek to find, the Friend ye need,
Has pled in vain from cradle to the grave.

W. S. In Spirit (Through S. S.)

HOW LONG?

How long, O King, must mortals serve and find no throne
can save
The wrecks of time their bodies are, thrown in uncoffined grave.
How long, Oh Lord, can this war last which speaks no hand of
Thine:
How long shall men serve but a king whose right is not
Divine.

How long shall life mean but a span of years from birth to
    death?
How long, Almighty God, must souls live for their mortal
    breath?

W. S. In Spirit (Through S. S.)

FOULING THE NEST

Birds make their nests and keep them clean,
Ne'er fouling them, but with their young:
Thus came to be a saying rare:
"No nests befoulded are birds among."
So 'tis in life with those who love:
Their own come first, and then the home:
Mankind can learn from every bird
The time to mate, or time to roam.
The spirit-world has long known this:
The feathered tribe are God's elect.
His coming ones at nightfall, aye,
Trust any branch He may select.
To be like these I plead thou canst:
To trust and make thy faith as sure:
Then coming hence, at eve, or morn,
No punishment must thou endure.

W. S. In Spirit (Through S. S.)

SUMMERTIME IN THE HEART

When the earth is all bare and covered with snow,
When the puppets of life hold no joy,
There is dearth of all things, a lacking of warmth,—
Life's gold is mixed with alloy.
'Tis the same with the heart when the summer of life
Is a season long past and gone by;
Though the warmth of affection it knew in life's spring,

Like the earth, is alive, cannot die.
'Neath the frost, beyond sleeping, all living awake,
In the warmth of God's love and caress;
. When the heart is aglow in its glad summertime,
Newborn in its beautiful dress.

W. S. In Spirit (Through S. S.)

THINE
(Song)

Make me Thy servant, Lord, or what you will.
Abundently with loaves the baskets Thou didst fill.
What need have I, thou, Lord, canst not supply.
"Thy Will Be Done," oh Lord,—and *not my* will.

Make me Thy spokesman, Lord, if lips of mine,
Exultantly can speak Thy love, Thy love divine.
What joy to be, Lord, messenger of Thee.
Increase my store, Oh Lord, and make me Thine.

Here in Thy vineyard, Lord, lab'rers are few:
Increasingly each day duties abound to do.
When all is done, Oh Lord, if at Thy feet
I am but Thine, at last, I am complete.

W. S. In Spirit (Through S. S.)

TAKE HIS HAND
(Song)

Lift up your prayer,—God will hear it:
Lift up your heart, He will know.
Lift up your eyes, He will see you;
Lift up your soul e're you go.

Lift up your hand: beg Him hold you.
Lift up your voice in His praise.

Lift up your cross, He will help you,
And spare, at the end of your days.

W. S. In Spirit (Throug S. S.)

COME TO ME

Would you lay your burden down? Come to Me.
Have you worn a thorny-crown? Come to Me.
Has the tempest tosst your soul.
Wrecked you on a desert shoal?
Come to Me.

Are you lost, with bleeding feet? Come to Me.
Would you know a Love complete? Come to Me.
Will you see Me at the door?
Hear Me calling o'er and o'er:
"Come to Me."

Can you try just once again? Come to Me.
Let Me ease your conscience pain: Come to Me.
Hear, I wait, and call to you;
Would you know a Saviour true?
Come to Me.

W. S. In Spirit (Through S. S.)

JESUS' WOES
(Song)

O tell the simple story o'er of Jesus' love for men,—
And let poor mortals seeking hope, revive their souls again.
O tell the aged of the cross their Lord has borne for them;
Let little children come and see His arms outstretched for them.
O bring the sinning Magdalenes to see the blood He shed,
That though they be as scarlet they can be white instead.
O fetch the men of wordly ways, who seek harvests of gold,
And let them find the only kind not to be bought or sold.

O keep the good Book open wide, and seek its well-worn leaves,
Upon which Jesus' woes are writ, —no word of which deceives.

W. S. In Spirit (Through S. S.)

ALL PRAISE TO THEE
(Song)

All praise be to Thee, Who gave us Thine own,
And made us joint heirs to Thy holy throne.
All praise be to Thee for Christ who hath shown
No life can be taken; no one be alone.

All praise be to Thee for Him crucified.
For Jesus Who came and suffered, and died.
All praise be to Thee, all love of my soul,
My heart, and my mind, Who maketh me whole.

W. S. In Spirit (Through S. S.)

THE SOUL'S CRY
(Song)

See me a penitent, here, in the dust.
Craving Thy pardon, Thy love, and trust.
Hear my soul's pleading cry,
Lord, do not pass me by,—
Thou wert despised as I—
Jesus, my Lord.

Behold, an outcast; I am unfit.
Promise of mercy, Lord, all mèn have it.
Even soul-beggars, then,
Can be restored again, —
And be as other men,
Jesus, my Lord.

Hear me, e're night decends. Lord, hear my woes.
Forgive my erring, e're my soul goes

Out on its homeward way,
Where there is night or day:
Thus for my sins I pray,
Jesus, my Lord.

W. S. In Spirit (Through S. S.)

IN THE CITY OF GOD

(Song)

When the harvest is ripe in the City of God,
And the reaper has gathered it in,
When the grain from the chaff is garnered at last,
And the toll has been taken of sin,—
Shall we stand with the saved whose ransom He paid,
When He gave up His life for us all,—
Or, outcast, and afraid, aside shall be laid,
With the heedless who heard not His call?

When the season is past, and we all view at last,
The field where our labors have been,—
When we see the poor soil or the riches of toil,
From which we have been gathered in,—
Shall we wish we had toiled in the vineyard of God,
The riches of soul there to win—
As we view the poor stubble of our barren selves (yield)
Shall we mourn for all we might have been?

Refrain:
In the City of God is the Kingdom;
In the City of God is the King:
In the City of God is the harvest;
In the City where God's angels sing!
In the City of God are the ransomed;
In the City of God are the blest:

Where the King, and no kingdom can vanish,
Is Christ, and His eternal rest.

W. S. In Spirit(Through S. S.)

TELL IT ALL
(Song)

Come kneel at His feet, and tell Jesus all.
He is waiting for you; do you not hear Him call?
He is speaking to You,—and all sinners who fall;
O come now to Jesus; oh come tell Him all.

Refrain:

Tell it all, tell it all, though as scarlet it be,—
O come now to Jesus, from sin be set free.
He will hear a faint whisper: say, "Jesus, take me!"
Tell it all—tell it all—"Come and see," "Come and see."

Come open the door, He's waiting outside;
He's knocking, He's knocking! . . Open the door wide!
He is calling on YOU,—even you He does call;
O bid Jesus enter; and then tell Him all.

Come sinner and saint; the table is spread;
God's wonderful table; Christ's wine, and Christ's bread.
He is waiting for You,—who died for us all;
O come to His banquet; oh hear, hear Him call!

W. S. In spirit (Through S. S.)

O KING DIVINE
(Song)

Oh come to the trenches my brothers,
And help in the fight to win
Souls for God's battle of "freedom"—
Freedom from sin,—from sin.
Oh come to the field of honor,

And help me bury the slain
Who were "lost" in the battle with Satan;
But "found" in His love again!

Oh come to the rescue my brothers,
Who serve but an earthly king;
Help in God's work of restoring
Souls that would joy, and sing!
Oh come let us swell the numbers,
Under the banner of God.
Singing His glad hosannas,
Bearing no mark of sin's rod.

Chorus: O King Divine, let Thy light shine
    Into this darkened soul of mine.
    Peace-of-the-World,, O Prince of Peace,
    Loosen the chain, from sin release.
                    W. S. In Spirit (Through S. S.)
(Or, A Message From The King)

OLD GLORY
(Song)
When the world is safe to live in,
For our children, and the lives
Of the yet unborn are not forlorn,
Nor Mothers, sweethearts, wives—
There's one thing you can tell them all
As you hold them to your breast:
Old Glory shared the victory
With France, England, and the rest!

When I've done my bit for Liberty
In the fight against the Hun,
Should the light of day be crushed away,
And my soldiering be done,

There's one request, and only one,
That's dearest in my breast:
Just wrap me in Old Glory
When you lay me down to rest?

> W. S. In Spirit (Through S. S.)
"For S. S."

ALONG WITH THE TIDE
(Song)

Tenderly over the billows, riding the mighty deep,
Many a craft is sailing, pilots the watchout keep.
Fitful and stormy the ocean, puny and fragile the craft,
Mortals are trusting to waves and tides, a sheltering haven
    at last.
Carelessly ever the boatswain, tackles the mast fore and aft,
"Where may the Captain be, steward?" somebody called, and
    laughed.
Riding a sea tempest-driven, riven by lightening in twain.
Strewn on the bed of the ocean, a wreck on life's sea again!

Rocked in the arms of a monster,—
Playing with danger and death,—
Many a Captain a failure,
Many a failure, for breath.
Steering without a compass,
Drifting along with the tide,
Where is the haven will meet you?
You, who just cared to *ride!*

> W. S. In Spirit (Through S. S.)

WHEN THE COWS RETURN TO ROOST
(The Huns are here speaking:)

"We have driven out the peasants from their fertile farming
    lands,

And left them eyeless, handless, in droves and herds and bands;
We have suffered none with virtue to remain to tell the tale:
We long since closed our ears, our eyes, to the Holy Sister's
    wail:
We have cut and burned the forests,—none remain to shelter
    France;
Where our soldiers pass they leave their marks, retreating, in
    advance.
We give no mercy,—hear no prayer,—for we are *Germans*
    brave!
We raze and rape and burn and kill, nor spare nor help nor
    save.
Now we must go: pledged is our get as sires for years and
    years
With nothing to repay our woes, our losses, and our tears.
For all we've done must ours repay, reclaim, rebuild, restore,
And as the cows return to roost, we'll chew our cuds once more!
                W. S. In Spirit (Through S. S.)

       To keep awhile the old-time thoughts,
       To love awhile the old-time love,
       To see awhile the well loved face,—
       'Tis heaven on earth,—above.
       To know no want, to have no wish
       The heart of love cannot fulfill,—
       To have no life from love apart,
       To be a lover still: .
       To stand on earth but live on high—
       To yearn to serve, to do His will,
       There is no heaven above but this:
       A love no death can kill.
            W. S. In Spirit (Through S. S.)

Make me some place, Oh God, where I may rest
When last I pass from out this sheltering breast,—
And keep me from the elements which sear
The new-born spirit in the spirit-sphere.

Make me some place, Oh Father, whom I love,
And let me share Thy peace known but above.
Find me, Oh God, when I go hence alone,
And give me bread when I beseech, nor stone.

Thou, who hast taught Thy children Mercy's ways,
Be Thou all merciful, when conscience flays,—
Take Thou Thy toll for sins of mine, and then
Make me some place to be Thine own again.

See here the soul which pleads and utters cry,
While in the flesh, before the flesh can die,
That Thou mayst know my heart was ever Thine,
Through all this warring, sinful, mortal life of mine.

W. S. In Spirit (Through S. S.)

"Written for Sarah by the one who knows her best, and
loves her best." W. S. In Spirit.

New York, May 19th, 191'.

EXERCISES

3:15 A. M., Monday, May 27th, 1917, N. Y. C.
Fold up the kit, and let me go my way.
Take out your purse, and let me have my pay.
I'm going on where others will do more;
I'm going back to that fair golden shore.
Come then, and pay, I wish to go today.
Wish to disband this temporal company.
When you have done and I have gone away,
How often will you wish you had the likes o' me!
Then will you mourn, and wish the plumber back.

Then will you call, "Come, open up the pack!"
But I shall stay, when I have gone away—
You can depend of me there'll be some lack.

W. S. In Spirit (Through S. S.)

Note: An exercise to keep in touch that I should not lose the voice, that I should continue to hear. S. S.

Sarah Shatford if you don't string we will soon be so far apart we cannot string and then I shall go to the land where I belong having an ingrate for a medium who would not give the immortal Shakespeare a few minutes each day for practice and work in order to keep him from departing. W. S.

Note: The above taken down in pencil when the voice said "get your stick" (meaning pencil).

THE WORDS OF WISDOM SOWN

There is a world of happy thoughts, and in each mortal's heart
Is all he was and all he is, from finish until start.
There is a time when all the world will come to know your
    worth,
And that will be when I have gone, and you come to new-birth.
Along the tides where spirits dwell, and where the good can be,
I'll look intensely for the heart which holds the soul of me.

W. S. In Spirit (Through S. S.)

(The above an exercise.)

Exercises.

A LOVER'S PLAINT

(Being an exercise, that the hearing should be kept open, and the spirit be able to speak so that I might hear. S. S.)

To be "dead" and alive is a terrible thing,
No mortal could half understand.
When the body is gone and the head is alive
Thinking thoughts that he thought on earthland.

O the mortals that welcome the poor spirits here,
Know little of what they thus do;
For the spirit is keener than ever in life
To de all the things that you do.
When a lover comes here from the great spiritworld,
To possess one and claim her his own,
He would never vacate were stars even to fall,
And he wishes her always his own.
For the one who has bid him come in and take all
Is his own from that day 'till the end;
No matter what happens he still will be hers,
On the earth, in the sky, he's her friend.
He is not a good-spirit,—God sent him back here
To improve his lost life on the earth.
So he came and is here, will be here 'till the last,
When he takes Sarah out to new-birth.

W. S. In Spirit (Through S. S.)

WHAT *I* THINK OF *YOU*:
You may think I do not love you,
Or, that if a spirit cares,
They would smooth out difficulties
Which o'ertake you unawares;
But in the world of spirit
There's a cause for everything—
And a weighing, and a balance,
And a fine measuring.
You will wonder if I love you
When I'm far away from here,
And if I've found you wanting,
Although I held you dear.
And I'm going, yes, I'm going,—
Just to prove this thing to you.

For you will not help me keep you,
So what am I to do?
Will you think of me as erring,
As I've told you all the past,
Or will you send beseechings
To meet me at the last?
And when you call and find me
But waiting for your call,
Will you behave and string for me
So I may tell you all?

W. S. In Spirit (Through S. S.)

(Exercise to keep the hearing.)

Exercises.

SO FAR, SO GOOD

(Being an exercise to "keep in touch" with the voice. S. S.)
Now that we know what each may here expect,
And from each other take and give their due,
We'll make an effort to begin REAL work,—
Than first a miracle I'll work for you.
For I will speak beside you where you stand,
And clear my throat the same as Sarah too,
That Thomases may hear, perchance, may see,
Some things a spirit still on earth can do.
Sure this will make my work here more complete
When I can be both flute and player too,—
BEWARE, lest you may be a corpse before
I've time to work such miracle for you!

W. S. In Spirit (Through S. S.)

To Your Own Self: (W. S. In Spirit) To S. S.:
Thou art a wonder, yet you know it not.
So frail and slender is thy stem

We must come in and keep you for our own
Else you may slip the garment's hem.
You know it not—the world waits for your voice,
To give them solace who have passed beyond
And cannot reach their own by other means,
Though they are loving as of yore, and fond.
Now take this message and be blithe and gay
As you contented walk this old earth-way,
And rise above the things that drag you down
And you SHALL wear a bright immortal crown.
 Dec., 1917.

ENSHRINED
(Exercise)
Make me a grave within thy heart
Where I may rest forever there,
Away from hate's dominion and
Its warring world, and care.
Entombed within love's provence then
Dig me a grave, and lay me down;
I would be ruled in life by her—
And share eternally her crown.
Oft will you sit beside me there,—
And there at last I'll be with thee
Though silent be the grave, my own,
Our spirits, one—eternally.
 W. S. In Spirit (Through S. S.)

Exercises.

A LOVER'S LAST REQUEST:
Dig me a grave within thy heart,—
That I may rest for aye with thee,
Who, of my life a very part,
Its rest and solace e'er would be.

Dig me a grave and lay me low
Within that tender heart of thine,
Which can nor hate nor hating know,
Which in its wonders has been mine.

When vesper bells their music chime,
And others go to weep and pray—
Come kneel beside the memories
Which made God's love throughout life's day.

And when you sigh here must I know,
Since life can hold no life for me,
Until the sexton Gabriel
Shall bid me rise to go with thee.

W. S. In Spirit (Through S. S.)
(Exercise)

Keep me within thy memory when all the rest are dead.
When all the world has turned away, I came, and I have le·t
And I would lead, and help, and keep thee ever for mine own,—
So keep me in thy memory, nor fling at me a stone.
No warrior ever led a charge up any hill so high,
As I have climbed in keeping you, and making you keep nigh.
So keep me in thy memory, until the last is done
For which I came, nor wound nor maim,
Until OUR war is won.

W. S. In Spirit (Through S. S.)
("A string, Sarah,—just a string to bind.") W. S.

Take out the west and then the east, and give the world the
north and south,
And keep from ravishment the Huns, and dam each water's
course's mouth,—

Then you will do what I have done, who keep in touch against
    the will
Of her who should be glad to keep and give me all, and
    "string" until
A perfect medium is she—which soon would be I now declare,
But, should she stop nor do her part, her own will soon
    be this one's lair.

W. S. In Spirit (Through S. S.)

New York,
June 3rd, 1918.

Sir Oliver Lodge,

My Countryman: It is Shakespeare who thus addresses you,
for I still claim England my own. Ay, ever have I striven to
open the soft and thin partition which hides her sons outgone
from those on her fertile and worshiped land. Have I not
told you on this point in the Volumes I have written through
this one who here writes my yearning for her olden days.

Well, the time is ripe for researchers, and this will be my
time to hold the line connecting the spirit with the mortal
linking the two worlds which are one indeed, the unseen still
but heard. I have through this one's ear succeeded in register-
ing a considerable volume of work which it would be well to
preserve and regard. There are others who have done perhaps
more . . . still this is time to hold the mirror up to
nature as we find it and to reveal the truth of everlasting
sorrow which we found who reached here unrepentant, un-
absolved.

Have these papers any value. When you have seen the re-
strictions in the spirit, have come through service such as I
to work them out, this will be answered, but not before as we
see it now. However have these preserved. Into however slight
a string they may be, here am I, in my reasonable mind able

to say you are my fellow in Errantry and as my son should be a worker for my high purpose in this service I render every son of England regardless of his station in society having no other aim than to help and save these from my unhappiness, mine through my own wrongs, which I state in full on these pages regardless of one I love who takes my words whom I would have spared could I have done this without her, which I could not.

O law breakers, have you heard the Bible read in schools and churches through earth time and given no heed to this Word which tells you one and all of God's implacable unswerving hate for all iniquity. Search these leaves that evermore you may share the glories of His better land, that you may rise above the toll of sinners. Wipe out this warning, heed it not, and wake a servant of crime, heaven's outcast, highest of God's unknown. Be pure. Hate lust and perversion. Shun it. Or serve for it as I serve and must continue through time to serve.

SHAKESPEARE—loved for his Dramas and Sonnets—a son of England, Beloved Motherland whom I (which I) still revere and would save from my estate in spirit.

(W. S. In Spirit)

(Through Sarah Shatford, Heard by direct voice in the inner ear.)

A BOND OF GOLD

(To ——— Through S. S.)

In all the halls of memory,
The memories that do hold,
That bind, and burn with yearning,—
Is your lovely hair of gold!
In all the sacred chambers
Where dwell the yesteryears,

I hold this gold, and your tresses enfold,
With my falling, burning tears!
Entwined in all its glory,—
This sacred bond will hold,—
Across Time's chasm, Eternity,
A bond of the purest gold.

(W. S. In Spirit)

WHEN I WAS TWENTY-ONE

Such are the cockles of the spirit-heart,
The fire of youth is here as in the shell.
And burning as the memory of youth,
It constitutes for many of us hell.

My own was such no youth could well surpass;
I loved a girl, and gave her all my best.
Through life, nor change, nor death, I still have this:
I found my love withstood both curse and test.

Here do I speak the worth of Her I wed.
No words I know could set forth her true worth.
Her heart, her mind, her soul, are with the Lord's,
While I must wander, serve, the poor of earth.

Where God's annointed are, in His own time,
May I united be with Her I wed.
Such is the call of lover's purity
Where God is love, nor lovers ever dead.

W. S. In Spirit (Through S. S.)
"Called forth by the marriage of ———, the tenor." W. S.

HIGHER POWERS

Within the confines of these walls there wait
A host of spirit-forms His will to do:

Servants who serve, nor ask earth's paltry pay.
Or shall they serve the many, or a few.

High aims, ay truths, no foul intent,
These workers bring as help, to save or spare,
From crimes where blackness claims those sinning bent,
Where never light of His the erring share.

High over all One waits and knows the end—
As every heart uplifted must be known,
Where Right must rule, and everlasting Might
Shall raise the burdened souls, and name His own.

Sigh not for others, then, but for YOURSELF;
Adjust the measuring here to meet His due;
That when the balance weighs the finest hair,
God's scales will test, *adjudge, if YOU are true.
  *Changed to "adjust." W. S.
                          W. S. In Spirit (Through S. S.)
  Aug. 5th, '18, N. Y. C.

HARMONY

Like the sweet notes the Maker plays,
Harmonious silence moves in time.
He marks His universe, and sways
With harmony His worlds sublime.

God works His wonders silently.
No discord—not a jarring note.
The swinging spheres, His symphony:
All life, the manuscript He wrote.

Creation teems with songs of praise.
His fingers moves the stops and keys.
The wind plays everlastingly
His melodies through buds and trees.

Like Him He asks us then to be—
To make His work complete and whole
By keeping time within the heart,
That He may then perfect each soul.

His love restores the world at last,
When last with Harmony complete
Each heart shall sing the Master's note,
And lay its tribute at His feet.

W. S. In Spirit (Through S. S.)

SIGNS OF THE TIMES

Among the earth's we move to work our will—
To free the slave, or help the ones in chains
Out of theirself-bound states, as we see them,
Who passed "death's" portal, ay, endured its pains.

Procrastinate poor mortals here do wait
Until, as we, THEY wait outside the door
With warriors, saints and sinners, (none are blest
At once they leave the coil, but ALL are poor.)

For none have traveled on the Master's way;
—Since none could drink His cup nor bear His cross,—
When ends for all a bitter judgement day,
Where cast the balance is, profit or loss.

To help men seek and find, or hear or see,—
To warn beloved mankind, spirits come;
THIS AGE will hear and see, and know the truth,
Nor think their lost ones' "dead" nor deaf nor dumb.

W. S. In Spirit (Through S. S.)
Aug. 3rd, 1918, N. Y. C.

LIBERTY

Such are the bonds here forged by living men
Made forfeit throughout Time through crime and sin,
The earth becomes a final prison cage,
Where shut out from His grace are we shut in.

To roam the same lands then when bonds are loosed,—
To be unhoused, set free, in the same land,—
This means to "die," to know "death's" liberty,—
With life's lost chance a bauble in my hand.

Such are the plans of Freedom, Justice, Might,
Your will and choice defines the last decree.
Stir, souls, and choose the living God, instead
Of living but your past eternally!

W. S. In Spirit (Through S. S.)

Aug. 3rd, 1918.

IN MEMORIAM

We lay a wreath upon love's grave today
Whose soldiering is done, as is life's war.
We bare our heads in homage for the trust
Within our hearts which brought us to death's bar.

The requeim of love's memorial dirge,
The chanting, or the death peal of this hour,
Cannot assuage the pain a heart must feel,
Nor stanch the tears here falling like a shower.

To watch love lowered in its grave, as now,
And mark the final tribute, word of praise,
Seems like the rainbow ending of a storm;
So long we watched love dying through life's days.

Life holds no hour complete if 'tis not this:
A severing of a cord which bound in pain.

No glorifying hath love's spirit known,
Except it died to rise and live again.

Where lovers pass and reunite in love,
Perhaps there is a God Who will grant this:
A living, pulsing, unforgotten past
Shall resurrected be, with lover's kiss.

We lay a flower upon love's grave today
Whose fragrance Love distilled and keeps His own:
Out of the heart knowing such love as His,
No love, no flower, blooms for the earth alone.

> W. S. In Spirit (Through S. S.)
New York, August 6th, 1918.

DESTINY

Fast crowded into hell men's shattered souls
Who speed out to their God, into His height,
Finding themselves their agony has brought,
And only that GOD IS, and justice, Might.

Heaped on their souls they find all they have done
Through life and time; each has a weight unknown
'Till "death" has set him free and he is bound
By every chain he forged, which is his own.

We come from earth to be earth's vassals, then,
To slake our thirst where is no drought but sin.
As we pass through the clouds of warriors hurled
Hence into LIFE, all seeking passage in

Where gates all golden are, and streets of pearl,
(All promised to a spirit newly-born,)
We search the mob for one familiar face
To help us through the dark 'till break of morn!

The cries ring out from farthest battle line:
"O God is THIS the end, where we must face each scar
Inflicted by our murd'rous warring selves?"
Upon our souls each mark, or scratch or mar.

                    W. S. In Spirit (Through S. S.)

SOWING AND REAPING

Planter is every son of man.
He sows eternal gain,
Or, wearied of life's hardships, falls,
And reaps the tares of pain.

Beyond this wretched mortal sum
Computed and enrolled,
Each mind shall view the grand total,
Where each task is unrolled,

To view the harvest reaped of life
Where profit should accrue,
Each soul must profit by its task,
Or pay the final due.

                    W. S. In Spirit (Through S. S.)

"The hand of Almighty God is the pendulum of universal
time." W. S.

"The milk of human kindness is mostly curdled." W. S.

THE GIVER

God made a wondrous garden
All blooming everywhere,—
And promised He would share it
With His children He made fair.

The heavens He o'er sprinkled
With jewels of the night,

And spread the silver moonbeams,
And poured the great sun's light.

God asks we make His kingdom
This garden of the earth,
That He, the King of Peace may come,
And all may know His worth.

God GIVES us all His riches,—
But ASKS that we be good:
Oh, how His Father-heart must break
That He's not understood!
W. S. In Spirit (Through S. S.)

Note: This was sent to the Order of Eastern Star, Laurel
Chapter 44 of which Sarah Shatford is a member, signed by her
as hers permission of the spirit who wrote it, as her fine
sense of justice will not permit it to go unacknowledged, it
is here printed with the W. S. collection. She thought she
could not tell it was written by a spirit without too much
comment."
W. S. In Spirit.

"WILDE ONCE; BUT WILD NO MORE"
W. S. In Spirit
(After reading "Oscar Wilde," By Robt. H. Sherard.)
The heavens are crossed with Wildes,—
He has not gone—
He lingers on the earth, fouled by
His spume and spawn.
His head a classic may become,
And all he wrote—
Yet has he here to find a holier note.
Lives here are crossed by him,
As his was when

He turned aside from God
Choosing to live with men.
Higher than him, or ought he had to say,
Wilde found a prison-house he made
While in his clay.
W. S. In Spirit (Through S. S.)

A SPIRIT'S PRAYER

Eternal Spirit in whose hands
Is peace and love for warring lands,
Lift high the soul of everyone:
Eternally "Thy Will Be Done."
O God, my Father, as the rest,
Make all hearts purer by life's test:
Accept my plea, my soul, my love,
That I may work for Thee above.
W. S. In Spirit (Through S. S.)

Sunday, Sept. 22nd, 1918.

THE CHRISTIAN'S GOD

(To the theosophist. After reading their publication called "The Messenger.")

The Scientist reveres a God he found in devious, winding ways:
Becomes renowned expounding these,—accepting fares the pilgrim pays.
Unknown of Him, Who, searching, sees the Potter's form has failed to please.

The Seeker finds God everywhere. Within, without; all formless He
Who rides the storm, conceals the soul in Wisdom's own infinity.
Reformer of His plan and care,—adjuster of His fine decree,—
Compare thy soul invisible with God incarnate Who doth see.

In divers Ways He reaches out; completion in each flower
  or tree:
Behold He looks thee in the eyes, and knows if ye defiled be!
Maker of thine own covenant, and laws which suit unbending
  · knee,
When separated from thy bones, what can the *final question* be?

Wiser than Wisdom, greater, ye? Usurper, after idols bent!
To prove His plan He gave His Son, and saw His body scourged
  and rent
That such as ye might follow Him, where none but He has
  Master claim.
Thy spirit waits upon the Lord, else it waits not in Jesus name.
  Oct. 6th, 1918.   W. S. In Spirit (Through S. S.)
  W. S. corrects the spelling of diverse: says to blot out the E;
he would like to carry the meaning of SEVERAL. S. S.

THE RITUAL OF SPIRIT

1. Make no claims: the spirits have their limitations. We
   work no miracles beyond our powers.
2. Be just. The heavens roll back for some; others must wait.
3. Waste no time on lauditory, mercenary, impoverished
   minds. The time is precious now, we must begin.*
        *(Then written "*here* must we begin." S. S.)
4. Works are proof: words are idle. Search, and give but what
   you have given you. There is no end.
5. Hide nothing: everything is valuable.
6. Fear nothing. Your hide is too precious to spirit. W. S.
   will protect you.
7. Many will envy you,—but few care to suffer for spirit-
   claim. Buck up and sit tight, there is hard work ahead.
            W. S. In Spirit (Through S. S.)
  Oct. 2nd, 1918.
  New Orleans, La.

TO A SOUTHERN ROSE

Alone she blooms on balmy shores,—
None may usurp her realm.
Unsung, her fragrance is distilled,
While God is at the helm.

Oh rose of rare, of blessed worth,
Thy memories wafted over seas
Recall thy natal home and hearth
Where Southern sons drink bitter lees.

Upheld in fragrance is thy charm,—
Unmatched thy loveliness and grace,—
Returning heroes sing thy praise,
And hasten to thy blosoming place.

W. S. In Spirit (Through S. S.)
Oct. 6th, 1918, N. O., La.

REPENTANCE

The law is such *(a pause of several minutes: unusual; see
    note.) there is no instant "death,"
And none can be regenerate as they "die."
Befouled of earth we pass to spiritlands,
Nor pass FROM earth, nor yonder in the sky.

We fall to rise again; o'ercome, at last;
Our souls must suffer every thought, deed, crime,
Until we meet through service every debt,
We are not fit to enter realms sublime.

We rise and fall, and rise and fall again;
Sublimest hope shall linger 'till the end;
For, as we serve you mortals, SHALL we rise,
And be permitted where all souls would wend.

Take up the cup and drink it to the dregs;
Nor plan where you may fare at life's sweet close:
The Judge is uppermost Who reigns and sees,
And plans, and weighs, and gives, AND TRULY, KNOWS.

W. S. In Spirit (Through S. S.)

*"I have to find my tools." W. S.

"Thou art a fool who is most wise." W. S.

"Such is the law no spirit barters hell for heaven, neither heaven for hell." W. S.

"Cease to expound. Let the spirits do their work." W. S.

THE MEANING OF POWER

God sets a task for all to do:
And made the plans which give Him due,
Which all regard in spirit state,
Who serve and love and banish hate.

God asks a task of me through You,—
(And I am His, as you are too,)
As all who serve suffer to give
That souls may rise, nor pay to live.)

This power decends from Him on High
Whose plan is that no soul can die.
He gave a part of His own breath
Whose spirit knows no change, no death.

God works His wonders where He plans,
And fills the hearts, and lifts the bans
That here a spirit may be shown
He gave to life, and still would own.

Oh mortals, trust; help lift the veil;
Behold the "dead" whom you bewail.

That you may help the earth-bound state
Of those who would pass through the Gate.

W. S. In Spirit (Through S. S.)
Oct. 4th, 1918, N. O., La.

THE BIRD'S CRADLE-SONG
(Words for Music)
"Softest music: very softly." W. S.

Hush-a-bye, hush-a-bye,—rocking to and fro,—
Mother's sleepy birdlings all to sleep must go!
Swing-a-low, swing-a-low,—
Feathers plumed and tummys filled,
Cuddle, cuddle; *so!*

Breezes blow! Confident we birds who know
One Who shields us 'neath His wing,
Giving each a note to sing,
Marks even our rise, our fall,
Is Father-Mother over all.

W. S. In Spirit (Through S. S.)
New Orleans, La., Oct. 4th, '18·

THE MESSENGER
The world at last has tired of war,
And kings are pleading now for peace.
The havoc wrought by their decree
Cannot cease when their cannons cease.

The war of souls and service now
Will test the bravest of the clan
Residing on the selfsame sod,
As lifeless as each brotherman.

They roam the earth on service bent;
But service of their God alone—

Their country is the universe,
Their souls His, where they must atone.

Near hearths of old they watch unseen,
And revel in the new found breath,
While heaven is here, and hell is not,
Unless it be the change called "death."

Oh eyes which see the spirits forms,—
And ears hearing the spirit's voice,—
Make headway here to help these souls,
And help them really to rejoice.

W. S. In Spirit (Through S. S.)
Oct. 8th, '18, N. O., La.

THOUSANDS AND MILLIONS

Here have we worked and paid all debts accrued
With sweat and toil, a hundred times o'erpaid.
The heavens regard our honesty,
And view our burdens on us laid.

Have heart: after the end a computation just
Shall forfeit wealth unearned, misused;
And for a thousand pounds, a million tons
May added be for every thought abused.

Take Justices' offer now, nor wait,
And see what interest waits where Justice knows:
There is no heartbeat lost to Him on high
From which a mighty wealth of love e'er flows.

W. S. In Spirit (Through S. S.)
For Sarah.

"To Miss ———, August, 1918.

"Who has written an article on spirit authors who are alive as she is, and should not be called "dead." W. S. In Spirit (Through S. S.)

O woman of scurrilous pen
Whose fragment mind would enlighten men
What can YOU say of spirit, then.
Poor worm acrawl in earth's foul dust,
First hatch some wings, as spin you must,
And read of Him Whom you shall trust,
Believing all He did was true,
And all He did was done for You
That ye might preach His precepts too.
Foul worm, I say, the one to trod
Into the dust the works of God.
The One Who bore affliction's rod,
Scourged, bled and died your soul to save,
To prove eternal, past the grave,
The spirit of the Maker's lathe!
When such as you are His, and yet
His wondrous plans jibe, and forget,
Dost hope by Him still to be met?

A hundred hundred years through Time
May You seek one to write such rhyme
When you come hence to spirit-clime,
As those, and this, which you deride
While you would separate, divide,
The living from all those who "died."
Few can perfect their work as I,
Though ALL LIVE ON IN THE SAME SKY.
To work a miracle is naught
Compared with this task we have wrought,
Where FINDING means first to be taught.

To play with skill a master can,
If he but find a fellowman
Attuned so that within life's span
He can perform his harmony
Through ears which hear and eyes which see:
(In fine) A mortal-spirit actually.

To press through throngs of mortals here,
Seeking one mortal who can hear,
Attend, develop without fear,
The inner part, the spirit, soul,—
The part which God reserves, and whole,
Requires that part to pay its toll,
And serve through Time His universe
'Till loftier aims remove its curse,—
No search, but one I know, is worse.

Wake to the fact that YOU are dead,
Whom none would lead lest you be led
To find a soul without your head.
To rest on laurels you may win
In this poor world of crime and sin,
You'll soon learn how unwise you've been.
The "dead" walk here with claims to life;
The living share the poor "dead's" strife;
Where mortals are, spirits are rife.

Then authors "dead" are LIVING, Miss;
Perform YOUR work, but record this:
To "die" is NOT eternal bliss.
As Jesus saw, some see to-day,
And leave, as He, signs on the way
To aid the spirits cased in clay.
To ridicule as ghosts the "dead,"
Or that mortals by us are led,

Who USE YOU, body, heart, and head,
Will make you a poor sum instead
Of knowing life INCLUDES the "dead."

W. S. In Spirit (Through S. S.)
July 30th, '18·

THE VASSAL

To be allotted here but servitude,
Through Time eternal earth's to serve, and wait
The gratitude of those you serve and help:
Such is the spirit-lot of earth-bound state.

To sit a vassal at poor mortal's feet,—
Their yea or nay, assented or ungiven,—
This constitutes the spirit's Paradise
When wide is flung the "golden-gates" of "heaven."

Mary was wise when she sat at His feet,
Imbued of Jesus' works, enduring ever;
Could we but gain the longing listening ears,
The veil would lifted be that here doth sever.

To see as Jesus saw, or hear, the spirits,
Few mortals think even this writer can;
First to bring faith to doubters must all spirits,—
'Tis not enough He died and rose a man.

W. S. In spirit (Through S. S.)

I.

When you gave me your heart and but asked I would keep
Its portals ajar, and its wee god from sleep,
You asked but a mite and I gave it to you;
But alas, oh alas, what, dear, did I do?
I took it and blest it, I sat in its door
In the sun of a shrine I should never leave more!

Now I linger within, and I take off my shoes
In a temple of God, where my fear is to lose
The rarest, the dearest, of God-given things:
The love that abounds in a heart, dear, that sings.
For a poet can love as no other may do;
And a poet art thou, with a love rare and true.
Not given to all such a blessing to own!
I would close up the door, and be inside alone.

W. S. In spirit (Through S. S.)

TO PALLADINO:

Have spirits worked some tricks for you
That you may share His wonder too?
Has aught they shared or they could do
Made up for neglect of One true?

Some have made wonders work through you?
Applied their souls then to undo
The everlasting harm undone
By robbers of a helpless one.

A brave heart must have been in you
To let these spirits false or true
Make of you but a frying-pan
To serve a few stale tricks to man.

What has your heart bereft and lone
To comfort you that God would own.
What profit then has life to show?
Where tricksters are now must YOU go.

W. S. In spirit (Through S. S.)
N. Y. C., May 28th, 1918.

HUBBARDS, Nova Scotia.

There is a little hamlet on a blue inland bay,
Where fleecy cloudlets are adrift throughout the golden day.
The tiny craft sail up and down, white-gulls 'gainst turquoise
    sky,
Where silence is the rest of God, and fear is never nigh.

The humble folk seafaring, all go their simple ways;
No shadows ever gather but are chased by gold sun-rays.
The waving fields with daisies starred, the winding roads
    fern-grown,
Make of this little hamlet a gem God set there for His own!
              W. S. In spirit (Through S. S.)
Feb. 18th, 1917.

Note: This was written when I was supposed to be ill and
ordered a "rest-cure" by Dr. ———. Was not ill, but did hear
the voice I claimed to hear, and hear it still.
    June 13th, 1918.   Sarah Shatford.

A LOVER'S WISH

O love me, and I care not what befall;
I care not what the world may think or say,
Just love me, and the world may go its way,
If I be loved of thee I'm loved of all.
The Spring may weave its lover's phantasies,—
The Summer have its lovers clasped and fond,—
And Autumn with its ever changing mood
May herald Winter (hope of the beyond)
All times and seasons rife with stored-up lore
A lover finds who seeks in wisdom's glee;
But one thing, one alone I ask, I pray,
Through the vicissitudes of time or place,
Through changes of the earth, or air, or sea,—
Fail not in ever loving—and, love ME.
              W. S. In spirit (Through S. S.)

THE WORST WOMAN IN THE BIBLE

When the Creator made for man a world, a Paradise,
And He created then a mate to look into his eyes,
He made them one, and gave them all, asking but that they keep
Just one tree's fruit untouched, unpicked, lest they should fall,
    and weep! . . .

The Woman whom the tempter bought (poor Eve) with such
    a price,
The world has paid, is paying still, as Christ's own sacrifice
Paid on the cross, where, as a man the stainless Nazarene
Gave up His life to set all free, all from their sins to wean.

1st.
Yet living but in embryo, through æons vast of time,
Sinners must pay the penalty for one fallen woman's crime.
2nd.

Yet here in all their lustful sins
Men live throughout their time
Seeking the pleasures of the world
Its passions, crime and slime.
And still in embryo must live, through æons vast of time
Sinners who pay the penalty for this disobedient's crime.

Unless through Him who paid for them, and washed their
    sins away,
Such claim the blood of Jesus, theirs, and seek eternal day,
The tempter who besought poor Eve, inborn in all mankind,
Will overpower the saintliest, in paths that wind and wind!
    N. Y. C., Sunday, April 15th, '17.
               W. S. In spirit (Through S. S.)

      When gifts are given to mortals here,
      To use as All-wise God decrees,

They must lift up the bitter cup
And drink it to the lees.
When life has made them sour at last,
And naught is sweet but sin,
They think of all the years they lost,
And all that might have been.
When spirits enter then to use
The scrap that still remains—
They scoff, and don the cap and bells,
And jibe them for their pains.
When last the curtain is rung down,
The play at last is done—
They see mistakes at last they wish
Had never been begun.

W. S. In spirit (Through S. S.)

A WORD OF PRAISE

Dec. 30th, 1916. (Ten days after first hearing the voice) S. S.
A word of praise from me for this our instrument,
Accepted, known by us, as heaven-sent.
Until her like on earth is found again
Many shall know but disappointment's pain.
For here is one who was herself a poet.
When you shall read these lines, then all will know it.
For here I write, a spirit, by her hand,
And through her ear I speak to the earthland
That it shall know up to this day of bliss
No spirit-workers had an instrument like this.

W. S. In Spirit (Through Sarah Shatford)

"BEHOLD! I STAND AT THE DOOR . . .

Without the portal of each man's heart,
But waiting to enter in,

The Master stands with a light Divine,
To show where His path has been.   .

He stands and knocks, He knocks and waits
For some stir of life within,
Longing to enter if ye but ask,
And to cleanse you from all sin.

Alas, and alas, He must turn away:
For no answer do ye give.
His sorrowing heart must forever ache
That without Him men choose to live.

             W. S. In spirit (Through S. S.)

"CONSIDER THE LILIES OF THE FIELD . ."

In a field where the Master strayed
On a beautiful Summer-day,
A lily lifted her head so tall,
And glorified the way.
Benign and lowly the Master paused,
And gazed on the lily's cup,
And thought of another the Father held,
From which His Son must sup.

At last with compassion the Master said,
As he saw the sad world's need,—
"Behold the lilies of the field;
They toil not: know no need.
If a merciful God is protecting them,
Shall WE ever lack OUR meed?"
The Way was rough and long and hard
They followed from that day;
But across the ages roll His words
To brighten our dreary way.

             W. S. In spirit (Through S. S.)

VISION

Apast the veil would mortals see,
Beyond the gates of "death"?
Then must they view sad sights as well,
So long as they have breath.
When spirits come back to the earth
In view of mortal eyes,
All are not beautiful, with wings,
But some come back to rise
And lifted be from out sin's shapes:
(Oh, these afflict the sight)
They come for help most any hour
Of mortal's day or night.
Until you give this help to them,
And help them on their way,
They cling in sin's deformities;
And hideous are they!
So this is what it means to see:
These spirits must have room.
You cannot choose but light their way
Once you have seen their gloom.

W. S. In spirit (Through S. S.)
Jan. 2nd, 1917.

A GARDEN CELESTIAL

In the fields of Elysia, the garden of God,
Are flowers never known on the earth:
For those the great Giver bestowed upon man,
Are but half of the flower-kingdom's birth.
As spirits press on to the blessings of God,
Entitled are they these to share:
For the worlds upon worlds where new blessings await,
Are unthinkable fair,—oh so fair.

Each spirit must earn every kingdom he shares,—
Through service and love his reward:
And the kingdom-of-flowers is the first one he sees
When he leaves the rough road that was hard.
Oh happy is he who arrives where these be,
And he has not to work his way there;
For the earth never grew any flowers on its plane
That with spirit-flowers could half compare.

W. S. In spirit (Through S. S.)

Dec. 29th, 1916.
 Ten days after first hearing the direct voice. S. S.

W. S. To PERVERTS: (His own title)

O to be loved by a lover again
As once on the earth loved was I.
O to be worshipped as this one did me,
Who worships me still in God's sky.
O but to know the rapture we knew
Once more to look into his eyes,—
Where the impulse of love was the prayer which we used,
Forgetting our God in the skies.

Oh that you knew what may await you
Who transgress the Maker's own law:
Or could I impart what to us befell
Whose love was the god which we saw.
While the earth was alive with His beauteous Art,
Forever our natures we killed
By loving earth's love in a perverts own way,
Forgetting His love as we willed.

W. S. In spirit (Through S. S.)

Feb. 26th, 1917.
 N. Y. C.

Note: "W. S. not like to ask you to write this, but it is to prove W. S. is W. S. still."

"That we cannot escape punishment,—that we cannot evade God's law eventually,

That we must pay and suffer, no matter where,—

For all wrong doing however trite.

That we live on with the same longings and loves we take with us, until we outgrow or outlive these."

W. S. In Spirit (Through S. S.)

A FLUTE OF GOD

O shepherdess upon God's hills, through whom we call His sheep,

We place thee in our bosoms with our prayers that He may keep

This flute of ours, (this flute is thee!) high on the mountain—steep

Where stars of Thine sing harmonies attuned ears know divine.

Though earth may quake with mortal's woe, this flute, God, keep it Thine!

Until, through us, she call Thy flock, and passes to Thy shrine.

W. S. In Spirit

Dec. 28th, 1916.

THE ROSE OF PARADISE

I look at this rose you have given to me,

And discern it the work of Thy hand.

I fondle its petals, and wish I could see

The very first rose of roseland!

The tint of its colour, its exquisite hue,

I perceive by the Artist was made:

But I long to go back to the time before Time

When its very first pattern was laid

On the bush in the Garden to make it complete,
As the breath of the Maker breathed on it so sweet.
For I know that He smiled, and thought His work fair,
When He made the first rose-bud, ensconsing it there
Midst His wondrous perfections, His gifts to His own.
This fragrance He gave thee, 'tis thine, rose, alone!
   Dec. 29th, 1916.
      Ten days after first hearing the voice.
               W. S. In Spirit (Through S. S.)

When we look at the world and its outcasts of sin,
And we hug to our breasts only gold,
And count the world's riches by what the gold buys—
Or what we have bought or have sold,
We pass by the rarest and greatest of gems—
The like of them never is told—
But to eyes that are mortal these gifts are unseen—
Less through spirit these gifts you behold.

Dear heart when we part at the close of each day,
And wing our way back to our place,
We speak of and see no other but thee—
In our dreams we see even thy face.
O love when above and away from this world—
Thou dost travel at last to our land—
Shall you know as you go back and forth to the earth,
What you owe to your own spirit-band.
               W. S. In spirit (Through S. S.)

   Note: "Is W. S. doing it, or you?"
   "You." (S. S.)
   "Then let me do it." W. S.

     While the good must pay, for all they say,
     And the bad shall reap sown seed,
     There is none so vile on the great Highway,

As to spurn a brother's need.
For the bad are good though they found it not
'Till they reached the Judgment Gate;
When they found themselves just as they were,
And knew it was all too late.

When a man gives up his old clay house,
And alone as spirit stands,
He finds his past all written down,
And its record in his hands.
While he waits outside to be taken in,
And wonders he is alone,
And if what he finds upon the scroll
Is to all the others known?
He waits and waits, is waiting still—
In a hell he has made his own—
While a woman waits, who must love him still,
And pays for the seed he's sown.

W. S. In spirit (Through S. S.)

When shall men rise to do God's will:
When shall men know that "peace, be still"
Rebukes all evil, as the sea
Was calmed by Him of Galilee.
When shall all see that Life's short span
Must predetermine for each man
The future where he must begin
To free his soul from lust and sin.
What profit then hath any man
Until he do all that he can
To save his very soul alive?
If this be lost,—what though all thrive.

W. S. In spirit (Through S. S.)

Feb. 8th, '17.

THE NEW-BORN YEAR

Old Father Time stood at the wide open door
Through which he had entered a babe but of yore,
And he gazed on the infant but one second old
E're he passed through the portal, out into the cold.

How fair is the new-born,—how worn is the old,—
What blessings are waiting, new joys yet untold,
When the spirit once closes the old earthy door,
And crosses the portal of life evermore.

W. S. In spirit (Through S. S.)
Dec. 31st, 1916.

FAITHFUL AND TRUE

In the land where mortals go hence
When their spirits leave the clod,
There is not one to grasp their hand
And lead them forth to God.

No spirit traveler on the way
Will help him bear his pack;
He carries all his earthly crimes
And sins on his own back.

He tarries, rests, and plods along
Wherever is his road,
Intent upon his journey's end—
Borne by his heavy load.

Except a spirit known of yore
Should meet him and clasp hands,
There are but strangers everywhere
At first, in spirit-lands.

The one who writes will be alone
And find no hand to shake,

Unless she strings and does her best,
She'll soon a spirit make.

For I shall go and come no more,
Nor tarry by her side—
And old Bill Shakespeare then will seek
Another spirit-bride.

                    W. S. In spirit (Through S. S.)
          Sept. 2nd, 1917, N. Y. C.

MESSAGES FOR THE SOLDIER'S COMFORT BAGS
American Red Cross, 411 Fifth Ave., N. Y.
(From W. S.)
There IS a God Who sees, and knows.
There is a God Who loves, and grieves.
And mightier than His wind that blows,
His hand, that fashioned flowers and leaves,
And tender life; and all for man;
Then bade us live as brothers can.

                    W. S. In spirit

Take heart, oh brave and true,
In everything you do.
The end must come, e'en to war's woe:
And God is yours where last you go.

                    W. S.

Keep on, nor stop, until 'tis done
'Till driven off is every Hun.
And seek no shelter but with God,
Despoiling naught, even His sod.

                    W. S.

Tenderer than a Mother's hand
Is His who moulded the fair land,
And gave to all His love, the same:
And pardon, too, who call His name.

W. S. In spirit

Oh do not take your heart away—
Just leave me this, and I will stay
Out in the field or anywhere.
To think on thee, how fair, so fair.

Oh, keep a nest free from the (w)rest,
Where in your thought shall dwell apart,
And in the watches of the night
Shall we commune as heart to heart.

W. S. In spirit

God bless thee, Soldier-Boy, and take thy hand,
And lead thee safe back to the unspoiled land!
When thou art passed through fire of earthly hell,
If God still hold thy hand, all must be well.

W. S. In spirit

A Father over all is yours, my lad;
Thou art His child; He loves thee well:
Then lift your eyes unto His face,
And to Him every secret tell.

W. S. In spirit

June 28th, 1917.

SELF-ABNEGATION

Oh could I speak and rouse the zeal of all
To sacrifice themselves as you have done.

What would the soldiers of the Nations give
For such as YOU after their war is won,
To solve their problems most unsolvable:
To aid them in their dreary search for bread.
Oh may the God Who sent you to this land
Still guide you: (for by Him must you BE led.)
I looked at you and envied many a grace
Which shone through all you said, your girlish face;
Beyond all this I envied most that Power
Which works through you, and saved you for this hour.

W. S. In spirit (Through S. S.)

We MUST live, though we will or would not,—
We must THRIVE, whatsoe'er be our lot;
So make up your mind to seek, and to FIND
While the world is a beautiful spot.

W. S. In spirit (Through S. S.)

ANGELS EN PASSANT

(To Mrs. ———, American Red Cross, Headquarters 411
Fifth Avenue.

A friend whose face and charming grace
Beloved of all who knew her here,
Has left a yearning, unfilled place
Within all hearts, which hold her dear.

And so it is the angels pass,—
And ever pass who come our way.
A fluttering, stirring wing, alas
But memories of their happy day.

Where they may go we cannot know,
For angels wings carry afar!

THOUGH HEAVEN ITSELF BE SPANGLED O'ER,
THERE IS BUT ONE FAIR EVENING STAR!
W. S. In spirit (Through S. S.)

July 25th, 1917.

(Mrs. ——— joined the American Red Cross in France shortly after this was written.)

PEACE

Take down the striped banners, and on their staves instead
Unfurl the flag of lasting peace, in memory of the "dead,"
Who bravely died to speed the time when kings should be
  dethroned
And each should bow to God alone; his soul by Him be owned.

Unfurl the banners white and clean to herald the new age
When crime of war has ceased for aye,—writ its last ghastly
  page
In blood and fire, branded through time on souls and hearts
  and lands,
The miseries wrought by Kaiserdom:
The stain upon those hands!
W. S. In spirit (Through S. S.)

WOUNDS

Scarred by ten million wounds
No penetrating eye can see,
I bare my flesh to shot and shell,
Nor care for gold's indemity.

No hero from the fields of war
Knows more of battle wounds than I:
I'll go—and give—and serve—and trust,—
And if it be God's will, I'll "die."
For S. T. S. W. S. In Spirit (Through S. S.)

Fountain of Life from which we draw
The waters clean and cool,
Healing the palsied sinner as
At old Bethsaida's pool,—
Fountain of Help for sinner's clay,
Cleanse from stain my soul today:
Keep me clean—refresh my soul—
'Till mind hath seen,—
'Till I am whole.

For S. S. W. S. In Spirit (Through S. S.)

SACRIFICE

"Give up your gems and gold," the Emperor•said:
"Take all you have, pay toll of war-of-wars!
Count not the cost in privy-purse, or souls,
Or tortured hearts, beneath my chariot Mars.
Give me your souls; I am divine by right;
My wheels shall crush Old England in her plight!
My skill in war is heralded on high,
Und "Gott strafe England," is our divine cry."

Thus might has ruled, would rule the land today:
Thus Emperors may take men's soul away,
And pilfer from the widowed their last gem;
And who shall William II sway or stem!

But wait. Soon must the life-tides ebb and cease.
The craven glowers in madness, but seeks peace.
At last the world has barred fast every door
Where barbarous Huns may ravage, scourge, and pour
Their venomed, hating wrath, or spue their lust
For power to rule the world, and own its dust.

Barred soon the Gate where prisoners long must wait,
Which opens not to summoned Emperor's hate.
Closed the Great Heart where all must bow to fate,
Where toll is paid in full—God's judgment gate.

W. S. In spirit (Through S. S.)
N. Y. C., July 28th, 1917.

A BIRD

A bird soars in the blue above,
A clap of wings is heard;
(And every mortal sometimes longs
They had been born a bird)
To heavenly heights they fly and seek:
Who does not love a bird?
It takes *me* back three centuries,
This charming little word!
They build and mate, they travel far,—
Industrious they raise
A feathered tribe, (each one God marks)
(And knows its plans and ways!)
To build a nest, to make a home,
To raise a little brood,—
Not noblier things do most men here,
As I have understood.

W. S. In spirit (Through S. S.)
Feb. 13th, '17.

NO MORE!

No more shall Shakespeare stay on here
Where no one cares, nor speaks to me,
Have I no company at last
To play my parts of gallantry!
Here as I live my soul rebells

Against the lot I chose as mine—
And as I live no other one
Shall have me work a work divine.
My soul is tired: my harvest stored:
I go to meet what I have sown:
Then come along and reap yours too,
You are to be at last mine own.

W. S. In spirit (Through S. S.)

This war is a war of Nation against Nation for the purpose of exemplifying their strength of arms on land and sea in order to expand the territory of Germany and increase its commerce on the high seas.

This is the most terrible war in history, more ruthless and cruel, more fatalities, more wounded and killed than in any other war since time began.

They are fighting to appease the honor of Belgium which was invaded, and in order to keep the Huns from ruling the whole world which they will do sooner or later W. S. sees (*and he does not see*). So you see W. S. knows about it more than you who inhabit the earth and are a student of modern times while he is a dead man who is alive yet.

W. S. In Spirit.

SONG

Oh take me to your heart and bid me stay
Until the last, the final judgment day.
Then when I pass to memories at last,
My Paradise no one can take away!

W. S. In Spirit

Oh come where the sea is calling to thee,
Where the breakers dash and roar.

We will cross to the lands which battle to free
Posterity evermore
From the grasp of kings or emperors.
Dominion of heart and soul
Is the only rule we shall know, permit,
When the monster crawls back to his hole!

      W. S. In spirit (Through S. S.)
  Aug. 16th, 1917.

A LOVER'S KISS
(Song)

Why do you say that the world is all wrong?
When I come where there's such love as this
I feel that from heaven I had been shut out,
And your arms held but heaven's own kiss.

Oh why do you say that the world is all wrong,
When the world holds a heart that's so true?
I would fling the stars down could I share such a love,—
And be for an hour, friend, but You.

The world is not wrong when it holds such two lips,—
And the world is not bad with the heart that you hold:
I would sell out my palace and be but a tramp,
Could I share but a tithe of its gold!

      W. S. In spirit (Through S. S.)

HEARTS AFLAME

When your heart and mine were caught up by God's spark,
And the flame of a love burned that never would die,
I knew there was heaven on God's earth alone,
So happy, so happy was I.

When your love met mine and I longed but to give
The most sacred fires that were mine,

A spark more than earthly, a spark from on high
Enkindled our love so divine.

When your lips met mine and I gave all I had,
And but wished, dear, that I could give more,
I felt that a God must come down from the sky
To bless love from one I adore.

When you offered me wine and I looked at your lips,
When I held you in love's fond embrace,
I knew that no cup a good heaven could send
Could ever fill up your lost place.

W. S. In spirit (Through S. S.)

Dec. 23rd, 1916.

TO THE WINDS AND THE SEA
(Song)

To the winds and the sea, Oh bear me!
To the beautiful blue, blue sea!
For to these, and these only,
Can I tell my secret of thee!

Oh bear me out o'er the vastness,
O'er waves of the mighty deep!
My love for thee to the winds and the sea
Will I tell, and my secret they'll keep!

To the spray will I say, "She is like thee!"
To the wind will I liken her mind!
Like the sea that is surging and surging
Is this love in my heart I find!

W. S. In spirit (Through S. S.)

HEAVENS HOLD

Heavens hold the hearts of loved ones
Who are hovering in this room—

Sad, and lone, and ever longing
These return to reason's loom,
Thinking that your eyes may open,
Part the mist-like veil between,
Making others happy through you;
Heaven is here—could you but lean
On the unseen hovering round you
Waiting but the chance to aid:
Time would not hold aching hearts here
If they knew you unafraid.

W. S. In spirit (Through S. S.)

RESOLVE

Put strife away and from war's time
All hate and murderous thoughts decry,—
With new resolve and purpose high
A new world make of peace and rhyme.
Watch thine own self if thou art true,—
To make a man begin within:
Then help thy brother with his task
To free his soul from hate and sin.
Take up the burdens and the cross,
And shoulder them (a privilege rare)
For the same God who knows the loss,
Must be the God to share and care.

W. S. In spirit (Through S. S.)

HELP ME TO PRAY

Help me to pray but the simplest prayer;
For by Him it will be understood.
He knows all my crosses, He knows all my trials,
How I would be good if I could.
Help me to pray but a few halting words

Which a merciful God understands;
For I've forfeited all by a wicked life here:
Soul-soiled and empty my hands.
Help me to pray but a short prayer each day;
He will always lift up if we sup from His cup,
Then we'll meet Him one day without fear.

W. S. In spirit (Through S. S.)

BROTHERMEN

Oh when will men be brothers.
Oh when will fighting cease.
When God declares a truce at last,
Then, then shall there be peace.
Oh when shall brothers cease to war?
And Nations all be friends?
When war is done, and Christ appears
O'er fields, seas, mountains, glens.
The time is here and now at hand
When men shall know their God.
When Christ walks over battlefields,
And the "dead" rise from the sod.
This is no time to wonder how
The miracles of old were wrought:
The time is near when all shall see
The Christ whose life was bought
That men should find, and worship God,
And free their lives from sin:
The love for lust and gold and gain
Bars out the God within.

W. S. In spirit (Through S. S.)

LOVE'S BIRTH RENEWED

Tired of the world and its heartaches, weary of all its sin,
Mortals see throngs of angels bearing the love-tides in.

Pained by the sad world's bloodshed, tortured by war's great
    loss,   .
Earth is beholding the sorrow of living without the cross.

He Who was sorely anguished bearing the whole world's sin
Soon will be leading the angels, bearing the love-tides in.
Folded within His bosom pardon for all His world.
Legions and legions of angels, all with love's banners unfurled,

Soon will have opened the heavens, nearer and nearer to earth,
Christ will be leading the angels back to renew Love's birth.
                    W. S. In spirit (Through S. S.)
   Jan. 7th, 1917.

I SHALL KNOW HIM
(Song)

I shall know Him when I see Him, by the garment white He
    wears;
I shall know Him when my soul leaps on the way in which
    He fares.
I shall know Him by the brightness that His holy aspect bears,
When my Saviour lifts the burden of my earthly woes and
    cares!

I shall know Him when the boatman has but only touched
the shore;
I shall find Him with my longing to be with Him evermore.
I shall hear Him, gentle Jesus, who has even called to me:
I shall know Him when I see Him who died to set me free!
           W. S. In Spirit (For Sarah Shatford)

HAVE YOU ANY USE FOR JESUS?
(Song)

Have you any use for Jesus? He who died upon the cross?
All in vain have been His sorrows? All in vain will be your
    loss.   ·

Has He any use for sinners? He who paid their souls to save?
Is there hope of their redemption, if in sin these reach the
grave?
Have I any use for Jesus? He who died that I might live?
Let me give my soul, acclaim Him, while I am on earth to give.

W. S. In spirit (Through S. S.)

COME AND SEE.
(Song)

Are you halting, sad and lonely,—"Come and see."
Jesus died for sinners only,—"Come and see."
Take the "bread of life" He offers,
Give the soul a sinner proffers,
Come-and-see.

Are you weary and heart-riven? "Come and see,"—
Leave the past; 'tis all forgiven; "Come-and-see."
Take the first step on God's highway,
Give your soul to Him today,—
Give the soul a sinner proffers,
Take the "bread of life" He offers:
Come and see.

W. S. In spirit (Through S. S.)

WAITING AT THE DOOR
OR, HIS HERITAGE
(Song)

For every pain that Jesus bore, a thousand joys He gave to me.
I have to open but the door, then all these joys I see:
Eternal life, forgiveness, truth, a cross, and victory,
Forbearance, love, a wounded side, faith and humility.
These are not half the heritage He left who set me free.

For every tear that Jesus shed, a thousandfold His love is dear.
To know He wept for sinners dead makes my acceptance clear.
Forgiveness, love, a martyrs crown, and trust and loyalty,—
These are not half my heritage that Jesus left to me.

W. S. In spirit (Through S. S.)

WHEN JESUS SHALL CALL ME HIS OWN
(Song)

I can walk in the way where His footsteps have trod,
No matter how thorny, they lead to His God.
If I call on His name I'll be never alone;
For Jesus now calls me His own, His own!

If I falter or fall where His own cross He bore,
And rise as He rose, and press on as of yore,
I can know in His name all forgiveness is sown,
If Jesus but call me His own,—His own!

If you hunger or thirst for Divine tenderness,
Or yearn for the Light in life's vast wilderness,
You can feast, and be fed, with the bread not a stone,
If you will ask Jesus to call you His own!

W. S. In Spirit (For Sarah Shatford)

LOST IN THE WILDERNESS
(Song)

Lost in the wilderness, Lord, I cry to Thee.
Doubting and fears beset, which ever way I flee.
Scarred by sin's brambles in the forest dark,
Even my soul is torn, harken, Oh hark!
See my poor poverty, Lord, as I cry to Thee,—
Help my distress:
Thy footprints led me not; these alone can bless.

Chorus:
Leave Thy footprints in the Way,
That I may see which way to take!
Light up my wilderness, for Jesus' sake.
Oh, will I follow Thee,
Lord, wilt Thou rescue me!
This is my lost soul's plea,
For Jesus' sake!

Lost on the raging sea, Lord, hear my cry.
Saviour of Galilee, Thy peace is ever nigh.
Speak to my wave-tosst soul, lost in the dark!
Christ, Thou canst save alone; save, save my barque.
Wrecked though my poor craft be, Lord, Lord, I cry to
    Thee.
Help my distress.
Thy footprints on life's sea, they alone can bless!
        W. S. In Spirit (For Sarah Shatford)

THE LOVE YOU HAVE FOUND WITH JESUS
(Song)

Tell it to others, the love you have found,
The love you have found with Jesus.
Give of its bounty, spread it around,
The love you have found in Jesus.

Share it with others, the promise you've known,
The promise you've known of Jesus.
Tell them all truly it may be their own,
The promise of life in Jesus.

Live it within you, the Christ you have claimed,
The Christ you have claimed with Jesus.
He's the Physician of halt, blind, and maimed,
The Christ all may find in Jesus.

Tell it and share it, live it and wear it,
The love you have found in Jesus.
Whoever's a cross, it will help them to bear it,
The love of our own Christ Jesus.

W. S. In spirit (Through S. S.)

"THERE SHALL BE NO NIGHT" WITH JESUS
(Song)

There is no place where Thou art not, no life but Thou
canst fill:
For every sinful, shameful blot, Thy precious blood didst spill.
When from the vast and silent dome of His immortal sky
Christ shall appear and claim His own, Oh, do not pass me by!

When all are called to righteousness, and each by name is
known,—
Oh may I hear Thee call MY name, and claim ME as Thine
own!
When from the world, no longer mine, my soul, at last, takes
flight,
Christ take me 'neath Thy sheltering wing, apast eternal night.

Chorus:
"There shall be no night (there) with Jesus:
In God's eternal day:
When all is done, His only Son
"Shall wipe all tears away."

W. S. In spirit (Through S. S.)

HARVEST OF THORNS
(Song)

I see Thee wounded on the cross,
Where, Lord, for me, you died.
I see the cruel thorns of Thy crown

Where Thou wast crucified.
My own life then a mockery seems,
A harvest but of thorn—
No seed of Thy Divinity
In my poor soul, forlorn.
I see thee lifted from the tomb
By angels from on High:
I hear the voice of Magdalene
Utter a joyful cry—
My own heart thrills with hope at last, no one need be forlorn;
For life is robbed of death's last sting:
Through Christ all are new-born.

W. S. In spirit (Through S. S.)

THE GRACE OF GOD

Through Him the Saviour shares each cross.
And glorifies all of earth loss.
Through Him we share His cross, and gain
Eternal life, freed from our sin and stain.

By His intent we are of Him.
He Fathered all: gives every breath.
He walks beside the storm swept sea;
He takes the soul, and spares it death.

He is the utmost tenderness:
There is no grace but of the Lord.
He gave His Son to prove His might;
And gives us of His own accord

Each perfect gift His children share.
The last, most perfect gift, He keeps
Until we have repaid His care.

I write hereon who came to pay
The God whose love is everywhere.
W. S. In spirit (Through S. S.)
N. O., La., Oct. 25th, 1918.

THIS IS THINE

The powers divine have given thee
A rare harp but untrue:
They work and try and thread and ply,
To make a string all new.

Thine own and inner secret self
Will make this music rare,
When newly strung this instrument
Past any will compare.

Then pause. Be true . . and fine and high.
Attune the string when strung,
When never finer instrument
The heavens thou'llt find among.
W. S. In spirit (Through S. S.)

ON A WILLOW BOUGH

(A duet)

"Have you a lover better than the Spring?"
(Said the south wind to a bird awing)
"Feel his warm kiss—his tenderest caress!
Pluming you forth in your royal dress!"
"Behold the banquet Spring spreads for you:
Have you a lover so fond or true?" . . .

(Birdie then rested on a willow-bough)
"Chirp-chirp!" called she, "Hurry, hurry-now!"

"Chirp-chirp-chirping, chirp, chirp!" chirped HE,—
"THIS is my valentine,—and, really, he suits ME!
          W. S. In Spirit (Through S. S. for Birdie S.)

SPRING'S JOYOUS NOTES
(Song)

Come to the woods, O come and meet with Spring!
Where every rivulet plays for the birds that sing!
Come seek the fairy-flowers, where lacy shadows fling,
Come where the building birds are on the wing!

Come to the woods, and watch the peeping things, —
Come where the wild-bird undaunted sings!
Let us forget! Cold winter now is past.
Spring's joyous notes, ring out at last!
          W. S. In spirit (Through S. S.)

CHRIST OF PEACE
(Song)

Come joy with me and sing a song:
Let anthems ring wide, clear and long,—
A babe Divine is borne to-day
Who will cleanse mortal's sin away!
And when men see the glorious sight,
'Twill make them long all wrongs to right.
In earth or sky there is one King
Whose praises all must one day sing!
'Tis He, the Christ of humble birth,
Whose peace must ring throughout the earth.
          W. S. In spirit (Through S. S.)

"A string, Sarah,—just a string to bind. June 12th, '17.)
          W. S. In Spirit.
Keep me within thy memory when all the rest are dead,—

When all the world has turned away, I came, and I have led
And I would lead, and help, and keep thee ever for mine own,—
So keep me in thy memory, nor fling at me a stone.

No warrior ever led a charge up any hill so high
As I have climbed in keeping you, and making you keep nigh.
So keep me in thy memory, until the last is done
For which I came, nor wound nor maim, until OUR war is won!
W. S. In spirit (Through S. S.)

Take out the west and then the east and give the world the
   north and south,
And keep from ravishment the Huns, and dam each water
   course's mouth,—
Then you will do what I have done, who keep in touch against
   the will
Of her who should be glad to keep and give me all, and
   "string" until
A perfect medium is she—which soon would be I now declare,
But, should she stop nor do her part, her own will soon be
   this one's lair.
W. S. In spirit (Through S. S.)

A LOVER'S LAST REQUEST

Dig me a grave within thy heart, that I may rest for aye with
   thee,
Who, of my life a very part, its rest and solace e'er would be.
Dig me a grave, and lay me low within that tender heart
   of thine,
Which can not hate nor hating know, which in its wonders has
   been mine.

When vesper bells their music chime, and others go to weep
   and pray—

Come kneel beside the memories which made God's love
 throughout life's day.
And when you sigh here must I know, since life can hold no
 life for me,
Until the sexton Gabriel shall bid me rise to go with thee.

W. S. In spirit (Through S. S.)

THE FATE OF POETS

A poet came to heaven one day, and sought his friends of yore,
He had not seen to welcome him when he reached heaven's
 shore.
He looked about and wandered far in search of those he knew;
But not a soul in sight of him but sought their old friends too.

At last grown weary of the search, he sadly sat him down
To watch the disappointed souls that hoped to find a crown
Bejewelled and awaiting them for all on earth they'd borne,—
And no reward, and not a friend,—Ah, these have been forlorn!

The poet then sought out a soul that seemed to be his kind,
And asked him where a new-born soul their relatives might
 find.
(This one I later learned was He Who came to earth to bless:)
"All poets," (said He to me, then) have earned but soul-
 distress.

"Thy friends, thy kind, you'll not yet find; but go thou on
 thy way,
And reparation make for all thy sins, and pay, and pay.
Thy sins were great, thy God was small; but here thou'llt find
 that God is All.
Take up thy burden, then, and go; and what you do our God
 will know!"

W. S. In spirit (Through S. S.)

BIRTH OF LIGHT

When I shall come again to earth, to wipe men's sins away,
No crucifixion and no birth I'll leave along earth's way.
But in the sky aflush with dawn the hosts of God and I
Shall sweep the world, open the eyes, and return to His sky.

When I shall come, as once I came, to speak my Father's word,
All eyes shall see me in His skies, all mortals ears have heard.
When I shall come, and pass once more along the ways of earth,
Men will look up instead of out, and all will know new birth.

W. S. In spirit (Through S. S.)

PRE-SCIENCE

The lighted lamp is turned down low, and in the shadowed
     room,
I seem to see another world, where is no wrong, or gloom.
My own reach out their loving arms, and wait to take me
     Home;
My life is just a little lane, where, lone, I had to roam.
I see a path, through future time which opens wide and fair,
Where never, never shall I find the one who left me, there.
The birds are singing, friends are rife; there is no one to hate;
Oh, I so long to travel on— how can I stay—and wait!
The dear ones go: I am alone: the lamp is burning still.
And yet, I know when I shall pass,—I'll praise the good God's
     will.

W. S. In spirit (Through S. S.)

BETHLEHEM'S STAR
(Song-words)

(I heard the voice on Dec. 19th and this was written Dec.
23rd, 1916.) S. S.

In a manger all so humble lay the babe wondrous, Divine,
While over Bethlehem's hills afar the shepherd's star did shine.

For humble, meek and lowly, was One now come to bless,
And save a world of sinners, and calm a world's distress.

In a manger 'mong the cattle, the Holy Mother lay
And presst the babe to Her meek breast Who would cleanse
  all sin for aye.
Among the lowly shepherds He taught the world to love,
And passing, left us Christmas, with Bethlehem's Star above!

     W. S. In spirit (Through S. S.)

SONG:

 Take but a part, and leave me, love, the rest,—
 Since when the heart is lost, all is, that's best.
 Leave but a pulse-beat in my loving breast,—
 Fluttering the love-bird's wings within its nest.
 Flown—flown at last,—no prison door can bar,—
 Into skies blue, and fast, it wings, afar!
 Love, love,—no chain is thine, free, free to sing,—
 All must thou take—and give,
 Soaring, awing!

     W. S. In spirit (Through S. S.)
  April 28th, 1917.

THE LATE ARRIVALS
(Cincinnati, Ohio, Aug. 29th, 1919)

With this one who inscribes my lines,
I come to bear her company.
Her form is still with flesh and bones,
While mine your eyes may never see.
We are related and in tune
So each word I impel is mine;
She is the writer and no more,
I am the author,—these are mine.

There is astonishment will come -
A little later she will see
Your own who've passed out of the case
Or shell, to His eternity. (First written "which was their
    mortal clay)
She works her wonder through my plea,
And never fails her work to do.
We will come forth in broad daylight
And carry on in front of you:
So be all ready when we come,
And do not shake, or scream with fear;
A long time here have I prepared
The way, and now I'm coming near.
This time next week, or any day,
You may behold my ruff· and me—
Your eyes then opened, rent the veil,
All other spirits must you see.
These may affright, amuse, attract,
They're here right now as we write on,
Hoping to use my medium,
And hopeful, wait until this dawn.

> W. S. In spirit (Through S. S.)

HEAVENS AND HELLS

All sane the men of earth live on,
While they pursue their insane way—
Despite the God of righteousness,
No word do they obey.
At last the heavens claim their souls;
Remorse their spirits shake:
While in the hells they chose themselves

Their thirst they cannot slake.
Yours is a hermits lot on earth,—
A kind of lonesome hell—
But heaven is nearer than you know,
Ay, all things shall be well.

                    W. S. In spirit (Through S. S.)

CHRISTMAS TIDINGS

When the world is wrung by hardships
Such as never were before,
And we find the angels waiting
But to serve outside the door,
When we hear the Christmas tidings
Joyful rung from shore to shore,
Hopeful promise fills our bosoms
Like we've never known before.
Christ is waiting with His angels
Waiting but outside THY door:
Will you open wide the portal
And accept Him evermore?

                    W. S. In spirit (Through S. S.)
        Dec. 24th, 1916.
(Being written five days after I first heard the voice.) S. S.

SUNDOWN

The light of day fast fades away:
Across the sky unfurled
The royal banners of sunset
On the regiment of the world.

The day is dying; ay, and thou:
Thy curtain must decend.

And through the night, the darkest night,
Thy pleading prayers must rend.

When thou shalt view thy ill-spent day,
Through which no prayer was said,
Willt thou, alive as spirits are,
Make up the only "dead."

W. S. In spirit (Through S. S.)

BE NOT AFRAID

Oh world in darkness, sit and wait,
Until the light doth shine
Which shall reveal Him to a world:
The One all His Divine.

Oh followers of His footsteps here,
Who watch and serve and lead
The halt and blind, the poor and sick,
Supplying every need,

Ye soon shall have new work to do
For Him upon the earth
Who will appear with angel bands
To give the old new birth.

Be not afraid, for it is He
Who died that ye might live;
Whose body hung upon the cross
That very life to give.

That ye might rise and look up high
And give your souls to God
Who, crucified, but died to show
They were not 'neath the sod.

W. S. In spirit (Through S. S.)

THE LIGHT OF THE WORLD

Through the black and dreadful night
At last the Light shall shine
Into men's hearts, and through the gloom,
The One Who is Divine.
When night is past, then morn is come,
The break of a new dawn
Which shall inspire with hope entire,
And draw the living on
To help, to rear, to worship here
The new-found Light of Love,
Who rules within each brotherman,
And Sovereign is above.

W. S. In spirit (Through S. S.)

WHEN MORNING BREAKS

When morning breaks across the sky
And God's own light appears
No more will men bow down to gold,
Nor give their lives to fears.
No more the sorrowing world will quake
To hear their own hearts beat.
The world will rise and look on High
Unto God's judgment seat,
Where One Who is Divinely just
Gives men their daily food,
And spreads the banquets in the hearts
Of all who would be good,
And serve and work and help and wait
Until He calls them higher
Where last His spark within their hearts
Will join His divine fire.
If men could see, if men could hear

God's voice of love within,
All men would rise and worship Him
Who cleanses from all sin.

W. S. In spirit (Through S. S.)

FAITH

(One of several sermonettes written by W. S. to keep the voice in the inner ear when it was first opened to spirit voice.)

S. S.

"Thinkest thou that I cannot now pray to my Father and He shall presently give me more than twelve legions of angels?" (Jesus)

When Jesus of Nazareth knew the scripture had been fulfilled and the time had come for which He came into the world as the beloved Son of God to save the world from sin, He proves to us His knowledge that He was not deserted or alone, as He seemed to those few of whom it is written, "they all forsook Him and fled." And it proves also that Jesus' communion with the unseen was not known or understood of His deciples. Was it for this reason they "forsook Him and fled?"

The hour was at hand, and He desired His own will to prevail. With a prayer to His Father He could save Himself. "But how then shall the scriptures be fulfilled, that thus it must be?" (Jesus) The scripture quoted proves this, as well as His immortal words, "nevertheless, Thy will, not mine, be done."

Prophecy needs no further records of divine communion than the words of Jesus uttered to the multitudes and His apostles both before performing miracles and afterwards; while Bible history would cease to be a divine record did it not relate the inter-communion of God the Father with His holy Son, Gabriel's conversation with the Virgin Mary, and also Elizabeth, and the warnings and councils of angels to the apostles and prophets.

Jesus had been betrayed by one of His own whom He had foretold would betray Him,—the hour for the supreme agony was come, yet He wanted all to know He was in touch with His heavenly Father, so near they could speak to one another, and that He would answer His every prayer, even were He to ask for "twelve legions of angels," would He send them "presently." "But how then should the scripture be fulfilled?" In other words: Should I have MY way, it would not be the will of my Father who sent me.

Who sent Him to die for the world God loved!

Thus we know Jesus had the council and help of the powers on High and foretold all things that were to pass, which are written and established as divine truth.

Jesus endeavored to establish His faith in the hearts of all who heard Him or saw the miracles He wrought. "I and my Father are one." "He that believeth on Me, though he were dead, yet shall he live." "I go to my Father and your Father, to my God and your God." "Whatsoever ye ask believing that ye shall receive."

Would mortals believe or consider the. Divine force which was with Jesus always, and recall "With God all things are possible," they would never argue the immaculate conception nor the miracles of God. For it was Jesus who assured them who led him forth "as to the slaughter with swords and staves."

"Thinkest thou that I cannot NOW pray to my Father and he shall presently GIVE me MORE than twelve legions of angels?"

O men of earth. Could you see the legions about you waiting to be recognized, and, as ye will, to aid you, or, "could ye bear now," the secrets Jesus kept; the "many things" He

could have told,—now differently would earth's miracles and
mysteries lead you, "Oh ye of little faith"! (Feb. 12, 1916,
N. Y. C. W. S. In Spirit.)

SPECTRES

Behold the spirits whom you cannot see
Who work their wonders here through thee
Who stand beside thee in this place
And lay their hands upon your face
Who wait and work and watch and pray
As you will too some future day
To move them by a single sign
To revelations most divine.

We have no shape ye earth ones say,—
You"ll not say this after today.
For minions here their work will do
That you the spirit's shapes may view.
Have you no sign to make for us
That we may see what we don't see?
Or do you think we play high-jinks
Who offer up a spirit plea?
"Please go and keep yourself in tune." W. S. IN spirit.
2:05 p. m., June 1st, '18, N. Y. C.
Note: The day and hour Dr. ——— tried out the spirit
writing these words. The above an exercise "to keep in touch."
Sarah Taylor Shatford.

TO MY SPOUF:

Written after ——— first sitting with W. S. (S. S.)
Such is my charge I keep
None may my right abuse.
Should any try these find I sleep,
While others I amuse.

To have such fine strung harp I own
What would the spirits give.
Should they attempt to rob me mine,
I'll prove how much I live.
How can I speak and give to all
A warning or a sign
To help, ay save, beyond the grave
The darkness that was mine.
This is the reason I am here
I still have work to do.
Be brave and help, and succour me,
For I shall reward you.
Make out the bill, Oh Spouf of mine,
Delighted will I pay.
I have so much this honour fine,
I'll work and work thy way.
Help on this work nor pause to war,
Thou shalt soon see the sky.
When we have done and you may come,
The Lord may not pass by.

W. S. In Spirit (Through Sarah Taylor Shatford)

RESEARCHERS

Some men here make pretense
To search for spirit sense;
To prove souls live and occupy
The same as 'ere they "die."

These write their musty tomes
Stored-up in marble domes;
And these do villify
The spirit, such as I.

Fine hairs are split, nails driven,
Solving earth is heaven.
Untold is half they tell:
There is no heaven—no hell.

Should these come to rehearse
The dead *living,* and curse
The fate of all who "die"
Alive, in earth's same sky,

They'll speak no more of "death"
Who live, and need no breath;
Who love, dream, ply the same,
But in the spirit name.

They'll dream their dreams, alas,
Wherever spirits pass!
Entering the doors ajar,
The souls ye thought were far.

We take the proffered place,
Looking you in the face!
And help you on—to rise—
When friendless in the skies.

There's better work to do
At once, on earth, for YOU,
Than measurements so fine
'Tween living, and dead-line.

We write who spoke to you:
The *doors* are oh, so few.
Lay down the pen: take up the *key,*
Help earth to see us *as are we.*

                    W. S. In Spirit
            (Through Sarah Taylor Shatford)
    New Orleans, La., Nov. 22nd, '18.

THE ORDEAL

In Flanders fields, the spirits walk
Who know their losses, and can talk
Of all that caused their loss to be
Such when their spirits were set free
On earth unseen to roam and stalk.

They are not dead. Nor can these die,
Though shattered, buried bodies lie
'Neath crosses where the poppies blow
    In Flanders Field.

Take up our crosses. Seek to know,
If ye do care, where we do go
Who sleep not, rest not, in a grave,
Whose spirits God makes His to save,
To live, and love, reap what they sow
    On earth's green fields.

              W. S. In Spirit
        (Through Sarah Taylor Shatford)
    Nov. 28th, 1918.
    New Orleans, La.

(Being a reply to the three poems "IN FLANDERS FIELDS,"
one by Lieut. Col. John McRae, (The Appeal), one by C. B.
Galbreath (The Promise), and one by Meigs O. Frost (The
Fulfillment). S. S.

THANKSGIVING
(The year of peace—1918)

Humbly we bow our hearts to Thee,
That we have won the victory.
That Thou hast set Thy people free
From monarch's rule, autocracy.

O give us grace to reap the lands
And peaceful fields with stainless hands;

Uphold Thy works, and see Thy plans,
Rejoicing in Thine own commands.

O make us one in peace to last,
With razed homes, and murders, past;
And, seeing Thee in each form cast,
Thine hand, the helmsman's, at life's mast

No man can slay a brotherman—
Nor rob him of earth's cherished span,
But, where is life, there, is God's ban,
With hope of Love's eternal plan.

> W. S. In Spirit
> (Through Sarah Taylor Shatford)
Nov. 28th, 1918.

THE LOST CHORD
(Song-words)

GOD is the Musicmaster:
His children are the keys:
His songs, the starry firmament,
The flowers, the birds, and trees.
His wonders are the works He wrought,
The soul, that cannot die:
While every note of harmony
Is HIS: as You, and I.
The Master searches every heart
To make His symphony:
Where love has failed to do *its* part,
A lost chord, there, *must* be.

> W. S. In Spirit
> (Through Sarah Taylor Shatford)

THE SONG NEVER SUNG
(Song-words)

There's a song in the heart that can never be sung:
There's music unpiped—from a heart never flung!
There are depths still unfathomed—
There are words yet unformed—
In the hearts that are wrung, there are songs, *never* sung!

There's a song of the soul that has never been sung.
There's a chord never touched on this harp all unstrung!
There is music undreamed—
Where each note is unlost:
In the soul that is wrung, there's a song never sung!

W. S. In Spirit
(Through Sarah Taylor Shatford)

A CHILD'S PRAYER

Heavenly Father, in whose care
The lambs are, in the wintry air,
Bless and shield the orphan fold
From the frost and bitter cold!

Take the lone ones to Thy breast;
Give them bread and strength and rest.
Thou art, Jesus, everywhere;
All are safe within Thy care.

W. S. In Spirit (Through S. S.)

"That's for my little child here, too." W. S.

(Written for the girls at the Poydras Orphan's Home where we went to nurse them during the influenza epidemic when called on by the Red Cross for volunteers.) S. S.

FROM WHENCE?

There is a form of murder penalized,
Which leaves no stain but does a hero make:

To wipe out armies then are murderers paid,
And worshiped for the sacred Law they break.

Where is adjustment for each broken law,
And murder is a crime as well as hate,
Adventure will prove less an ecstasy,
Where murderers bemoan abiding fate.

W. S. In Spirit (Through S. S.)

TO THE AERIALISTS:

"From the immortal Shakespeare who reveres their achievements, knows their success, and looks on wondering when he, too, may fly." W. S. In Spirit.

We have scouts who sail the horizon
Here where we spirits dwell,
Some bound for the equator,
(A firey place of hell)
Or, on celestial errands,
To mend, make sound or well.
We sail by our volition,
Ay, fast or slow at will:
We never ride in hatches;
We swerve from plain to hill.
But, near the land we trod in boots,
We grind God's grist at mill.
We see YOU sailing overhead,
(Some of us long to fly)
Who hitched our wagons to the stars,
Time lost, that passed us by.
Thus do we spirits envy you
Who skim the clouds on high.

To you, who rise nearest the stars,
And glimpse these globes of night,

Where silence is the voice of God,
And vastness is His height,
How puny must these iron wings seem,
When poised, you view HIS might.
To you who look God in the eyes,
Who sees you if you fall,
Who gathered up the fragments here
After we heard Him call,
O shall *you* rise above His clouds,
And meet Him, one and all?

                    W. S. In Spirit (Through S. S.)
     Feb. 20th, '19.

TO SCIENTIFIC RESEARCHERS PSYCHICAL:

Halt, in your bellowing after truth
Who KNOW the truth, proclaim it NOT,
While fetish savage has done more
Than you who write to boil a pot.

No welcome waits on any shore
For blind pretenders who can see
Yet silence keep, though speaking worlds
Deny that spirit dies when 'tis set free.

Until the armies of the dead
Can burst through portals, none can rise:
But all must serve where now I serve,
To bring to men spirit replies.

Ye can go forth with lamp untrimmed
Where none abides to share their oil;
Then parting with intelligence
Ye seek for gain, renown, and spoil,

You carry forth a blasted crop,
Belittled by your every breath,

While pondering here the multitude
You gave SO LITTLE before "death."
                    W. S. In Spirit (Through S. S.)
    N. Y. C., July 29th, 1919.

ONE KING, ONE THRONE

War's harvest here in spiritfield
Stands thick as ripening grain.
No laurel gleams, nor voice acclaims,
But ripening souls reap pain
Where never king or monarch rules
But One Who claims His due:
Then here my spirit warns and pleads
Ye serve your God anew.
                    W. S. In Spirit (Through S. S.)
        July 12th, 1919.

BRITAIN'S DAY

(December the 7th, 1918, U. S. A.) Set aside by Congress to
celebrate England's victories, and the part She took in the
world war.) W. S.

ONE dead alive acclaims in British name
Revered immortal England's poet-son,
Her task, though Herculean, is well done:
Aye, where HER domains are, HER heart is one.

Send then a trumpeter to blast afar
The ebbing tides again do lap the shore:
Unseen, or seen, they'll work for England's cause;
Abide WITH Her, to count Her victories o'er.

The dead walk everywhere the living are:
The loved ones sit companioned by their own;

Her skies unlost, no crepe hangs at Her door;
Her part well played by Her who stands alone.
                    Wm. Shakespeare In Spirit
                    (Through Sarah Taylor Shatford)
        Dec. 7th, 1918
        New Orleans, La.
"This will end the written work of W. S. In Spirit." W. S.

TO SEARCHERS OF GOD'S WISDOM

A fool is he who thinks I came
To work a wonder in His name
Inside a form of flesh and bone:
Such is not Wisdom's plan, I own.
To suffer for a cause Divine
I came to plea, accept as mine
A current on which I could ride.
Magnetic current needs a hide.
But spirit needs *mind* tuned and fit:
Else my words here could not be writ.

The jargon snivellers think and write,
They may bewail in spirit's night.
We now affirm, and make it *plain,*

Your hides are bound, and bound in pain,
When ye come hence and know the truth
From spirit's sockets, aye forsooth,
That ye but frittered time away
Who served through life to pry His way.
Ye can adjust *naught* lest His scales
Weigh all the lot. Your mauling, trails,
Lead to black forests where no game
Ye ever bagged in Science' name

Can measure in God's balance true.
Ye'll find there all ye *failed to do.*

Past mortal's vision, as I write,
His elements of day and night!
Past solving ever and for aye,
Unless God brush the veil away.
To lands unseen but near ye float:
No river, boatman, nary boat:
But each must push their own canoe,
And work their way. And God's way, too.
Each stands revealed without a coat.
The old saw of the sheep and goat
We do not smirk as here we quote:
But feel such pain we are remote
From God's elect, where He must be,
Who saves this goat, this soul of me,
To be revised, unmade, restored,
Whose life of ennui was too bored
To pay his God one tithe His due.
Thus am I here. Thus I warn you.

To all earth's men whose Godless ways
Lead where for crime through time each pays,
I lead with lantern true, alight,
Who venture here with power, ay might,
To brush for aye the veil aside:
To claim hell's current foul and wide
Leads DOWNWARD: NEVER upward, nay.
I claim from God just spirit pay.

W. S. In Spirit (Through S. T. S.)
Aug. 21st, '19.

TO GOD'S ELECT

We stand on His eternal shore
Who must still bear the woes of earth,
And straining, yearning, pulse alert,
We kneel, now humbled, sing His praise,
As all should speak through all their days.
We look aloft where every light
God poised on His eternal night
When by His word He swung these spheres
And gave my soul repentance, tears,
And see His way, His hope, His plan,
Who saves each soul, Himself, in man.

I serve Him now in my poor state,
Who, to save souls for Him relate
The way I came as here I speak
To save my brothers. Souls are meek.
No flaunting praise for us who write
Can fling our star a guiding light:
But what, as spirit, without clan,
My God elects, in spirit span
Shall be my due who paid my debt;
And by adjustment is mine met.

To you who lean upon His breast,
And wear His robes, I make request:
As here I send from my soul's past
The lust and crime which bound me fast,
Endearing for God's cause His Law,
And worshiped Him in all I saw,
Would ye but help my soul to plead
The Bread of Life, the spirit's need?

W. S. In Spirit (Through S. T. S.)

Aug. 22nd, '19.

THE FINAL WORD

The world at large is gaping for the truth my leaves will disseminate shortly. I never trod the boards more short of breath nor pulse alert than now I stand here on the stage of spirit where souls play their parts well or poorly let me add, as all is known, applauded, criticised truly, venomously as ever too, for souls are opinionated and do not agree that I (but I should not puff my part.) 'Tis here, and well received, applauded yea or nay, my soul's production is my best and underscore the word.

To all who snivel at my marvel would I add: Let them come forth and do the work as well. Then give me time to criticise their leaves as spoken on a human wire between two worlds where but thin air divides, and my soul's word I'll pen their praise unstinted by the poison of a sting.

To the woman who hears and gives her time, energy, funds, service royal let me add, I mouth a final plea. Go forth to God where soon you too shall stand as I, with my small taper in thy loved, ay treasured hand, and stand on the steeps of Eternal Time having here performed in the flesh-body the highest miracle since Jesus' time. Be true. Let time prove all I say. My words are writ as true as God's purpose was to send me here to find the one who could undo my vile earthtime (regardless of what others think or speak or pray) and this my plea and final word to you:

A paltry plea, a paltry plea
To one who has served God for me.
When all I asked she tried to write,
Perform, to set with God aright
My soul, that I might rise and go
Where are mine own, and His I know.
O do I hope where swings His spheres
Apast earth's crimes and spirit's tears,

There is adjustment at His word:
As all must know thoughts seen are heard.
Then shall my plea reach to my God
Who spared my soul past earth's cold clod
To speak, repair, and make anew
A work of praise which gave Him due.
So here my leaves are justly fit
Which bares my soul, the all of it,
That I might save for all of time
Souls for their Maker pure, sublime,
Whose stage is set where here I play
My part for God to point His way.

(Put up the pen.)

W. S. In Spirit (Through S. T. S.)
August 17th, '19.

FINIS

Lightning Source UK Ltd.
Milton Keynes UK
UKOW01f0721250717

305996UK00011B/495/P

9 781334 679940